WHEN GOD AND MAN FAILED

WHEN GOD AND

Non-Jewish Views

MAN FAILED

of the Holocaust

EDITED BY **Harry James Cargas**, Ph. D.

MACMILLAN PUBLISHING CO., INC.
New York

COLLIER MACMILLAN PUBLISHERS
London

FOR KATHY AND ED BURDULIS:

How can one show gratitude
for a quarter of a century
of love and understanding?

Macmillan Publishing Co., Inc.
866 Third Avenue, New York, N.Y. 10022
Collier Macmillan Canada, Inc.

Library of Congress Catalog Card Number: 81-15568

ISBN 0-02-521300-8

10 9 8 7 6 5 4 3 2 1

Printed in the United States of America

Contents

Preface

ix

Acknowledgments

xi

Contributors

xii

1

A Visit to Majdanek

Frank S. Parker, S.J.

1

2

Help Me to Remember: Three Personal Prayers

Harry James Cargas

13

3

The Transcendental Anti-Semitism of Hitler's Third Reich

Robert F. Drinan, S.J.

15

4

The Crucial Importance of the Holocaust for Christians

Eva Fleischner

28

5

Ethics After Auschwitz

Franklin H. Littell

38

6

A Theodicy of Protest

John K. Roth

51

7

A Visit to Belzec

William Heyen

74

8

Simple Truths

William Heyen

78

9

The Holocaust as a Problem in Moral Choice

Robert McAfee Brown

81

10

Anti-Zionism and the Christian Psyche

Edward H. Flannery

103

11

Holocaust

Bernard Lee, S.M.

116

12

The Holocaust: A Technological Triumph

W. Robert McClelland, S.T.D.

131

13

Holocaust Day: 1975

Jack S. Boozer

141

14

Auschwitz and the Nurturing of Conscience

Robert E. Willis

147

15

What Are They Saying About Christian-Jewish Relations?

John T. Pawlikowski

168

16
Holocaust Literature: Today's Burning Bush

Harry James Cargas
179

17
Art and the Inhuman: A Reflection on the Holocaust

Thomas A. Idinopulos
184

18
Modern World Literature and the Holocaust

Harry James Cargas
196

19
How German Thinkers View the Holocaust

Alice and Roy Eckardt
202

Epilogue
Harry James Cargas

212

Bibliography

220

Preface

Too many Christians remained silent while Holocaust atrocities were being perpetrated and too many are still silent about that awesome event today. Nevertheless, both then and now a small band of individual consciences raised their voices. Even if they were barely heard, those who did speak out were men and women who thus preserved their own moral integrity. This is no small achievement, whether we are talking of the World War II period of mass hysteria or the contemporary time of mass apathy.

This collection of essays on the Holocaust is an attempt to bring together some of the most eloquent insights by some of the finest Christian students of the Holocaust in the United States. These are men and women who have seen the Holocaust as one of the most significant Christian tragedies of history. I think that each of the authors included in this volume, whether consciously or not, is deeply troubled by the historical problem that the Holocaust poses, from a theological point of view.

Traditionally, Christians have been taught that "history is the revelation of God's plan for mankind." The Holocaust challenges this teaching. How can the deliberate extermination of some eleven million people, perhaps six million Jews and about five

million non-Jews, be a part of any divine plan? How does the
massacre of a million Jewish children under the age of twelve
glorify God? How is it that people who claimed to be followers
of the Prince of Peace, the God of Love, could have perpetrated
such crimes or been absolutely silent while these atrocities
were being committed? Indeed, what is history from a Christian
point of view now, after the Holocaust?

The question is, of course, rhetorical. No answer seems available to us, but that does not imply that we must not continue to
attempt to find a solution to the problem. We must ask ourselves,
beyond this, how Christianity will have to be different so that a
comparable event will not be possible in the future.

Each of the contributors here has wrestled with the above
problems either indirectly or head on. Each is a pioneer approach-
ing the dark forest of a terrible truth, perhaps fearful of what
will be found there, but following the path of personal obligation
wherever it may lead. For these priests, ministers, and scholars,
the pursuit is, at times at least, a lonely one. Nevertheless, it is a
necessary pursuit of immense importance.

Lest the above remarks seem self-serving, and lest, too, my dis-
claimer be of the "he protesteth too much" variety, let me merely
thank all of the contributors to this volume for their continuing
good work and let me tell them each, individually, by telling
them all publicly, how proud I am to share in this publication
with them. Our struggle indeed is right, our cause indeed is just.

HARRY JAMES CARGAS
Webster College, St. Louis
Member, United States Holocaust
Memorial Council

Acknowledgments

My SPECIAL THANKS to Jerome B. Agel and S. Arthur Dembner
for their assistance and cooperation in bringing this volume into
existence.

My ongoing debt to the work of Elie Wiesel, to his leadership
in causing many of us to confront the Holocaust, and for his
friendship, must be expressed, regardless of the limits of vocabu-
lary. Let me use the words which Herodotus put into Darius'
mouth in *History*:

There is nothing in all the world so precious as a friend who is at
once wise and true.

Contributors

JACK S. BOOZER is professor of religion in the College and Graduate School of Arts and Sciences at Emory University, Atlanta, Georgia. He received the B.Ph. and B.D. degrees from Emory University and a Ph.D. from Boston University. The Holocaust has claimed his interest in the last ten years because of its unparalleled human suffering and its implications for Western culture and for Jewish-Christian relations. His writing has been in theology and ethics, with an edition of Rudolf Otto's ethical essays to be published by C. H. Beck in the fall of 1981. He continues to be a member of the team teaching a course on the Holocaust at Emory College.

ROBERT McAFEE BROWN has taught at Union Theological Seminary, Macalester College, Stanford University, and is currently professor of theology and ethics at Pacific School of Religion. His many books include *Theology in a New Key* (1978), *The Bible Speaks to You* (1978), *Is Faith Obsolete?* (1974), *Religion and Violence* (1973), *The Pseudonyms Of God* (1972), and *The Significance of the Church* (1956). He serves on the editorial board of *Theology Today, Christianity and Cross,* and *Journal of Ecumenical Studies.* Dr. Brown is a member of the United States Holocaust Memorial Council.

HARRY JAMES CARGAS is professor of literature and language and professor of religion at Webster College, St. Louis, Missouri. He is a member of the United States Holocaust Memorial Council, serves on the Board of Directors of the National Christian Leadership Conference for Israel, and on the Board of Directors of the Holocaust Remembrance Foundation. Among his twenty-one books are *A Christian Response to the Holocaust* (1981), *Harry James Cargas in Conversation with Elie Wiesel* (1976), *The Holocaust: An Annotated Bibliography* (1977), and *Encountering Myself: Contemporary Christian Meditations* (1977). He has over one thousand publications to his credit.

Jesuit FATHER ROBERT F. DRINAN was the first Catholic priest ever elected to the United States Congress (D. Mass). Prior to serving five terms in the House of Representatives, Drinan served as Dean of the Boston College Law School for fourteen years. He is currently affiliated with the Georgetown University Law Center after obeying a directive from the Vatican not to seek reelection in 1980. Among his numerous publications are two books: *Vietnam and Armageddon: Peace, War & The Christian Conscience* (1970), and *Honor the Promise, America's Commitment to Israel* (1977).

ALICE and ROY ECKARDT are both professors of religious studies at Lehigh University, Bethlehem, Pennsylvania, where Roy chairs the department. Alice, who has been a research associate in the Rockefeller Humanities Program, has lectured widely and published in various periodicals, including *The Christian Century, Evangelische Theologie*, and *Shoah*. Roy is the author of *Older and Younger Brothers: The Encounter of Jews and Christians* (1968). He has published in *Religion in Life, The Christian Century, The Dialog*, and numerous other magazines and is the editor of *Journal of Bible and Religion*. Alice and Roy Eckardt are co-authors of *Encounter with Israel* (1970).

FATHER EDWARD H. FLANNERY served for many years as the executive secretary of the American Bishops' Secretariat for Catholic-Jewish Relations and is a member of the Vatican Secretariat for Promoting Christian Unity. He has served on the faculty at Seton Hall University in New Jersey, and more recently in his diocese of Providence, R.I.

His writings have appeared in *Thought, Journal of Ecumenical Studies, The Jewish Digest*, and elsewhere. Flannery's book *The Anguish of the Jews* (1964) is a history of anti-Semitism.

EVA FLEISCHNER is a professor of religion at Montclair State College in New Jersey and has published and lectured widely on the Holocaust. A member of The Grail, Dr. Fleischner has written *Judaism in German Christian Theology Since 1945: Christianity and Israel Considered in Terms of Mission* (1975) and edited *Auschwitz: Beginning of a New Era? Reflections on the Holocaust* (1977). Her articles on the Holocaust have appeared in numerous periodicals, including *Engage/ Social Action, Face to Face, Horizons*, and others.

PROF. WILLIAM HEYEN teaches English at the State University of New York at Brockport. His volumes of poetry include *The Swastika Poems* (1977), *Depth of Field* (1970), and *Noise in the Trees: Poems and a Memoir*, which was honored by the American Library Association as a Notable Book of 1974. He has edited *A Profile of Theodore Roethke* (1971) and *American Poets in 1976*. His poetry has been published in *American Scholar, Quarterly Review of Literature, Poetry, Southern Review, The New Yorker, The Ontario Review, The American Poetry Review*, and other periodicals.

DR. THOMAS A. IDINOPULOS is a professor of religion at Miami University, Oxford, Ohio. He has written for *The Christian Century, Cross Currents, Soundings, Middle East Review, Journal of Religion, Process Studies, Intellect, Encounter, The Journal of the American Academy of Religion*, and many other journals. His book, *The Erosion of Faith: An Inquiry into the Origins of the Contemporary Crises in Religious Thought*, appeared in 1971.

PROF. BERNARD LEE is a Marianist priest who now teaches in the School of Theology at Saint John's University at Collegeville, Minnesota. He formerly taught at Maryville College in St. Louis. A frequent contributor to journals of theology and religion, Lee is particularly active in the field of process theology. His books include *The Becoming of the Church* (1974) and *Religious Experience and Process Theology* (1976).

PROF. FRANKLIN H. LITTELL chairs the Department of Religion at Temple University, is president of the National Christian Leadership Conference for Israel, and is a member of the United States Holocaust Memorial Council. He has lectured throughout the world on the Holocaust and has written on the subject extensively. His volumes include *The Crucifixion of the Jews* (1975), and *The German Church Struggle and the Holocaust* (1974).

W. ROBERT MCCLELLAND is currently the minister of Hope United Presbyterian church in St. Louis. He has served on the faculty of Illinois College in Jacksonville, Illinois, and Maryville College, St. Louis. Dr. McClelland is the originator of the experiential-content method of teaching embodied in the *Come Alive* church school curriculum published by Hope Church Publications. He is the author of several books: *And On This Rock* (1975), *You And Me, Lord* (1976), and *Here I Stand* (1974). His most recent book, *God, Our Loving Enemy*, is soon to be published by Abingdon Press.

FRANK S. PARKER, a Jesuit priest, is a professor of real estate and of international management at Boston College School of Management and is an adjunct professor at Boston College Law School. A former Senior Fulbright lecturer in Africa, Father Parker is the author of three books and of numerous articles that have appeared in publications such as the *Cornell Law Review, Real Estate Review, Commonweal*, and *America*.

JOHN T. PAWLIKOWSKI, a Servite priest, is professor of social ethics at Chicago's Catholic Theological Union. A member of the United States Holocaust Memorial Council, Father Pawlikowski is also on the Advisory Committee of the Secretariat for Catholic-Jewish Relations of the National Conference of Catholic Bishops and on the General Board of Christians Associated for Relationships with Eastern Europe. He is also co-founder of the National Interreligious Task Force on Soviet Jewry. He has published in *National Catholic Reporter, Journal of the American Academy of Religion, Journal of Ecumenical Studies*, and elsewhere. Among his books are *What Are They Saying About Christian-Jewish Relations?* (1980), *Sinai and Calvary* (1976), and *Catechetics and Prejudice* (1973).

DR. JOHN K. ROTH is chairman of the department of philosophy and religion at Claremont Men's College, where he is Russell K. Pitzer Professor of Philosophy. A former fellow at the National Humanities Institute, Roth has published widely in magazines in the United States and Europe, including *Journal of the History of Philosophy, Ultimate Reality and Meaning, Idealistic Studies, Shoah, The Princeton Seminary Bulletin, Americana-Austriaca*, and many others. His books include *A Consuming Fire: Encounters with Elie Wiesel and the Holocaust* (1979), *God and America's Future* (1978), *Problems of the Philosophy of Religion* (1971), *American Dreams* (1970), and *Freedom and Moral Life* (1969).

REV. DR. ROBERT E. WILLIS, an ordained United Presbyterian minister, is professor of religion at Hamline University, St. Paul, Minnesota. He is a former president of the Midwest Region of the American Academy of Religion. He has been on the faculty of the College of Emporia, in Kansas, and Macalester College, in Minnesota. His publications include *The Ethics of Karl Barth* (1971) and articles in *Journal of Ecumenical Studies, Religious Studies, The Christian Century, Scottish Journal of Theology*, and *Religion in Life*, among others.

WHEN GOD AND MAN FAILED

1

A Visit to Majdanek

•

FRANK S. PARKER, S.J.

IN ADDITION TO MY UNIVERSITY TEACHING schedule, I am in the final stages of writing a legal treatise concerning the extradition of Hermine Braunsteiner-Ryan from the United States in August, 1973. This Queens, New York, housewife was returned to West Germany, against her will, to stand trial on charges of assisting in the World War II concentration camp extermination of 5,000 inmates during her tour of duty as an SS Führerin at the Majdanek Camp near Lublin, Poland. Braunsteiner-Ryan still sits in a Düsseldorf jail awaiting trial.

In the course of my research it was necessary to familiarize myself with the history of Nazi concentration camps in Poland. Thus, the following item in the *New York Times* for Sunday, November 3, 1974, caught my eye:

Oswiecim, Poland—Nearly 30 years after Auschwitz concentration camp was closed down, the underlying horror of the place seems diminished by the souvenir stands, Pepsi-Cola signs and the tourist-attraction atmosphere.

Despite chilling autumn rain, thousands of Poles and some foreigners visit Auschwitz every day. Most are modishly dressed and obviously too young to remember World War II.

Reprinted with permission from *Judaism* 25, no. 2, 1976, pp. 158–166, copyright © 1976, the American Jewish Congress.

They troop through the former prison barracks, gas chambers and crematoria, looking with interest at such gruesome displays as an enormous showcase filled with some of the human hair the S.S. used to make into cloth.

Then the visitors often stop for a snack in the noisy, cheerful cafeteria or a snack bar in the building that once housed Nazi guards, a few hundred feet from the nearest crematory.

The indirect lighting, modern facilities and movie auditorium in the building, plus the crowds of young people, create an impression vaguely reminiscent of weekends at New York museums.

At the souvenir stands, visitors can buy a selection of Auschwitz lapel pins in Polish and German, or picture postcards showing gas chambers and crematoria, or even souvenir Auschwitz ballpoint pens which, when held up to the light, reveal similar pictures.

For visitors wishing to stay longer, there is a hotel in the building.

"All that seems to be lacking," one disenchanted visitor remarked, "is a stand selling souvenir bones and ashes."

The piece caused me some thought. I have not visited Auschwitz, but I did spend a day at Majdanek less than two years ago. No doubt, current conditions at Auschwitz are as the article recounts. If so, they bear little resemblance to those that I experienced at the former camp which is still preserved on the Russian border-end of Poland. I left Majdanek thinking that every man, woman and child in the world who considers himself concerned with his fellow man should have the opportunity to witness what went on there. Therefore, I cannot welcome the trend to commercialize Auschwitz. Some day, it will happen at Majdanek. One more opportunity for man to learn from his past mistakes will be gone.

At the end of the Second World War, the Polish Government decided not to destroy Majdanek Concentration Camp. Instead, the government dedicated it as a memorial to the courage of the Polish people and declared it a national museum. Because of the political situation in that country, few people from other nations have visited it, and a great many Poles, understandably, prefer to write off World War II as a bad dream. They don't want reminders, so Majdanek is not heavily patronized by natives, either.

Now that Poland is starting to assume a more active role in the world community, there may be a change. Tourism should increase. A new restaurant and guest house are being constructed.

I visited Majdanek on a beautiful morning in May. The weather was warm, the sun shining. Two miles away, people thronged the streets of Lublin. In Majdanek, all was deserted. Traffic sped by on the main road. The occasional beep of an automobile horn was the only reminder that one remained a part of the real world. Perhaps, more accurately, one was still in sight of the real world.

There is no way to prepare adequately for Majdanek. Reading about it, seeing pictures, talking to survivors, all these count as fragmentary attempts. For the brutality and horror one is ready, but not for the efficiency. It could have been a Mercedez-Benz factory. Everything was so neat, clean and functional. In one case, the starting material is a hulk of metal, cloth, wood and other materials; the end product turns out to be a shiny roadster. In the other case, the starting material was a healthy human being guilty only of displeasing the Nazis. The end product turned out to be the ashes of a totally worked-out, recently dead cretin. Something about Poland must have inspired the German planners. There exists a slickness of design there that was never matched in the camps built in the Fatherland.

If Majdanek had resembled an American prison of the same era, it would not have seemed so disturbing. Places of misery that they are, the San Quentins and Sing Sings can be rated as functionally and architecturally ridiculous. Wasted, impractical mountains of concrete abound. Very little space is productively utilized. Large numbers of guards are needed to supervise prisoners. The American prison architects must have been misfits. Designing an outhouse appears beyond the capacities of most of them. Majdanek is in a different league. Every inch of space was utilized. Every building there was placed in logical functional succession. Intelligent men constructed it. Many of the same men today build houses, roads, and hospitals in Germany and Austria. Clearly, their on-the-job training helped.

Dividing the spoils must have been easy in Majdanek. The prisoners stripped on entry. Clothes in one pile, shoes in another, glasses in a third, money and valuables in a fourth. Anything that a person treasured enough to carry with him on his last journey was taken away. Even hair fell to the onslaught. Each pile of merchandise went into separate warehouses, and these were so arranged that trucks could easily come to pick up spoils and depart without having to mix with prisoners. The SS thought of everything.

The first selection took place at the unloading platform. Those healthy enough to work were led to the barracks at the left. The unfortunate were dispatched to the gas chamber, just a few feet away. The close proximity could not be an accident. It must be remembered that there were hundreds of prisoners to each guard. Sloppy arrangements could encourage revolt. If the sick and aged were marched half the length of the camp, suspicion would arise. However, moving them just a few feet for a "bath" would appear ultimately reasonable.

Months later, the prisoners who had been led off to the left would be back at the forming area. This time they would continue across to the right and take their own last bath. By now they would be as sick and as aged in body as the first group had been in years. A month at Majdanek was the equivalent of a year in normal life. Virtually no one lived through two winters.

Even after death, Nazi efficiency was not done with the corpse. The route from the gas chamber to the crematorium was all downhill. It is a lot easier to push dead weight than to pull it. Before burning, the body was passed through a dental inspection room, where all gold in the teeth was removed. Then burning began. The SS, like a good housekeeper, wasted nothing. Ashes were collected and stored in large bins. A letter was sent to relatives of the deceased. "We regret to inform you your relative died from typhus at Majdanek. To prevent the spread of the disease, it was necessary to burn the body. The ashes have been saved for you. Order them by sending 20RM to us." Of course, the ashes were comingled. No possibility existed of receiving a relative's own ashes. A last heartless abuse of the prisoners was being practiced. Their relatives were tricked into paying the expenses for their death.

Two buses stood alone in the parking lot on the day that I visited Majdanek. The one hundred passengers, all high school students, fanned out from building to building. I was not the only one stunned by the sights. Two girls passed me, tears streaming from their eyes. These teenagers had just visited the warehouse containing the pile of infants' shoes taken from them moments before death. If these Polish high school students had been born fifteen years before, their shoes might well have adorned this pile. The shoes of uncles, aunts, and cousins probably did.

One small group of male students had something else on their minds: specifically, the butt of their very feminine tour guide. The smirks and wisecracks provided a pleasant relief from the normal camp tone. The minuscule blonde, well aware of the attention that she was receiving, wiggled some more. I, too, welcomed the distraction. Life and health in the jaws of death. In time, however, even the blonde could not keep her pursuers from forgetting what had happened at Majdanek. By the time we reached the huge concrete memorial, her comments were being treated in a state of silence. Even her physical charms took second place to a display of uninterrupted evil.

I made two small experiments in order to get some feel of what had gone on at Majdanek. The first was to spend five minutes in a barracks. The door to the outside remained open. Within two minutes, I found myself moving toward the air current. The musty smell and lack of oxygen were sickening. My stomach churned and my head throbbed. All I wanted to do was escape to the sunshine. To think of 1,500 people jammed together in this small wooden enclosure for hours on end filled me with horror. I could not stand five minutes' worth all alone.

My second experiment was to walk from the city train station to the camp. As the crow flies, it is two miles, but winding through the narrow streets doubles this distance. The last three-quarters of a mile are straight uphill. The grade is extremely steep. I am in reasonably good shape and often walk five miles without much effort. On this particular trek I stopped at least five times. At the top of the hill, I headed for the small cafe like a homing pigeon coming back to base. The Majdanek prisoners had no beer break. They were scared, tired, sick and starved. One stop could bring death by gun shot. As I drank my beer, I felt very lucky to have climbed the hill as I did, under such different circumstances.

Steep as the hill is, beauty abounds on either side of the road, adding to the shock awaiting at the summit. Suddenly, barbed wire and gun towers are everywhere. I thought immediately of William Holden in *Stalag 17*. Just one look at Majdanek was enough to swear me off of Hollywood prison escape fiction forever. It would take a miracle to escape from Majdanek, but two hundred such miracles occurred in four years. Interestingly, almost all of the escapes happened while prisoners were on work details away from the camp. The Germans took great pains to keep down the numbers leaving home.

Each visitor to Majdanek must come away with one particularly strong impression of horror. Mine came from recalling something I had read in Braunsteiner's first statement to the Vienna police at the time of her 1946 arrest. The words "Roman Catholic" had been typed by the police officer in the space asking religious persuasion. This fact kept passing through my mind. How could a follower of Jesus Christ take part in the activities of this camp? Did His death mean anything to her? Did the teaching of His Church lead her to stronger reactions than a mere displeasure at what was going on? Did she ever beg His forgiveness for what she had done to Jews, yes; but also to thousands of Catholic Poles? I suppose, as a Catholic priest, the shame that a member of our church did this was stronger for me than it might be for others. Braunsteiner was by no means alone in the Majdanek persecutions, but each one must account for his or her own guilt. I wondered if she had.

Near the magnificent medieval tower in the old city there is a rundown building which houses the Majdanek Relief Center. Every day, from 10 a.m. to 3 p.m., it is jammed with former concentration camp inmates. A small amount of special government aid is available to them. All look older than their years. Yet they lived when 350,000 died, so that their strength must have been, at one time, awesome. The woman sitting next to me told of back pains and "liver spasms" that, for years, have prevented her from sleeping a full night. Her husband, another Majdanek inmate, has been in and out of hospitals two dozen times. He has been partially blind since a female guard struck him between the eyes with a stick that she wanted to break in two pieces.

The whole room was filled by people with similar stories. Reparation payments and soft words by the West German government notwithstanding, many Polish people still suffer from the effects of World War II. West Europeans among concentration camp inmates are in a different category. For the most part, their imprisonment is but a black memory. Good food and a booming standard of living have divorced them physically from the past, but not mentally. The West European and Israeli survivors are far less reluctant in their hatred of Nazis than are their Eastern counterparts. It is the Western victim who demands punishment even now. This is understandable. Life has become good; if it were not for the Nazis, it always would have been good. A Polish inmate never had a good life and still does not. Nazi persecution was worse than what has followed, but only quantitatively. Condemnation of Nazis is lost in a "what's-the-use" attitude. The fate of Braunsteiner-Ryan does not particularly interest the Poles. It interests Western inmates vitally—perhaps too much. Their desire to have her punished is not appealing when it is so nakedly exposed. Polish indifference is more appealing because it comes in the midst of hardship. The outside observer wishes to vindicate them even if they do not desire vindication.

Before seeing Majdanek and its victims, I felt much more sympathetic toward Braunsteiner-Ryan than afterwards. My doubts about the accuracy of some witness testimony remains unabated. The 30 year hiatus before arrest seems excessive. The casualness of American judicial review disturbs me. Giving her to West Germany for trial appears wrong. Nonetheless, I can not comprehend how any human being could have worked for the SS at Majdanek. That people could, and seemingly treat such work as just another day's labor, proves that bestiality lurks close to the surface in the souls of many citizens who, under other circumstances, never would dream of committing a crime.

Although Lublin residents try not to think any more concerning Majdanek, its effect on their lives still is transluminously present. Spend one day in Lublin and you know that something is out of whack. Humans treated like cattle for five years can not shake off the effects in one lifetime. Russian domination and Communist administration of Poland are beyond the scope of this article, as well as surpassing the knowledge of the author, and what degree of the blame the Russians must accept for the present isolation and poverty of Poland, I do not know. Whatever the true answer, the Communists took over in the midst of utter desolation. Braunsteiner and company did not leave much behind with which to rebuild. To the Poles' credit, they have rebuilt themselves, at least, partially.

Before the time of the Nazis, Lublin was an agricultural center of 100,000. Today, more than 250,000 people live within the city limits. A large majority work in the automobile and farm machinery plants in the area. The city has two universities, including the only official Catholic university presently permitted in the country.

Understandably, Poland became less interested in the West after World War II. Russian occupation was in large measure accountable; but the aversion went deeper. The West had not intervened effectively on Poland's behalf, either in 1939 or later on during the course of the war. Even the Russian-controlled Eastern Zone had no appeal, because the residents spoke German. Poland shut its borders and its mind. The schools taught Russian as the second language and western tongues were never heard.

A foreigner not speaking Polish can survive today in Lublin only if he resigns himself to talking with no one under forty years of age, and can speak English, French and German. Before the war, many Poles had worked or travelled in France, Germany or

England. Although the rust shows, they still can communicate in these languages. Among the young, Romance and Germanic languages are almost totally unknown. Perhaps this will change, but thirty years of contact with, and learning from, the West is irretrievably lost. Until recently, brain surgeons and piano movers were paid the same wage in this most fundamental of Communist nations. No inducement to learn other languages existed. Job promotions were based on party connections, not language knowledge.

Two hotels of the better commercial variety are the best bet for travelers to Lublin. These are western in appearance; a bath comes with each room. From the outside they look successful and urbane. The first shock comes on seeing five clerks doing the work of one. Shifts are twenty-four hours long and then the tired worker has forty-eight hours free. If the western visitor is lucky, one of the female clerks will speak a bit of German, assuming that she is not so weary that she has forgotten it all. Otherwise, registering for a room and getting a key is an adventure carried out in sign language. The restaurant is worse. Words such as water, coffee, whiskey mean nothing to the help. Ten dollars worth of a Polish bill sends everyone running in circles looking for change. A request that the restaurant bill be added to the room bill is greeted with bewilderment. The local tourist information office is no help. "We speak English, French, German and Russian," the sign proudly proclaims. It must have been composed before the present occupant arrived. A stunning beauty, she flashed a smile which would launch seven nuclear navies. Then she shook her head negatively to my basic inquiries in English and German. Momentarily, French looked more promising. However, when the first five questions all brought the response "*Je ne comprends pas*" (I don't understand), I gave up and staggered on my way.

I mention the "provincialism" in Poland to illustrate that World War II is not yet finished. I do not mean to poke fun at the Polish people. Kindness and helpfulness can be expressed without words. People walked blocks out of their way in order to be sure that I reached my destination. Old ladies handed me bus tickets when I didn't know enough Polish to ask the amount of the fare. Taxi drivers never cheated me. Government officials gave me full assistance. As a visitor, I was wonderfully treated by one and all. The shame is that they have so little but are willing to give so much. In the advanced West, we have so much and give so little. Maybe Poland is not so badly off after all. At least, the choice to be selfish should have been their own to make. The Wehrmacht deprived them of this opportunity.

Poland has rebuilt its economy, slowly, and inefficiently, to be sure. Nonetheless, the country now can begin to enter into the East-West trade goldmine that their Eastern bloc neighbors have found. However, it is going to take them so much longer to succeed because of their quarter-century sleep. Premier Gomulka never visited the West in his life. His successor has, if only as a worker in Belgian coal mines. Reentry into the world community will be painful. The average citizen of Lublin is poorly clothed, poorly fed, poorly housed. True, things were worse ten years ago; but this only prevents revolution. However, thirty years after the Germans ran home westward, Poland still has not recovered. When World War II started, life in Germany was five times better than in Poland; today the gap is double. Only the highest of Polish functionaries lives in a manner equivalent to the poorest West German. This, after Germany destroyed Poland and left 10,000,000 dead.

If, as well may occur, the concentration camp at Majdanek loses its essential character at some future date, the loss of Jewish identity in the Lublin area will have become total. At the present time, Lublin is *Judenfrei*. The spirit of anti-Semitism which resurfaced in the post-war Peoples Republic of Poland finished, in a non-violent manner, the work started by Hitler in a violent fashion. It is unlikely that even 100 Jews live today in Lublin.

The final disappearance of Jews from Lublin ends a bittersweet residence extending over 600 years. 1318 C.E. is the first recorded reference to Jews living in this city, 109 miles southeast of Warsaw. Even then, Jews were not welcome, and were forced to live in the dangerous confines outside the walls of the city. In 1375, King Sigismund III lifted this restriction.

During the next five centuries, Jewish people were an important, if not always appreciated, part of area life. Always active in trading and commerce, by the nineteenth century Jewish management and workmanship caused the leather and cigarette manufacturing factories to flourish.

Intellectually, Jewish physicians from Poland were considered, for many centuries, as being among the best in the country. Similarly, Lublin became renowned as a center of rabbinic wisdom and the observance of Jewish practices. During the middle ages, the city was the site of a semiautonomous Jewish legislative body.

As Lublin grew, so did the number of its Jewish inhabitants. By 1857 they numbered 8,747, 56% of the total population. During the next 80 years, the population of Lublin spiralled uncontrollably. Thus, the Jewish percentage of the city slipped at the same time as the absolute numbers rose significantly. By the start of 1939, over 39,000 Jewish people resided in Lublin. Soon this was all to change.

Duplicating the earlier actions of Cossacks and Tatars, the Nazis conquered Lublin. This event occurred on September 18, 1939. Almost immediately, the Jewish population was devoured. 30,000 Lublin Jews were shipped to Belsen, many dying on the journey; most of the others died soon after arrival. A fate of terrible suffering and death at Majdanek or Majdan Tatarski awaited the other Lublin Jews. No matter where they were sent, chances of survival were most minimal. The very few who did live, returned to a Lublin which did not welcome them. What happened to this handful is difficult to say; but they no longer live in Lublin.

As could be expected, the present authorities pay no attention to the history of the Jews in their city. The uninitiated would have no way of knowing that they ever lived in Lublin. This oblivion is occurring even at Majdanek. In the whole day that I spent at Majdanek, not once did any of the camp-museum officials emphasize the enormous number of Jews among the dead. At all times, the dead were referred to as Polish citizens. Although true, this statement could lead to a wrong impression, since specific mention was made of Jewish inmates from Slovenia and Greece. It would be easy to assume that Polish Jews were sent elsewhere. My direct questions on this matter were answered in vague generalities.

If the Jewish suffering at Majdanek follows Jewish history and Jewish presence in Lublin into a state of suspended animation, much of whatever lesson that the Holocaust can provide for future generations will be lost. To make a Disneyland fantasy of Majdanek, as has occurred at Auschwitz, would be the last straw.

2

Help Me to Remember
Three Personal Prayers

•

HARRY JAMES CARGAS

I AM STUNNED by a photo of this prisoner who killed himself by throwing his body against the electrically charged barbed wire of his death camp. Does this man need our prayers because of the despairing manner of his death? Or is it we who need his prayers? Creator of the universe, You who made this unfortunate creature, we trust in Your mercy for this sufferer and we implore Your mercy on ourselves.

Enlighten us and thereby spare us and our children, so that we may make a world devoid of persecutors, of victims, a world filled with women, men, and children of good will.

Teach us to learn to disagree without injuring each other. Help all of us to see what it means to be born in Your image and likeness and therefore somehow to share in Your holiness.

I have seen the bones of mothers, fathers, and babies, of rabbis, laborers, and doctors bulldozed into heaps of infamy. How far from You have we strayed, Lord, that this could have happened? How long will You allow us to continue in existence if we in-

Reprinted with permission from *Face to Face* VII, Winter 1980, copyright © 1980, B'nai B'rith Anti-Defamation League.

sist on treating human beings in this way—sometimes even in Your name? How can we overcome the sins by which the moral atmosphere of a world hungry for sanctity has been damaged? Is our earth a fit place for a Messiah? Is my own soul such a place? Am I praying and working to help purify the world from hatred, from bigotry, from the kind of ignorance that would produce the Holocaust? Dare I pledge, in prayer, a lifelong commitment to fight evil everywhere in Your name?

Maker of the universe, can we be forgiven for having invented ovens for human beings? Should we be forgiven? Is any penitential act of separation possible to balance the scales of justice and love over against the fact of these instruments of annihilation conceived, constructed, operated, and maintained by actual people? In the names of the nameless victims of Dachau, Dora, Auschwitz, and Buchenwald, I must ask myself what I am doing to see to it that such monstrous events do not occur ever again— whether in Somalia, Yemen, Brazil, Cambodia, on reservations, or wherever. My God, help me to see my responsibility, to understand it, and to act on it.

3

The Transcendental Anti-Semitism of Hitler's Third Reich

•

ROBERT F. DRINAN, S.J.

CHRISTIANS FAMILIAR WITH ANTI-SEMITISM before the rise of Adolf Hitler cringe at the quantum leap in hatred of Jews that is revealed in *Mein Kampf*. A Christian seeks to disassociate his religion from the ravings of the fanatic Fuehrer. After all, Hitler wrote in 1919 that "Jewry is without question a race and not a religious fellowship." He continuously described Jews not in any language that classical Christian anti-Semitism had used but in terms of filth and disease. Hitler, furthermore, appears to have virtually overlooked the Christian period and sets forth his vision of human existence as a conflict between the Aryans and the Jews.

But the understandable and persistent desire of contemporary Christians to disavow any responsibility for the heinous form of anti-Semitism created by Hitler cannot deny or explain away the fact that Hitler's depiction of the Jews as the carriers of filth and disease had its implicit origins in the Middle Ages when Jews were accused of poisoning the wells and spreading the plague.

On the other hand, it does not appear to be just to say that the grotesque excesses of anti-Semitism that were put into practice in

Reprinted with permission from *Honor Thy Promise* (New York: Doubleday & Co.), copyright © 1977, Robert F. Drinan.

the Third Reich can be attributed exclusively or even principally to Christianity. After all, the Christian churches had been ousted as the moral leaders of Europe several generations before Hitler came to power. Neither Catholic nor Protestant leaders, with or without the concurrence of their congregations, could deter the horrendous injustices brought about by unbridled industrialism. Nor did the churches have any overarching influence in curbing the exploitation of underdeveloped nations by the European colonial powers. Assuming, therefore, that the Christian churches would not necessarily have been in a position to deter the rise of Hitler's *ersatz* religion of anti-Semitism, the question nonetheless recurs as to whether or not the churches could have done more to prevent the rise of that anti-Semitism which was incorporated into the platform of the Nazi Party as early as 1920. That document called for denial of citizenship and public office to Jews, the expulsion of all Jews who had come to Germany since 1914, the exclusion of Jews from the press, and the designation of all German Jews as "foreigners." In Italy for many decades Catholics had been forbidden to join political parties which refused to recognize the rights of the Holy See. There is no indication that any suggestion was made to Catholics that they could not join the Nazi Party because of the injustices against Jews proposed in the platform of that political party.

The anti-Semitic bias was of course everywhere in Germany before and especially after the First World War. Lucy S. Dawidowicz, in her 1975 definitive book, *The War Against the Jews, 1933–1945*, states that in the years of 1907 to 1910 in Vienna "Anti-Semitic politics flourished, anti-Semitic organizations proliferated, anti-Semitic writing and propaganda poured forth in an unending stream." That was the atmosphere the young Adolf Hitler absorbed when he lived in Vienna during those years. It may be, therefore, that any answer to the haunting question about what Christians did to blunt the escalation of anti-Semitism in the 1930s in Germany should appropriately be directed not to the Christians of that decade but to all of the Christians in previous decades who had acquiesced in the propagation of ideas about the

Jews which were contrary both to the Scriptures and to basic natural justice. The heresies and the hatreds which Christians had permitted for some nineteen hundred years could hardly be excised or even cauterized during the dozen years of the Nazi nightmare.

Hitler's extravagant assaults on the Jews were, however, different in a significant way from anything that had preceded them. Hitler's anti-Semitism was transcendental, all-purpose, and final. In the view which he made the policy of the Third Reich, neither baptism nor the renunciation of Judaism could alter the status of the Jew. As early as 1919, Hitler had written that "rational anti-Semitism" must have as "its final objective" the unswerving "removal of the Jews altogether."

Christians should certainly have known that the proposed extermination of the Jews, however veiled, was contrary to the very essence of Christianity.

Christians should also have been able to discern the perniciousness of Hitler's association of the Jews with Russian Bolshevism. If such an allegation had any credibility, the conclusion that Hitler drew from it lacked any shred of plausibility. Hitler added: "In Russian Bolshevism we must see the attempt undertaken by the Jews in the twentieth century to achieve world domination."

Christians will almost certainly continue to resist any unilinear argument that the ideas and events which led to the holocaust are traceable to Christian teaching or practices. But after all of the distinctions are made and the inferences drawn, one still has to accept the fact that both Luther and Hitler were obsessed with fantasies about the Jews. Luther wrote that "next to the devil life has no enemy more cruel, more venomous and violent than a true Jew." Hitler echoed these sentiments in *Mein Kampf* in words not rejected by the religious leaders of Germany: "I believe that I am today acting in accordance with the will of the Almighty Creator: by defending myself against the Jew I am fighting for the work of the Lord." These statements, issued four hundred years apart by the theological father and the political dictator of Germany, made it possible and perhaps inevitable for millions of Germans to accept and believe in the lies set forth in the *Protocols of the Elders of Zion* which was translated into German in 1920. This fantasy purports to be a plan for a conspiracy of Jews and Freemasons to ruin Christendom and found a world state ruled by Jews and Freemasons.

All of these factors worked together to produce in Germany in 1932 a nation intoxicated with hate, obsessed by paranoia, searching for a national unity that would restore dignity at last to the German people, and prepared through some insanity to believe that the elimination of the alleged Jewish conspiracy would bring about the consummation of all of the aspirations of the German people.

Drastic steps against the Jews were taken within a matter of days after Adolf Hitler became Chancellor of Germany in 1933. But the development and execution of the "Final Solution" under Adolf Eichmann and his fellow executioners came many years later. Consequently, the nagging question remains and recurs: could not the other nations of the earth have done much more than they did to prevent the murder of six million Jews? There is, of course, the question of how much knowledge the outside world was permitted to obtain; Hitler's agents sent out deliberately obfuscating and untrue reports about the evils being planned and fulfilled against non-Aryans in Germany. The number of Jews in Germany, furthermore, diminished very sharply in the first four years after Hitler came to power. This exodus presumably gave rise to the feeling in world opinion that the most vulnerable Jews had been able to flee before the Austrian house painter could carry out his barbarous intentions. Nonetheless, one must still wonder whether some apathy toward the fate of Jews or even some covert anti-Semitism prevented more nations from adopting affirmative action to make places available for any Jew who desired to flee from the foreseeable and foreboding wrath that was to come.

The United States has traditionally welcomed political refugees whose lives or safety were endangered in their country of origin. During the years after Castro came to power in Cuba, for example, the United States accepted at least 400,000 Cubans simply on their undocumented statements that they would be in danger if they remained under Castro's Communism. The welcome given to Cubans harks back to the Displaced Persons Act passed by Congress immediately after World War II. In the thirty years from 1946 to 1976, the United States accepted at least 1.2 million persons as permanent residents on the basis of their being political refugees.

One must wonder whether the United States in the late 1930s lived up completely to its proud tradition of giving haven to the "huddled masses." The generosity of the United States after World War II was extended by statute to those individuals who were political escapees from Communist countries; but Congress understood that the vast majority of these people would be Christians. It is not clear that the Congress or the country extended the same generosity to the victims of the Nazi regime who were known to be Jewish.

The same doubt exists with respect to the congressional resolution of 1922 that approved the idea of a homeland for the Jews in Palestine. A question can be posed about the total sincerity of this resolution in view of the fact that in 1921 the Congress had enacted a new immigration law which, because it discriminated invidiously against persons living in eastern and southern Europe, made it much more likely that non-Jews rather than Jews would be able to emigrate to the United States.

Almost no group, Christian or otherwise, can boast of its role in preventing, postponing, or alleviating the holocaust. The usual way most Christians treat it is to ignore it. When pressed or challenged, Catholics can point to an encyclical by Pope Pius XI in 1937 entitled "With Burning Sorrow"; this document was delivered secretly to the German hierarchy by then Father Francis Spellman. Again, when challenged, Catholics can assert that Pope Pius XII was not as silent or unconcerned as he was portrayed in the famous play *The Deputy*.

Both Catholics and Protestants have at least a few heroes who stood up against the Nazi onslaughts. Catholics can be proud of

Cardinal Faulhaber of Munich while Protestants can rightfully proclaim Pastor Niemöller and theologian Dietrich Bonhoeffer. But Christian passivity in the face of the enormity of the holocaust can be explained only by that strange, unfathomable, and humiliating unconcern with, or unconscious rejection of, Jewish suffering which has characterized the Christian centuries.

It may be that the concern of Christians in America for the slaughtered Jews can be measured against the level of involvement which Americans have for the victims of other tragedies, such as those inflicted by the United States in Nagasaki and Hiroshima. Even then comparison is misleading, however, because the vast majority of Americans have never come to the conclusion that the use of nuclear weapons by their own nation was immoral in these two instances. If most Americans so believed, it might be possible to compare the depth of their compassion for these Japanese victims with the intensity of their feeling for the Jews killed by the Third Reich—killings which hopefully all Americans would deem to be unjustified.

The Catholic Record in Germany on Anti-Semitism During the Third Reich

The evidence on Catholic resistance to and rejection of the cruel anti-Jewish policies of Hitler is not entirely one-way. But the silence of Catholic leaders on the slaughter of Jews is hardly edifying or commendable.

On July 20, 1933, the Nazi government concluded a concordat with the Vatican which guaranteed the freedom of the Catholic religion and of its schools. The agreement, signed by the then papal Secretary of State, Monsignor Pacelli, later Pope Pius XII, was violated by the Nazi government almost immediately after it had been ratified. Nonetheless, the concordat almost certainly gave the Hitler government some very valuable prestige at a moment when the first extreme actions on the part of the new regime in Germany had elicited world-wide repudiation.

Although Catholic resistance to Nazi excesses grew during the 1930s, no Catholic authority or author appears to have repudiated the wisdom of the concordat. Gordon C. Zahn, in his volume *German Catholics and Hitler's Wars*, raises the question of why the Catholic Church in Germany did not "make a total break with the Nazi regime." Dr. Zahn, an articulate Catholic pacifist, agrees with the opinion of Pope Pius XII, who in 1945 stated that the concordat had spared the Church in Germany a far greater measure of hardship and persecution than that actually suffered by it during the Nazi years. Zahn goes on to raise this fundamental question:

"Is it enough for the leadership of any national segment of the Catholic Church to limit its concern to its own institutional interests or the personal welfare of its own membership?"

He concludes that in Nazi Germany "the areas of open Catholic resistance were almost exclusively those directly affecting" the institutional interests of the Church. These included the secularization of religious schools, the closing of convents, the suppression of Catholic organizations, and the pressures upon those who aspired to civil service to renounce their membership in the Church. Dr. Zahn concludes sadly that "only the heroic resistance to the infamous euthanasia program and the more direct Nazi assaults upon traditional family values went beyond these self-centered interests to a more general level of moral concern."

He documents this conclusion by reviewing all of the relevant annual statements of the German Catholic hierarchy made in Fulda from 1933 until the demise of Hitler. In virtually all of these documents the Catholic hierarchy reaffirmed its judgment that the German Catholic population had a moral obligation to obey the legitimate authority of the National Socialist rulers. After the war began in 1939, there was hardly a mention of any possibility of sincere conscientious objection on the part of a German Catholic to what Hitler was doing.

Episcopal statements in Germany during this period, along with other documents revealing the Catholic mentality at the time, demonstrate that, aside from several condemnations of racism, there was little sustained objection to or protest about the crescendo in anti-Semitic actions by the Nazis.

Guenther Lewy, in his book *The Catholic Church and Nazi*

Germany (1964), concluded that the Catholic Church in Germany "shared the widely prevailing sense of nationalism and patriotism." This author adds that the "bishops, many of the lower clergy and their parishioners concurred in certain Nazi aims."

Professor Lewy describes the passivity of the German episcopate as in marked contrast to the often heroic conduct of the French, Belgian, and Dutch bishops, all of whom sought to use their high position to condemn the barbarous treatment of the Jews by the invading Nazis. The situation was, of course, different since the conduct of the Catholic leaders in the invaded nations was almost universally regarded as signs of patriotism and resistance.

Dr. Lewy summed up his study of the attitudes of the German bishops and the Holy See toward anti-Semitism in these words: "But once the Nazis were established in power, the pontiff, like the German episcopate, seemed to have limited his concern to Catholic non-Aryans." Lewy notes that the Holy See repeatedly took issue with the Nazis' glorification of race but that "the Jewish question specifically was never discussed." Even in Pope Pius' encyclical "With Burning Sorrow" of March 1937, the myths of race and blood were rejected as contrary to real Christian truth, but the document neither mentioned nor criticized anti-Semitism as such.

It is very easy to be harsh and one-sided in concluding that German Catholic leaders did not do all they could to impede the advance of anti-Semitism and the opening of the first death camp for Jews on December 8, 1941. One is almost tempted to weight the evidence in this direction so that there will be a solemn warning to all Christians never again to temporize or compromise with a ruler or an organization that preaches anti-Semitism. But even the minimal effort to be fair to those persons involved requires that we seek to evaluate whether or not they really believed that the Nazis were exterminating Jews—as subsequently became known; whether in addition they thought that their protests might have some value or, on the contrary, whether they thought their protestations might bring about even greater evils for both Christians and Jews.

But even when all the extenuating circumstances are set forth, the mind comes back to the conviction that the silence of the Catholic bishops in Germany was reprehensible. A contrary policy would surely have brought about the imprisonment of thousands more priests and nuns than actually were confined during the Nazi period. It seems safe to conclude that countless Christian leaders in Germany were deterred from speaking out because of the amorphous and ambiguous theological premises which they had inherited from their training. Even the brilliant Catholic author and theologian, Karl Adam, defended the preservation of the German people's pure blood as a justified act of self-defense; he theorized that the physiological basis of all thinking and feeling was blood and that, as a result, German culture and history would be decisively shaped by the preservation of that blood. If a great mind like that of Karl Adam can be deceived by a gross lie about Aryan blood, one can imagine the falsehoods which would be accepted at lower levels of the Church!

The worst possible interpretation of all the facts can probably be seen in the conclusion made by Guenther Lewy, who wrote as follows:

When thousands of German anti-Nazis were tortured to death in Hitler's concentration camps, when the Polish intelligentsia were slaughtered, when hundreds of Russians died . . . and when six million human beings were murdered for being "non-Aryan," Catholic Church officials in Germany bolstered the regime perpetuating these crimes. The Pope in Rome, the spiritual head and supreme moral teacher of the Roman Catholic Church, remained silent. In the face of these greatest of moral depravities which mankind has been forced to witness in recent centuries, the moral teachings of a church, dedicated to love and charity, could be heard in no other form but vague generalities.

The same indictment is reflected in the question the young girl in Max Frisch's *Andorra* asks of the priest: "Where were you,

Father Benedict, when they took away our brother like a beast to the slaughter, like a beast to the slaughter, where were you?"

Could the Holy See Have Been More Effective Against Hitler's Anti-Semitism?

The entire Western world might well have been liberated from its anti-Semitism if everyone had subscribed in 1945 to Pastor Niemöller's avowal made in that year:

Nobody wants to take the responsibility for the guilt. Nobody admits to guilt but instead points to his neighbor. Yet the guilt exists, there is no doubt about it. Even if there were no other guilt than that of six million clay urns, the ashes of burnt Jews from all over Europe. And this guilt weighs heavily on the German people and on the German name and on all Christendom. These things happened in our world and in our name. . . . I regard myself as guilty as any SS man.

As the Christian looks back at the horrors of Buchenwald, Dachau, Maidanek, Belsen, and Treblinka, he wonders whether there was in fact any Christian resistance to the madness of Hitler. Of what relevance is it that some three thousand priests died in these death camps? Is there any place to hide from the accusation that the Christians of Germany and the nations which it conquered betrayed the Jews by silence and by neglect? Perhaps some consolation can be obtained by reflecting on the accepted view that the intellectual and cultural classes did far less to save the Jews than did church groups. A rare tribute to the Catholic Church was enunciated in 1940 by Albert Einstein in these words: "Only the Catholic Church protested against the Hitlerian onslaught on liberty. Up until then I had not been interested in the church, but today I feel a great admiration and a great attachment to the church which alone has had the courage to struggle for spiritual truth and moral liberty."

Critics seeking to understand why Christian resistance to Hitler's genocide of the Jews failed so badly have understandably turned their attention to Popes Pius XI and Pius XII. The evidence for and against these pontiffs is summarizd in a 1967 volume by Pinchas E. Lapide entitled *The Last Three Popes and the Jews*. The volume gives the unmistakable impression that Pope Pius XI, who died in 1939, and Pius XII did more to protect the Jews from the wrath of Hitler than is commonly assumed. At the same time, the author makes clear in a 40-page section those things which Pius XII did *not* do. It would seem that the emergence of a consensus on any culpability to be attributed to these two Popes and particularly to Pius XII will be difficult because of the vehement rejection by the Catholic community of the blunt charge by the Protestant playwright Rolf Hochhuth in *The Deputy*. The harsh criticism in Catholic circles of this dramatic charge of the sin of silence against Pope Pius XII derives from the enormous and unshakable veneration for the person of the Holy Father which Catholics cherish.

It is uncertain whether Catholic or world opinion with regard to the actions of Pius XI and Pius XII will ever advance beyond that state of doubt and ambiguity which now characterizes them. As more evidence is discovered and additional information becomes available, Catholics will probably feel like the famous French Catholic author, François Mauriac:

We French Catholics, whose honor was certainly saved by the heroism and charity shown hundreds of Jews by so many bishops, priests, nuns and monks, but who never have the consolation of hearing Galilean Simon Peter's successor clearly condemn the crucifixion of these innumerable brethren of the Lord in plain terms, not diplomatic allusions . . .

Those who would have liked the Holy See to speak in such unambiguous terms are fearful that the world will believe what Father Riccardo says in the fourth act of *The Deputy:* "A vicar of Christ who has the deportation of Jews under his eyes, and who keeps silent for reasons of state . . . such a pope is a criminal."

It may seem self-serving for a Catholic to demonstrate that Pope Pius XII did more to resist anti-Semitism than any previous

Pope of any age. The genocide of six million Jews seems to contradict such a possibility. In addition, it seems hard to theorize that, but for Pope Pius XII's intercessions and interventions, the slaughter would have been worse. Nonetheless, there is cogent evidence that Pius XII did all within his power and the power of the Holy See. In his Christmas messages, for example, of 1939 through 1944, Pius XII condemned racism in unmistakable terms. His Christmas message of 1942 pleaded for the lives of "the hundreds of thousands, who, through no fault of their own, only because of their nationality or descent, are condemned to death." The words "nationality or descent" so clearly referred to Jews that the message was withdrawn from publication by the Nazis. Similar evidence is manifest elsewhere in many places. But the shadow of the holocaust is so mind-numbing that the genuine and persistent heroism on the part of the Holy See during the nightmare of Nazism may rest in obscurity for the foreseeable future.

In November 1975, American author Robert Katz was found guilty of defamation by an Italian tribunal for his 1973 film *Massacre in Rome*, which alleged culpable Vatican inaction in the face of forthcoming atrocities by the Nazis at the height of the war. Katz, in his film, postulated that Piux XII overlooked the atrocities of the Nazis because he saw the Germans as a lesser enemy than the Communists.

In 1976, Pope Paul VI issued Volume IX of his multivolume history of the wartime activities of the Vatican. Volume IX reveals and documents scores of Vatican attempts in 1943 to help Jews in Rumania, Bulgaria, Poland, Yugoslavia, and Italy.

A total of six books have to date explored the question of whether Pope Pius XII could have done more to save six million European Jews from extermination. A 1975 volume on this question, *The Race for Rome* by Daniel Kurzman, contended that the Pope feared that he himself might be kidnapped by the Nazis and the Vatican destroyed if he spoke out publicly against Hitler's atrocities. Volume IX of the Vatican's own history of the war tends to confirm the rumors of such a kidnap plan in 1943.

More facts are emerging all the time about the activities of Pius XII in the difficult and desperate years when the holocaust was taking place. Perhaps the following evaluation by Professor Guenther Lewy is about as balanced as one can expect:

Given the indifference of the German population towards the fate of the Jews, and the highly ambivalent attitude of the German hierarchy towards Nazi anti-Semitism, a forceful stand by the Supreme Pontiff on the Jewish question might well have led to a large-scale desertion from the church. . . . The pope knew that the German Catholics were not prepared to suffer martyrdom for their church; still less were they willing to incur the wrath of their Nazi rulers for the sake of the Jews, whom their own bishops had castigated as a harmful influence in German life. In the final analysis, then, the Vatican's silence only reflected the deep feeling of the Catholic masses of Europe.

Whatever one might conclude about the Holy See's attitude toward the holocaust, it is unfortunately impossible to conclude that the Holy See gave very much encouragement to the next struggle of the world's Jews—the establishment of Israel.

4

The Crucial Importance
of the Holocaust for Christians

•

EVA FLEISCHNER

LET ME AT THE OUTSET clarify the meaning of the term "Holocaust," for even thirty years after the event we cannot yet presume general familiarity with it. There are those who have never heard the word; others will use it for any disaster—whether World War II, Hiroshima, Vietnam, or an earthquake. In this article the word is used in the new and symbolic meaning it has acquired over the past twenty-five years in the English-speaking world as what I consider its primary meaning: the murder of six million Jews by the Nazis, carefully planned and meticulously carried out.[1] I shall approach the subject via three main topics: 1) The problem posed for Christians by the failure of the churches during the Nazi era; 2) the roots of this failure in Christian tradition; and 3) the challenge to the very heart of faith posed by the Holocaust—faith in the redeeming God of biblical revelation.

The Churches' Failure During the Holocaust

In the spring of 1973 I taught a seminar on the Holocaust at Montclair State College. One day, after I had discussed the role

Reprinted with permission from *Engage/Social Action*, copyright © 1976, *Engage*.

of the churches in class, a Jewish student asked if he could address a question to the Christians present. "How can you, in the light of what happened, remain Christians?" Because the question was asked without hostility we did not feel attacked or put on the defensive, but were willing to struggle for answers (which differed in each case).[2]

This semester I am again teaching the Holocaust to a mixed class of Christians and Jews. Recently one of my students, a Catholic, came to see me. He was deeply disturbed. "What about Matthew 27:25?" he asked ("His blood be upon us and our children"). How was this text interpreted by the early church? Did it contribute to the development of that Christian anti-Judaism that we had been discussing in class? The student had intended to do his paper on the attitude of the churches during the Holocaust. Now he felt a growing hesitation: could a deeper investigation of this subject be a threat to his Christian faith? Much as I would have liked to be able to reassure him that his fear was groundless, I could not do so. All I could tell him was that, after years of studying the Holocaust and through times of real crisis in my own life, I am still able and willing to call myself a Christian today.

These two experiences point up what I would call the first level of the impact of the Holocaust on Christians; first, not in the sense of deepest or most important, but most immediate and obvious. Let me call it a soul searching, an examination of conscience, about the role that Christianity has played in the deliberate murder of six million innocent Jewish women, men, and children.

It is a well-known fact today that not only did Hitler never repudiate his Catholicism, but that many high Nazi officials repeatedly stressed that they were "good Christians." Among the thousands of lesser officials were some who had been theology students, even pastors and church officials (such as Ernst Biberstein, who was placed in charge of one of the mobile killing units that rounded up and shot by the hundreds, and thousands, Jews in occupied Soviet territory). On a broader scale, there is the phenomenon of the "German Christians," who joined with millions of other Germans in acclaiming Hitler as savior of Germany and pledged him their whole-hearted and undying fealty. There is, finally, perhaps best known and still the subject of controversy, the silence of Piux XII who, whatever his personal efforts to save individual Jews, never publicly condemned or excommunicated Hitler.

It is without doubt a dismal and shameful record. Yet it should be pointed out that the darkness is not without rays of light. The Dutch hierarchy, in a pastoral letter ordered to be read in all churches after the German occupation of Holland, called on Catholics throughout Holland to protect Jews wherever possible, because their Christian faith demanded nothing less. The bishops on this occasion threw prudence to the winds, prudence that continued to silence Pius XII. Seen pragmatically, the Pope would appear to have been more circumspect. For the Germans responded to the bishops' pastoral letter by rounding up and deporting not only all the Dutch Jews that could be found, but also Christians of Jewish ancestry (it was on this occasion that the philosopher and Carmelite nun, Edith Stein, was sent to Auschwitz where she perished). But if we ask, who were the true Christians?, where was the church's prophetic voice to be heard?, it is the Dutch bishops, and not Pius XII who are vindicated.

Holland, the Confessing Church of Germany, and acts of heroism on the part of individuals notwithstanding, I find it impossible to avoid the conclusion that the churches as a whole failed shamefully to speak out on behalf of Jews. This poses a problem for Christians today. What does being a Christian mean and demand, not only of the individual, but of the church as an institution, since it is precisely at this level that the church claims to carry on the work and mission of Christ? Have the churches lost their claim to credibility since the Holocaust? And if so, what makes many of us able still to call ourselves Christians?

One possible answer is that the church is not confined to the Pope or hierarchy, but includes the wider body of Christians. Yet this does not solve the problem, since so many members of this "wider body" also betrayed the Gospel. It seems to me that here we are brought face to face with the "mystery" of the church: "the bride without spot and wrinkle," yes, but only in the eschaton; meanwhile, here below, a muddy mixture of sanctity and sinfulness at best.

There is still a more painful aspect for Christians, however. Not only did the churches by and large remain neutral, an attitude that in itself is reprehensible enough. We have abundant evidence of strong anti-Semitism on the part of some highly placed church officials. For example:

In 1942, the Nietra Rebbe went to Archbishop Kametko of Netra to plead for Catholic intervention against the deportation of the Slovakian Jews. Tiso, the head of the Slovakian government, had been Kametko's secretary for many years and the Rebbe hoped that Kametko could persuade Tiso not to allow the deportations. Since the Rebbe did not yet know of the gas chambers, he stressed the dangers of hunger and disease especially for women, old people and children. The Archbishop replied: "It is not just a matter of deportation. You will not die there of hunger and disease. They will slaughter all of you there, old and young alike, women and children, at once. It is the punishment that you deserve for the death of our Lord and Redeemer, Jesus Christ— you have only one solution. Come over to our religion and I will work to annul this decree."

There are literally hundreds of similar anti-Semitic statements by individual people reported in Holocaust literature. As late as March 1941—admittedly still before the full destruction was unleashed—Archbishop Grober (Germany) in a pastoral letter blamed the Jews for the death of Christ and added that "the self-imposed curse of the Jews, 'His blood be upon us and upon our children,' has come true terribly, until the present time, until today." Similarly the Vatican responded to an inquiry from the Vichy government about the law of June 2, 1941, which isolated and deprived Jews of rights . . . "In principle, there is nothing in these measures which the Holy See would find to criticize."[3]

Such anti-Semitic statements did not materialize out of thin air.

Christian Tradition of Anti-Judaism[4]

Statements like those quoted above (and hundreds of others could be cited) can be understood only against the background of nearly nineteen centuries of distorted Christian teaching about Jews and Judaism, a distortion that the twentieth century French historian Jules Isaac has labeled the "Teaching of Contempt"[5]: Because Jews killed Christ (which soon became the infamous deicide charge), and persevered in their blindness, they are eternally punished by God, doomed to wander homeless over the face of the earth, a sign of reprobation to all God-fearing people.[6]

While I consider it a distortion of fact to say that the Holocaust was the work of Christians—even though, as already pointed out, many of its perpetrators were Christians in name, their Nazism *de facto* made a mockery of Christianity—I believe there is ample evidence that the centuries-old Christian anti-Judaism prepared the soil for modern anti-Semitism and the Holocaust; that the Holocaust could not have happened if Christians of Germany, Europe, the world, had taken an unequivocal stand against the Nazi program of persecution and eventual extermination of the Jews. The reason why no such stand was taken, why so few prophetic voices were raised, is the strong anti-Semitism of the West, one of the roots of which I perceive to be in Christian teaching.

Anyone studying Christian anti-Judaism will eventually have to confront what for many of us is the most difficult question of all: is anti-Judaism part and parcel of Christian dogma? Are its seeds to be found in the Christian scriptures and in our Christology, rather than in the fourth-century church fathers? This is the theology of a number of Christian scholars today.[7] It raises profoundly disturbing questions, which touch the heart of Christian faith. Is anti-Judaism endemic to Christian theology? Did the early church's effort to define its identity lead to a downgrading of the people of God whose place it now claimed to occupy, a downgrading and hostility that are reflected in the New Testament itself? (Particularly in the treatment of the Pharisees, who are frequently portrayed as hypocrites and the natural enemies of Jesus, and in the Gospel according to John, where with rare exception "the Jews" are the implacable enemies of Jesus, scheming almost from the first to bring about his death?) These questions, which cast a shadow on the very foundations of Christianity, are more painful by far than the discovery of the virulent anti-Judaism of a Chrysostom and other church fathers. For saints, after all, are people of flesh and blood, different from the rest of us in degree only, and their sermons and letters are not part of our Canon. But what if the scriptures, the Word of God, is tainted?

I can do nothing more here than raise the question, and leave it to readers to pursue the matter further.[8] However painful the question for us, we owe it to ourselves, in a post-Holocaust world, to confront it.

The Holocaust: A Challenge to Faith

Judaism and Christianity are both religions of redemption. That is to say, the central faith experience of each rests on a saving act of the Living God: for the Jews, the Exodus and Sinai; for Christians, the death and resurrection of Jesus Christ. Are these root experiences of salvation endangered, or even blotted out, by the overwhelming destruction of the Holocaust? I do not personally think so, but I understand those who do. Where was God at Auschwitz? Was his "absence" only one more instance of his "hiding his face" for a little while, or had he ceased to care, and thereby ceased to be the God whom Christians and Jews worship and in whom they trust? Can we still speak of human dignity when millions of human beings were not only brutally murdered by their fellow human beings, but their hair was used for blankets, their skin for lampshades? (Richard Rubenstein, in *After Auschwitz*, speaks of the Nazi effort to reduce the camp inmates to excrement, a theory recently brought into sharp focus by Terrence Des Pres' *The Survivor*.) In the summer of 1944 Jewish children in the death camps were burned alive to save the two-fifths of a cent it would have cost to put them to death by gas.[9]

Even if we are still able after Auschwitz to believe in the biblical God who cares, who cherishes his people, and in whose sight human life, all of human life, has incomparable value, such affirmations no longer come easily to us—if indeed they ever did or should have. Those of us who take our faith seriously, whether Christians or Jews, must struggle with these agonizing questions. Perhaps Irving Greenberg points the way here—not toward a resolution of the tension, for I believe none is possible, but at least toward a way of bearing it. In the paper already referred to, Greenberg speaks of "moment faiths." Since Auschwitz, he suggests, there are times when "the flames and smoke of the burning children blot out faith," but these are interspersed with moments when we glimpse anew the vision of redemption.[10] Since Auschwitz our life of faith is lived in the dialectic of this polar experience. The difficulty this entails may eventually lead to a more authentic faith, won by doing battle with God as Jacob did long ago (Genesis 32:23-33), and as an Elie Wiesel is doing in our own day.

Here, then, are what appear to me to be some crucial questions with which the Holocaust confronts Christians. They are hard questions, and some of us may wonder whether there is any way out for us. Can one still be morally a Christian after Auschwitz, asks the Christian theologian Alan Davies.[11] Has the betrayal of Jesus' teaching by Jesus' followers impaired Jesus' own beauty and greatness? Has Nietzsche's prophecy that God is dead at long last come true?

Let me suggest some ways I perceive whereby these hard questions may lead—not to a rejection of Christianity, and even of God, but to a purer life of faith and a deeper bond with our Jewish sisters and brothers and, perhaps, the building of a world "where justice and truth may embrace."

1. If we are willing to confront the sins of our churches, to work through the initial—and I believe inevitable—reaction of guilt, we may hope to come to a new sense of responsibility. Guilt that remains guilt—"a giant mea culpa," in the words of Harvard historian Yosef Yerushalmi—is not only paralyzing but dangerous. For it may in the end turn upon the victims once

more, as a means of ridding itself of its burden. Responsibility, on the other hand, will lead to commitment, to the determination to do everything in our power that another Holocaust will not occur. It will lead us to make our own the slogan, "Never again."

2. Our willingness to confront the Christian past may bring us to a truer, more realistic, and humble understanding of the church: an institution divinely instituted, we believe, but rooted in human hearts and minds, shaped by history, hence subject to all its vicissitudes; frequently denying the very love it claims to embody; yet somehow continuing to struggle to give witness to this love. I do not see how, in the face of the Holocaust, we can continue in our arrogant Christian claim of superiority. What is called for are compunction of heart and confession of our sinfulness, in knowledge that God's love and mercy are infinitely greater yet, and can indeed transform our hearts of stone into hearts of flesh (Ezekiel 36).

3. Not only our faith in the church, but our faith in God will be purified if we suffer the impact of the Holocaust (unless, indeed—and we must admit this possibility—it is destroyed). A glib, easy affirmation that God is good and looks after us all, that all suffering has a deeper purpose, that good always comes from evil—such cliches are no longer possible after Auschwitz. Does this mean that faith in God is no longer possible? I for one do not think so. But such faith will henceforth be lived in alternating moments of darkness and light. Perhaps it has always been so with authentic faith—the "night of the soul" is, after all, no twentieth century invention. But the Holocaust accentuates this aspect of faith.

4. The Holocaust is one of the three major catastrophes in the nearly 4000-year-old history of the Jewish people. Even if the Exodus experience still remains central to Jewish faith, the trauma of the extermination of one-third of the Jewish world population—and the sometimes real fear that the Jewish people might not survive at all—have indelibly seared the Jewish soul. To the extent that Christians begin to have some insight into this experience which, while uniquely Jewish also transcends Judaism and

has universal proportions, genuine dialogue between Christians and Jews becomes more possible. Some insight into the Holocaust will also give us a better understanding of the centrality of the State of Israel for Jews today. For if, as Buber suggests, the Holocaust was the veiling of God's face from his people, the establishment of the State is experienced by many as God's renewed pledge that he is still with his people.

5. Finally, awareness of the Holocaust may heighten our sense of responsibility and sharpen our sensitivity to suffering and injustice wherever they are found. A study of the Holocaust cannot fail, it seems to me, to lead us to ask: How would I have acted? Would I have been among those who were silent, or looked the other way, whether through fear or apathy? Might I, unthinkable as it may seem, even have been among the murderers? Do I look on today in silence as human beings are oppressed, discriminated against, killed? Do I excuse myself on the grounds that my actions don't count anyway? This is the level of questioning my students reach sooner or later, and which I find to be constructive and hopeful. The Holocaust happened more than thirty years ago; but if we relegate it to the past we are dooming the future. It has lessons for us today, for people of all time. As the German poet Georg Buchner has said, "The human being is an abyss, and I turn giddy when I look down into it." If we are willing to bear the giddiness, perhaps it will eventually give way to sanity and a greater humaneness.

Notes

1. See Fleischner, Eva, *The View of Judaism in German Christian Theology Since 1945*, Scarecrow Press, 1975, pp. 20–21, for a more detailed discussion of the term.

2. See Fleischner, Eva, "Holocaust Seminar at Montclair State College, Spring 1973," *Journal of Ecumenical Studies*, Vol. XI, No. 2, Spring, 1974, pp. 321–328.

3. Irving Greenberg, "Cloud of Smoke, Pillar of Fire: Judaism, Christianity, and Modernity after the Holocaust," in *Auschwitz: Beginning of a New Era?* ed. by Eva Fleischner, KTAV 1976. An abbreviated version of this essay is to be found under the title "Judaism and Christianity after the

Holocaust," *Journal of Ecumenical Studies*, Vol. XII, Fall 1975, No. 4, pp. 493–551. The various references appear in Greenberg's essay but are not given here.

4. See Fleischner, *Judaism in German Christian Theology*, pp. 23–26.

5. Isaac, Jules, *The Teaching of Contempt: Christian Roots of Anti-Semitism*. New York: Holt, Rinehart and Winston, 1964.

6. For the most recent and detailed treatment of this subject see Ruether, Rosemary, *Faith and Fratricide*. New York: The Seabury Press, 1974.

7. See the articles by Rosemary Reuther, Gregory Baum, John Pawlikowski, and Claire Huchet-Bishop in *Auschwitz: Beginning of a New Era?*

8. Literature on this subject is constantly growing. Malcolm Hay's *The Foot of Pride*, recently republished under the title *Your Brother's Blood*, was the first work by a Christian to examine this subject; Edward Flannery's *The Anguish of the Jews* signalled another step forward, by a Roman Catholic priest; Rosemary Ruether's work has already been cited; John Pawlikowski's *Catechetics and Prejudice* is available in paperback; the late Bernard Olson's *Faith and Prejudice* is an exhaustive study of the subject in Protestant religious texts.

9. Greenberg, *op. cit.*

10. *Ibid.*

11. Alan Davies, "Response to Irving Greenberg," in *Auschwitz: Beginning of a New Era?*

5

Ethics After Auschwitz
A Covenant Between Christians and Jews

•

FRANKLIN H. LITTELL

TEN YEARS AGO, in an address to an audience of German students, Peter Lotar, author of *Das Bild des Menschen*, raised the question of how the years of the Third Reich's power and crimes shall be dealt with.

How can we build the future when we are not finished with the past? How can we avoid the old mistakes when we don't even recognize them yet? We have a choice: do we intend to freeze fast in self-deception? or do we intend to carry through the cleaning up of ourselves and thereby grant ourselves and our children a full, new life?

At first glance this would seem another simple, if somewhat blunt, demand that a people mend its ways. We remind ourselves that ten years ago the *Bundesrepublik*, years after the *Deutsche Wunder* was the talk of the world, was still trying to come to terms with the sources and nature of its "old mistakes." This dimension of the statement was not unimportant for a society which, especially among youth and students, was beginning to live through many of the ideological and practical crises of the encounter with

Reprinted with permission from *Worldview*, September 1975, copyright © 1975, *Worldview*.

sectarian Marxism. The Baader-Meinhof gang and its activities still waited in the wings, but already the universities and *Gymnasien* were beginning to experience the conflicts many in England and the USA had worked their way through in 1936–40, years when Germany had cut itself off from the chief intellectual currents and mainstream of historical events. To this day—and this is one of the high prices the Germans are paying for the "lost weekend" of 1933–45—the struggle with issues raised by "United Front" theories and sectarian Maoist, Stalinist, Fidelist, Trotskyite, and other groups has not been resolved among German youth and students. To a person coming from the West much of the intense political conflict of the left-wing youth and student organizations in Germany seems like a memory of a bad black-and-white movie suffered through forty or thirty-five years ago. The anti-Semitism of the German "New Left" dredges up vivid memories for those who have not undergone a lobotomy of the memory circuits, memories of the *Hitlerjugend* (H.J.) and the *Bund Deutshcer Mädel* (BDM).

But the substantial question raised by Lotar (author of one of the best morality plays of this generation, a play based on encounters with conspirators rounded up after the July 20, 1944, attempts on Hitler's life) has to do with the meaning of life itself: "How can we build the future when we are not finished with the past?" We must attend to that question if our decisions in the present and actions for the future are to be as critically enlightened as possible. Contempt for history and ecstatic embrace of the present sensational moment distort many of the communities—including academic communities—in which we live. We must therefore make a covenant, both personal and professional: We will study those times. We will remember.

In America the first academic seminar on the Holocaust was taught by Marie Syrkin at Brandeis University in 1957. The first academic seminar on the Church Struggle was my graduate seminar at Emory University in 1959. The first scholars' conference that brought together students of the experience of the two communities, Jewish and Christian, under the assault of Nazism was

our International Scholars' Conference at Wayne State University
in Detroit in 1970. I mention these facts partly because a conference was held in New York City in 1974 that claimed to be the
first interfaith conference on the Holocaust, and the record
should be kept straight. More important, however, we should be
aware that we are no longer working, as individuals or as a group,
in an unoccupied hall in which the echoes of our own voices
reverberate against the walls and empty seats. A recent survey
turned up some three hundred institutions holding occasional
courses, classes, seminars, and research programs on the Holocaust and related phenomena.

"Related phenomena"—there the theoretical issue is raised. How
shall we understand "related phenomena"? Are the Holocaust and
the Church Struggle so related, or are we in truth trying to
harness two separate and distinct sets of phenomena, as has been
suggested. A letter from Eberhard Bethge, Bonhoeffer editor and
biographer, is reassuring on this score. Bethge states that the study
of the Church Struggle cannot today be carried forward except
in the context of the Church's relation to "the Jewish question"
and its resolution in the Holocaust. Robert McAfee Brown has
noted that the difficulty of relating the two fields of study today
is related to "that very failure, namely, that during the Nazi
period the connection between the church struggle and the
murder of the Jews was not clearly perceived." That is precisely
the point: Any further consideration of the Church Struggle,
neglected as it still is in most seminaries and by most church publishing houses, would simply result in a spirit of triumphalism
were it not yoked unbreakably to the experience of the Jews in
the Holocaust.

The two events were not symmetrical. This must be said forthrightly and be strongly maintained against all peddlers of "cheap
grace" (for example, A. C. Forrest, who has attempted to use the
martyrs of the Church Struggle to absolve Christendom of its
guilt of commission and omission during the Holocaust). There
were six million Jewish victims and, at most, twelve thousand who

perished as Christian resisters in the Nazi concentration camps. Eberhard Bethge recently stirred considerable controversy by pointing out that even the Confessing Church, the backbone of such resistance as the German Protestants offered, lost over 1,200 activists during the military campaign against Russian "Bolshevism," and less than fifty as clear-cut opponents of the Hitler regime. At Barmen (May, 1934) the resisters made no mention of the Jewish issue, and even in the Stuttgart Declaration of Guilt (October, 1945)—when the opening of the Death Camps had already informed the world of the enormity of the Holocaust—there is no mention of the crime against the Jewish people. After years of work on the Church Struggle, and with all admiration and affection for those courageous persons in the Christian minority—some of whom I have been privileged to count as friends—who did not apostatize with most of the *Kulturchristen*, I have been forced to the conclusion that the "Alpine event" (Bialik's term) was the Holocaust; the Church Struggle was a footnote to it. I speak of Christian history, and not just something that happened to the Jewish people. As Gerd Korman put it, quoting Elie Wiesel, in his *Hunter and Hunted:* "Today we know that all roads and all words lead to the Holocaust. What it was we may never know; but we must proclaim, at least, that it was, that it is."

We come to the matter of telling the story, of why the event must be remembered, and why it must be told to coming generations. Of this idiom, the story, men like Elie Wiesel and Abba Kovner are masters, but academics too have a part in storytelling. Unless we remember with understanding, unless we are brought to direct encounter with our present, our scholarly research is mere "sound and fury, signifying nothing."

As we study in a mood of moral earnestness, as well as with intellectual discipline, what we find hits us at many levels and in many ways. A German Catholic resister, Joseph Ernst Füst Fugger von Glött, tells the story of one of his own experiences. Before 1933, before the Nazi accession to power, he visited a friend in

Italy. His friend complained bitterly of the corruption and of Mussolini's brutal, fascist government. Whereupon Fugger responded, "Why do you put up with it?" and commented that such a thing could never happen in Germany. Relating the story years later Fugger commented that he had yet to learn what Germany was capable of.

I agree with those who warn against facile analogies in the study of history, and I agree too that USA 1975 is not Germany 1933. But there are other ways of breaking the morale of a people besides a lost war, inflation, depression, massive unemployment, and a solitary burden of war guilt. One of those "other" ways might very well be a lost war, inflation, depression, massive unemployment, and a painful, never successfully suppressed sense of guilt. In time of crisis a great deal depends upon the basic loyalty and integrity of those who exercise the stewardship of power and decision-making. Here too we have had our own American experiences.

Of course analogies are easy, and in this case they may confuse rather than inform. The Holocaust—Nazism's supreme achievement—was unique. In a technical sense the Holocaust was but one major event in the twentieth century, the Century of Genocide. If we speak only of "genocide," what of the fate of the Kurds today? From what we know of the fascist clique that runs Iraq, the current reports of genocide are quite credible. It would be easy to subsume the whole matter of the destruction of European Jewry under the rubric "genocide," particularly since the term "genocide" as well as the Genocide Convention of 1948 arose out of the Holocaust. For example, how shall we handle this year's sixtieth anniversary of the Armenian massacres? Armenians maintain, not without ample evidence, that the "first Holocaust" of the twentieth century was experienced by the Armenians. In its dying throes the Holy Muslim Empire deliberately slaughtered over half of the inhabitants of Armenia, the most ancient Christian nation in the world. Michael Arlen, Jr., has pointed out in his survey of that tragic episode published in the *New Yorker* in February, 1975, that the genocidal policy of Enver Pasha was made possible by modern technology. The telegraph enabled wholesale murder to be launched simultaneously throughout the Ottoman Empire. The telegraph also made it possible for lying reports to be issued to the outside world, in several languages, denying the facts. To the telegraph, the Nazis added the misuse of radio. Now we have TV.

But the method of analogy, like generalizations and abstractions about "man's inhumanity to man," is morally unacceptable. Scientifically there are analogues; morally, the generalization is false. Jacob Katz refers to the Holocaust as a "novum"; Uriel Tal, after a review of its antecedents, calls it "unique"; Roy Eckardt calls the Holocaust "uniquely unique." The point is that sociological or historical analysis may lead to the conclusion that the Holocaust was simply the most appalling activity of a genocidal era, and morally such a generalization is obscene. As Wolfgang Gerlach puts it in an unpublished dissertation on the subject, to treat the Holocaust as one manifestation of a general problem misses the main point:

. . . It would be to argue in lively fashion something like a husband who has difficulties with the spouse entrusted to him and now wishes to claim that he is experiencing "the problem of women"—since his wife is a woman. He has obviously not noticed that at the point when he married this one woman the question which arose for him was the problem of marriage. Thus the relationship of the peoples of the world to the Jews is something quite different, for example, from the relationship of white Americans to the Negroes.

The Holocaust may be a "plumb line" held for comparative purposes against other cases of mass murder. It may not be bracketed finally with them.

We are brought back forcibly to the original point: The Holocaust compels each of us, and expecially those with membership in the Christian church, to ask where he was and where he is in relationship to the Holocaust. Six million Jews were murdered efficiently and scientifically by baptized Christians in the heart of Christendom. This is an event comparable in holy history to the Exodus, Sinai, Golgotha, the profanation of the Temple by Titus, the fall of Rome, the fall of Constantinople. To treat it as merely another vivid illustration of the effects of race prejudice, anti-Semitism, or neopaganism ("secularism"?) is both banal and spiritually blind.

The closest thing to "the Holocaust," at least so long as Israel can keep standing off the Muslim crusade of the Arab League, was what happened in 1894 and 1915 to the Armenians under the Turks. But even the sixtieth anniversary of the Armenian massacres does not entitle us Christians to flee again into generalizations and abstractions. There are, to be sure, certain important parallels between what Christendom in decline did and allowed to be done to European Jews and what the "Holy Muslim Empire" in collapse did to over half of the oldest Christian nation in the world. The inability of a unitary Islam to deal rationally and fairly with a "foreign body" in its midst is not unlike the inability of a unitary Christendom to cope with the rational claims of modern pluralism. But the problem of a militant, nationalistic Islam is not our first concern here. We must set our own house (Christendom) in order, and hope for the emergence of Muslim scholars capable of analytical and self-critical study of ideological massacres and crusades. Martin Buber, speaking as a Jew, commented in the early years of Nazism that "the significant fact that this hour is a test of Christianity is not our concern; what concerns us is that this hour is an ordeal by fire for Jewry."

Our immediate problem is not Islam, but Christendom, although Israel is a "crisis of faith" for both Muslims and Christians of traditional type. Speaking as a Christian historian and theologian, I find my problem precisely in the fact that in the time of temptation and testing most Christians apostatized and went over to the Adversary. My immediate political problem may be the ruin of the U.N. and its tributaries by the reckless politics of the Communist and Arab League alliance and their bloc voting; my theological problem is closer to home. There was only one other period of church history with a comparable measure of mass apostasy, and that was the period when, in the eighth and ninth centuries, millions of Christians in North Africa and Asia Minor (the heartland of Christendom) went over to a militant and colonialist Islam. Some Christians were martyred; more dug in and wintered through; most of the baptized apostatized and accepted Islam as the final revelation and Mohammed as the last of the prophets.

The easy way to deal with the rise of Nazism and the enthusiastic response it for years evoked from baptized Christians is to interpret what happened as a return to the Age of Persecution. In this vein apologists now describe Nazism as "neopaganism," refer to the sufferings of the churches under Roman Emperors Nero, Valerian, Decius, and Diocletian, and paint a picture in which European Jewry suffered terribly, to be sure, but the Christian churches also bore repression and persecution. That was not the way the great majority of churchmen saw it at the time, and it is no act of good faith to try now to discern a pattern of apologetic excuse along those lines. Most of the baptized, including most top leadership in the churches, enthusiastically supported Hitler's self-portrayal as an enemy of "atheistic Communism"; most of them made no protest against terrorism, sadism, and mass murder.

On November 8, 1938, according to a conservative report, 191 synagogues were burned, 76 more were fully destroyed, 815 Jewish businesses were destroyed, 7,500 businessmen plundered, and 171 houses were burned. On July 17, 1939, Bishop Otto Melle of the German Methodist Episcopal Church told a group of visiting American Methodists: "Hitler is God's man for Germany." It is a hard thing, if needful, for a Methodist to have a memory! The first problem of twentieth-century Christianity is not persecution but wholesale apostasy. Until we face that truth neither our Christian education (or reeducation!) nor our periodization of history (including eschatology) will be sound.

The typical faces of this age of Christianity are the lawless policeman, the disloyal general, the corrupted scientists, the sadistic surgeons—apocalyptic types produced by a Christian community that has lost its rudder and has no life and authority as a counterculture. When the salt lost its savor in Germany, the fate of the Jews was sealed. In a sound Christian profession after Auschwitz it will be acknowledged that the vast majority of the martyrs for the true Lord of History in the twentieth century were Jews.

Already in 1933 Dietrich Bonhoeffer commented that on the Jewish question many of the keenest minds among the church people had "lost their heads and their whole Bible." The practical question for the churches is how to find their way back to the center, and it will take something vastly more powerful than "civil religion," "natural epiphanies," and other fads and fancies to accomplish that earthmoving job. It is a task for heavy equipment, as it were, and so far most of our efforts have been confined to isolated individuals of good will, working with shovels and buckets.

Reflecting upon the horror of the Holocaust and meditating upon the benefits of the Church Struggle, one is inclined to start with the pledge that it must not happen again. From the decent and humanitarian concern we move back to the old stance: that the little minority of Jews needs the Christians, in order that the gentile world may stay its hands from innocent blood. But this is the wrong *blik*, however well meant; it leaves the Christians in a position of strength, with the Jews dependent upon their good will and definition of terms. Actually, religious and cultural vitality is far stronger in the Jewish community today than among the Christians. The truth is far more basic; the Christians need the Jewish people, not only needed them in the past for the foundations of the faith, but need continuing interaction with the Jewish people for the sake of authenticity today. It may be that Jewish self-definition requires no distinction between "Christians" and "gentiles"; Christian self-definition cannot be achieved without continuing reference to the Jewish people. Whenever a Christian self-definition has been attempted without that reference, as in some other ethnic and cultural setting apart from the Jewish, Christians have slipped into heresy and from heresy into great wickedness. Today, after the worst rebellion and denial of God in our entire history, we Christians desperately need to go up to Jerusalem again.

Just as it is dangerous for Christians to seek severance from the essential Jewishness of Christianity, so even the study of the Church Struggle ought never to be pressed without major attention to the Holocaust and its meanings.

Although we salute and praise cooperation between Jews and Christians, also in study of the Holocaust and the Church Struggle, we cannot get away from the truth that our relationships to the event are vastly different. Even the tones of voice that are options for us may differ.

A Jewish scholar, particularly one who is himself a survivor, has the moral right to pursue studies of the Holocaust in the mood and style of clinical objectivity. (Whether or not clinical reportage is a useful form of communication is a technical question not here at issue.) Like Emmanuel Ringelblum, assembling the documents for his chronicle of the last days of the Warsaw Ghetto, *Notes from the Warsaw Ghetto*, a Jewish scholar may be as "clinical" and "objective" as he or she pleases, for his or her own life has been pledged to give a bona fide. Not all Jews would agree. Dr. J. Presser, when he had finished his great work, *The Destruction of the Dutch Jews*, concluded: ". . . one thing has become clear to me while writing this work: no single Jew who has lived through that period can think dispassionately about the events here recorded." But a Jew has the right, I would maintain, to try to do so if he wishes.

I question whether a Christian has the moral right to adopt that stance, just as I question that the various familiar rubrics of generalization and abstraction have offered ways of telling the truth about what happened. The Christian scholar may not forget Søren Kierkegaard's story of the professor who was driven above all by a quest for "objectivity." If he could have observed the crucifixion of Jesus he would have asked, if possible, to have it repeated so that he could be sure to give as accurate and detailed a description of the event as humanly feasible. We who are professing Christians may not deal with the crucifixion of European Jewry in such a way. The Holocaust is a river of fire that flows across our whole history, both communal and individual, and it compels us either to keep silent or to begin anew with totally fresh categories of thought and ways of acting. To continue with Kierkegaard, a Christian auditing is needed—and the auditor is himself a condemned man.

Do you now know that there comes a midnight hour when all must unmask?
Do you suppose that life will forever suffer itself to be treated as a joke?
Do you suppose that one can slip out a little before the midnight hour?

That life is a joke is the testimony of the twelve major denominational publishing houses studied by Gerald Strober over a ten-year period, 1961–71, in his book, *Portrait of the Elder Brother: Jews and Judaism in Protestant Teaching Material.* The story of the Holocaust, the most important event in recent Christian history, is simply suppressed. Henry Friedlander, in his major study of college and university textbooks, published in *The German Church Struggle and the Holocaust, 1933–1945,* showed that the major textbooks in modern European or twentieth-century German history also, and again almost without exception, suppress the subject. Professor Friedlander, from his position, was able to expose the lack of proportion, the neglect of scientific attention to evidence, the failure of true balance and objectivity revealed by such suppression. A scholar who is also a Christian, however, must ask whether many of these writers of textbooks are simply gentiles who share the embarrassment and averted gaze of perpetrators and spectators, or whether some are Christians who cannot yet bring themselves to deal with an event that challenges the credibility of Christianity as has nothing else in two thousand years.

Study of the Church Struggle and Holocaust must be built around two foci: (1) a commitment to the most strict canons of research, analysis, and writing that the various academic disciplines of the modern university can mount; (2) a commitment to let the stories of our recent history play upon our minds and consciences to the improvement of our moral earnestness and actions. In advancing such study, ours is not a solely antiquarian and antiseptic interest, one more of the games academics play. Nor do we meet as concerned persons to moralize with sweeping analogies, or even to pass resolutions, comparing what has happened since 1969 in America to what happened during the last days of the Weimar Republic. But we would be blind indeed who, remembering the subversion and destruction of Weimar, did not shudder to reflect upon contemporary revelations of illegal and disloyal activities by, for example, the FBI, the CIA, the Attorney General, and the former President of the United States. They took oaths to uphold the Constitution "against all enemies, foreign and domestic," and they broke their oaths. To some this may be at the level of "stealing chickens," as one columnist recently put it. But to the less frivolous it is an ominous development.

We have the right as concerned citizens, which was our condition before any of us ever consciously associated with the university or the church (or synagogue), to nourish the hope that our work will help to bring the era of genocide to an end. But we must first let the documents and the stories speak fully to us before we assume we have the data fixed in time and space.

Consider a story that sets a seal of moral responsibility upon our study of the Holocaust. In the last days of World War II Rabbi Samuel Rose, eighty-nine, of Denver, Colorado, received word that his son, Major General Maurice Rose, had been killed in Germany. Rabbi Rose sat down heavily, grasping his cane, and said: "It is well that since this had to be, it happened in the week of Passover. As Jehovah said, 'When I see the blood, I will pass over you.' He spoke not only to the Jews but to all peoples—to the gentiles, to Americans, to Germans, to all peoples. And so, may Jehovah accept this sacrifice, and see the blood and pass over all peoples for their sins, at this Passover time, for my son's sake."

In the name of the Isaacs for whom no rams were caught in the thicket, in memory of the six million for whom the waters refused to part, in respect for the few thousand Christian martyrs who gave some of us here a right to speak, if not too loudly, about the past, let us dedicate ourselves to clear thinking and responsible research, but above all let us dedicate ourselves to this covenant: We will remember, the story will be heard, we will tell it to our children and children's children.

6

A Theodicy of Protest

•

JOHN K. ROTH

"Jesus gazed at them. 'For men,' he said, 'it is impossible, but not for God: because everything is possible for God.' "
—Mark 10:27 (The Jerusalem Bible)

"He is almighty, isn't He? He could use His might to save the victims, but He doesn't; So—on whose side is He? Could the killer kill without His blessing—without His complicity?"
—Elie Wiesel, *The Trial of God*

"And the Lord repented of the evil which he thought to do to his people."
—Exodus 32:14 (Revised Standard Version)

We Are Consumed

SEVENTY MILLION HUMAN BEINGS have been uprooted, enslaved, or killed in the twentieth century alone. Albert Camus made that estimate when he published *The Rebel* in 1951. What the figure should be today, God only knows. It is all too clear, however, that wars persist, scarcity continues to take its mammoth toll, and human misery, so graphically written on the faces of refugee children, rages unabated. Granted, even if the twentieth century is one of unprecedented mass death, it is not different from others that have gone before. But that fact gives no comfort, especially if one cannot escape the conviction that such

This essay first appeared in Stephen T. Davis, ed., *Encountering Evil: Live Options in Theodicy* (Atlanta, Ga.: John Knox Press, 1981). Copyright © 1981, John Knox Press, reprinted with permission.

waste is wrong, either because it is contrary to God's will or because it reveals life's fundamental absurdity.

Usually "theodicy" refers to human vindications of God's justice in permitting evil to exist. Most theodicies of the Protestant Christian variety belong in that tradition. The outlook developed here is related to it, too, but the breaks with classical Christian Protestantism are no less important than the lines of continuity. My approach underscores God's sovereignty. It allows for his disappointment with human life gone wrong. It also holds out for the possibility of grace experienced through faith and for the hope of God's salvation. At the same time, and precisely because the accumulated devastation of history is so vast, this perspective echoes voices that are Jewish as well as Christian, some of them far older than those of Martin Luther or John Calvin. The Jewish voices belong to a dissenting spirit that quarrels with God over *his* use of power. That confrontation is rooted not so much in rejection of God but rather in recognition that such defiance is crucial in struggles against despair. Jewish insight, ancient and contemporary, calls for men and women—particularly Christians—to consider a theodicy of protest.

What does "evil" mean? That question itself is a crucial element in the problem of evil. The word often functions as a noun, suggesting that evil is an entity. In fact, evil is *activity*, sometimes *inactivity*, and thus it is a manifestation of power. Evil power displays are those that *waste*. That is, evil happens whenever power ruins or squanders, or whenever it fails to forestall those results. Evil comes in many shapes and sizes. The kind that concerns us here ignores and violates the sanctity of individual persons. Everyone inflicts that sort of pain and yet some individuals and societies are far more perverse than others. The measure is taken by the degree to which one's actions waste human life.

Prior to death, and perhaps beyond, existence is in process. Because things move and change, waste may not be simply waste, nor evil simply evil. Capitalizing on that fact, some writers mute screams of pain by hearing them as *instrumental*. Destruction then becomes a means to what is new and better. Or, if not all havoc readily fits that scheme, ruins may still provide occasions for atonement, forgiveness, and magnificent attempts at redemption. To the extent that evil can be interpreted as instrumental, as somehow transcended by a better situation overall, power's waste is rendered less radical.

Eschatological hopes hinge on some version of an instrumental view of evil. They differ, however, in their optimism about evil's being overcome by good. Most Protestant theodicies affirm that this overcoming, at least from a divine perspective, will be complete. A protesting theodicy affirms that any overcoming of this kind, at least from a human perspective, should be less well regarded. The reason is straightforward: Too much has been lost.

Theodicy consists of fallible options. That result is unavoidable because we are dealing with thoughts, emotions, and choices organized by finite human minds. It is equally true that such minds exist only in social contexts that decisively influence what they are. Therefore, it is not accidental that I speak of a theodicy of protest. Before proceeding with a more detailed discussion of points only mentioned thus far, let me note some factors that produce this personal outcome.

My father was a Presbyterian pastor. I was raised in a home where God was alive, and his reality abides with me still. Early on I was introduced to theology and philosophy in my father's sermons, which emphasized human responsibility, social justice, and the sovereignty of God. Later encounters with Søren Kierkegaard would do much to deepen my understanding—and my questioning—of those ideas.

In the latter half of the 1960s, while I was in my late twenties, the "death of God" was bandied about. Although I could not agree with the facile optimism that proclaimed God's demise as a joyous event signifying humanity's freedom and coming-of-age, I was profoundly moved by Richard L. Rubenstein's *After Auschwitz*. This book and its Jewish author placed the Holocaust, the mass murder of the Jewish people during the Nazi era, firmly on the American theological agenda. Rubenstein affirmed the death of a traditional God of history, but he neither rejected all views of God nor saw that the "death of God" was any cause for celebration. If Rubenstein's constructive proposals did not always persuade me completely, his straightforward insights about the religious crisis lurking in the Holocaust sent me on a quest. Could my own religious and philosophical experience muster a response that would work better for me? My journey is still under way.

Other currents were touching me as well. The finite, limited Gods of William James, A. N. Whitehead, and other "process theologians" offered some appeal. But as I wrote about American religious thought with my colleague Frederick Sontag, I became disenchanted with the sanguine assumptions about human nature and history that are required by those outlooks if trust in redemption is warranted.[1] Nonetheless, religious hopes remained in my bones, as they still do, and thus my convictions about human frailty and failure forced me to reconsider the power of God.

As it happened, the context in which that reconsideration took place was again provided by the consuming fire of Auschwitz, seen this time through the writings of a Jewish survivor, Elie Wiesel.[2] Wiesel's authorship shows that life in a post-Holocaust world can be more troublesome with God than without him. And yet Wiesel will not let God go, any more than he will give up on humankind, although he has good reason to do both. Instead he dissents, seeking to check despair not by acquitting or ignoring God but by putting him on trial.

The verdict reads "guilty," but that word is not the end. Wiesel's thought has a method, and the method is that of a protestant. Never failing for questions, he keeps asking. "What is the next step?" Reaching an apparent conclusion, he moves on. "And yet? And yet." . . . "In spite of this, something more must be noted." . . . "How is one to believe? How is one not to believe?" . . . Those are the forms of his thinking. They enable Elie Wiesel not to discount the waste that indicts God, but to stand with Moses in acknowledging God's sovereignty even as he argues against God for the sake of his people.

Wiesel's point is not to locate a divine scapegoat, nor does he think that any problems are solved by blaming God. On the contrary, his work demands human responsibility. And yet Wiesel understands that much also depends on God's reality or lack of it, on what God can and cannot do, will and will not do. More than once Elie Wiesel has said that he opposes two things: indifference and absurdity. Religiously speaking, his aim is to map out boundaries of meaning in the wake of Auschwitz. To deny God outright could go too far. But to affirm his total goodness, to apologize for God, to exonerate him on grounds of weakness—these steps go too far as well.

The quotations at the outset of this essay were chosen with care. A protesting theodicy puts God on trial, and in that process the issue of God's wasteful complicity in evil takes center stage. The God interrogated is one for whom everything is possible, an awesome biblical announcement. According to the gospel narrative, when Jesus made that claim he did so where entry into the Kingdom of God was at issue. One implication of that discussion is that God can bring about good ends that are completely beyond human energies. I agree, but not unequivocally For those ends to occur in the fullest measure possible, human repentance will have to be matched by God's. Even then there will be too much waste left over. Unlike some theodicies, this one is *not* too good to be true.

How Long, Lord, Before You Relent?

History   Protestant theology usually holds that God cares about history. My theodicy of protest begins by probing that assumption, and it does so by agreeing with Hegel: History is "the slaughter-bench at which the happiness of peoples, the wisdom of states, and the virtue of individuals have been sacrificed."[3] Granted, that appraisal does not contain all that should be said, but that fact itself produces more problems than it solves.

According to Genesis, God called his creation good. In some sense, everyone agrees. Corrupted though the world may be, our lives are not without optimism. It persists in the experience that life is worth living. If it were not, nobody would bother with theodicy. We do not inhabit a perfect world, but neither is this one the worst that might be. Therefore, questions about history's meaning and destiny loom large. One way to summarize those questions is to ask: If creation is good, and yet history is largely a slaughter-bench, how "cost-effective" are God's decisions?[4]

Theodicy must reckon with God-as-economist, and the question posed above deals with his waste. When Jews and Christians say that history should be understood in terms of creation, they imply that God's purposes affect what comes to be. So consider a dilemma: Either those purposes necessitate every jot and tittle of history, or they are compatible with alternatives that would reduce the slaughter-bench qualities of human life. On all counts there are good grounds for protest.

In the former instance, for example, God's economy might be without waste, but the issue of whether God was bound to pursue only those particular purposes, with their exact and horrendous historical consequences, surely calls into question the freedom—divine and human—so central to the biblical records. On the other hand, if God is not so determined, his purposes permit multiple routes to their achievement. Indeed the purposes themselves may have a flexible quality. Such largess, however, is not merely lavish. The slaughter-bench makes God's luxury wasteful. And one point more: No matter what horn of the dilemma is seized, any ways in which God could rationally justify his economy as purely cost-effective in pursuing goodness that we can appreciate . . . well, those ways are beyond imagining. This result testifies that such a wasteful God cannot be totally benevolent. History itself is God's indictment.

Responsibility Most people want a totally good God or none at all. In religious circles, then, it has not been popular to put God on trial. For centuries human beings have taken themselves to task in order to protect God's innocence, and not without reason. Even at the price of an unwarranted guilt trip, the desire runs strong to separate good and evil neatly. Life is simpler that way, and so theology puts Father in the right and his children in the wrong. At least that tendency held until the idea of sin was replaced by an "I'm OK, you're OK" psychology.

A protesting theodicy finds both of those views wanting. Nobody is OK. Otherwise the slaughter-bench would not be so drenched. And when one says "nobody," God is included as well as humanity. Whether considered in terms of violation of God's will, or simply in terms of goodness that is known and left undone, sin abounds in human life. But Camus is also correct: "Man is not entirely to blame; it was not he who started history."[5]

It is irresponsible to assign responsibility inequitably. God must bear his share, and it is not small unless he could never be described as one for whom all things are possible. God's responsibility is located in the fact that he is the one who ultimately sets the boundaries in which we live and move and have our being. True, since we are thrown into history at our birth, we appear in social settings made by human hands, but ultimately those hands cannot account for themselves. To the extent that they are born with the potential and the power to be dirty, credit for that fact belongs elsewhere. "Elsewhere" is God's address.

Do not take lightly what God's responsibility entails. It means: In the beginning . . . Auschwitz, Hiroshima, and the words of a nine-year-old girl, one of the Vietnamese refugees, who recently was heard to say, " 'I prayed that my death would be quick and merciful.' "[6] The point is not that God predestined or caused such events directly. Some theodicies have taken that position, but not this one. It rejects such conclusions because it assumes the reality of human freedom. At the same time, that freedom—much as some thinkers would like—does not remove God from the dock.

Freedom   Richard L. Rubenstein's penetrating study of the Holocaust, *The Cunning of History*, makes the following observation: "Until ethical theorists and theologians are prepared to face without sentimentality the kind of action it is possible freely to perpetrate under conditions of utter respectability in an advanced, contemporary society, none of their assertions about the existence of moral norms will have much credibility."[7] The inference I want to draw from Rubenstein's assertion is this: Human freedom has been used as God's defense; in fact, it is crucial in his offense.

Using freedom as a defense for God is a well-known strategy. Moving from the idea that freedom is a good, the argument has usually been that God gave freedom to human life in innocence. The gift, to be sure, did include a capacity for self-perversion. God knew that fact and perhaps even that liberty would be abused. Still, the apology continues, God's gift is justified. Only with the freedom we were given can men and women truly be the children of God. Moreover, where sin infests us, God's own freedom is gracious enough to offer forgiveness and love that can release us to try again and also rectify every wrong. On all counts, apparently, God's benevolence is validated even as humanity's is not.

Already the cost-effectiveness of God's creative acts has been challenged. In that challenge a critique of the gift of freedom was implied. To make the critique explicit, the nature of our freedom must be focused. In a word, our freedom is both too much and too little. It is far more an occasion for waste than a defense of God's total goodness can reconcile.

On one hand, freedom constitutes an insufficient defense for God because of its paucity. Two areas of life make this fact evident. First, as Descartes emphasized long ago, human ignorance wreaks havoc everywhere. In his optimism about human reason, however, Descartes underplayed his hand: Too often our freedom is helpless to dispel ignorance in time to save countless victims from their tragic fate. Cancer, for example, kills thousands every year. If we could, we would use our freedom to stop its waste, but a shroud of unknowing is more than the powers of our freedom can presently penetrate. Granted, that situation may provide an opportunity for us to use freedom nobly in a struggle to obtain knowledge or in a battle with pain and death. Meanwhile the mound of corpses rises.

Evidence of the paucity of freedom is not restricted to our struggles against natural forces that can kill. It also exists in the social structures that bind our lives. Rubenstein's example of the Holocaust offers a telling case. The Holocaust was no sport of history. When the fury of Auschwitz was unleashed, the powers at work there were so deeply entrenched that none of humanity's countervailing energy, individual or collective, could halt them before millions perished.

To think of millions, however, may not make the point sharp enough. Consider, therefore, *Sophie's Choice*. Sophie Zawistowska is a Polish survivor of Auschwitz. As William Styron tells her story, his brilliant novel becomes a commentary on the powerlessness of individual freedom as it faces overwhelming forces of social domination. For a time, Sophie has been a privileged prisoner, assigned to secretarial duties in the house of Rudolf Hoess, the commandant of Auschwitz. Urged to use her position to assist the underground resistance movement, Sophie will try to steal a radio from Hoess's house.

Sophie knows where one can be found, a small portable that belongs to Hoess's daughter, Emmi. She passes the girl's room every day on her way upstairs to the office where Hoess does his work. Once she tries for the radio, but Emmi catches her, and Sophie is nearly undone. Her sense of failure runs deep, only less so than the realization that she will never regain her courage to steal the radio again. Sophie knows "how, among its other attributes, absolute evil paralyzes absolutely."[8]

She knows the frailty of freedom not simply because of the incident with the radio, but because of the setting that surrounds it. And nothing is more important in that setting than her children, Jan and Eva. Jan is alive somewhere in the children's camp at Auschwitz. Hoess has promised that Sophie can see him, and her attempted theft took place with the knowledge that she would jeopardize her chance to embrace the boy whose life gives hers a reason for going on. Sophie is not without courage, far from that, but once is enough. She cannot put the radio ahead of her need for Jan.

Who could blame Sophie, especially when Eva is remembered? Eva is gone, gassed. And Sophie's freedom, or the lack of it, shows how pathetic a "free-will defense" for God can be. Eva's life was lost because Sophie was left free to choose. As she disembarked from the stifling train that brought her and the children from Warsaw to Auschwitz, a selection took place. An SS official— Styron calls him Dr. Jemand von Niemand—decided to make freedom real, dreadfully so, by forcing Sophie's choice. Instead of losing both Jan and Eva to the gas, which was the fate of most young children there, Sophie could pick one of hers to live. " '*Ich kann nicht wählen!*' she screamed."[9] I cannot choose . . . and then, so as not to lose them both, Sophie let Eva go. Sophie's choice stayed with her. She experienced liberation in 1945, but only fully in 1947 when she gave up her own life—also by choice.

It is only a story. But there is truth in it because paralysis and untimely death are results of freedom that is allowed, like Sophie's, to be too little. Of course there was heroism in Auschwitz, hers not least of all, and ultimately the death camps died. The price, however, was horrible, and even to suggest that there could be no adequate display of human virtue—or no sufficient glory in heaven—without such testing odds . . . well, that proposition mocks the victims far more than it honors them. Sophie's choice accuses God and rightly so.

The matter does not end there, however, because the freedom God gives us is also too much and too soon. That fact follows as a corollary from what has gone before. So often the waste of human life is our own making. Cancer illustrates that we are free to abuse our bodies until things go too far, and the Holocaust shows that human beings can and will do anything to each other. We have more power, more freedom, than is good for us. Perhaps there was an Eden where all the factors of freedom were in healthy equilibrium. In present history, however, that dream is at best a myth. Our condition smacks too much of the feeling that we are "damned if we do, and damned if we don't"—not in some hell to come, but here and now.

Freedom's defense for God looks more and more like a ploy by the devil's advocate. That defense cannot avoid saying: Only if freedom has the potential to be what it has become can there be a chance for the highest good. But can the end justify the means? That is the question. A protesting theodicy is skeptical because it will not forget futile cries. No good that it can envision, on earth or beyond, is worth the freedom—enfeebled and powerless—that wastes so much life.

Excuses Perhaps Stendahl was right: God's only excuse is that he does not exist. Not so, suggest some contemporary voices. God, they say, has been mistakenly viewed as all-powerful. In fact, his creative activity reveals limitations in his existence, and thus the claim that he is totally benevolent can be preserved. In effect, then, this God's excuse is that he always does the best he can. Originally, he brought order out of chaos—uncreated, primordial, resistant—and fashioned a world of beauty and richness. Within that setting he lured humanity into existence, endowed with freedom to choose. But if God's authority can minimize the confusion that we produce with our liberty, it is also true that he cannot both intervene directly and still retain the integrity of free human creatures. This God holds his breath, as it were, while we act . . . and then the best he can do is to pick up the pieces so that survivors can try again.

Such a view would be fine if the pieces were not so many and so bloody. This God of weakness may indeed be excused, not least because he is hardly worth bothering about. He is simply too ineffectual to forestall waste decisively, unless of course one holds that he has some heretofore unwitnessed potential for eschatological power. On what ground, however, could such a claim be based? Most versions of Jewish and Christian faith would locate that ground in historical events: the Exodus or the Resurrection, for example. But to speak of a God who leads people out of bondage or who raises persons from death is surely *not* to speak of a God who, by history's ongoing testimony, is always doing the best he can.

If God raised Jesus from the dead, he had the might to thwart the Holocaust long before it ended. Coupled with the view that resurrection is not merely the release of an immortal spirit from a lifeless physical body, but rather the re-creation of a person for whom all life has ceased, that premise governs a theodicy of protest. In doing so, it makes God harder to excuse. But that fact, in turn, leads us to ask: Why should anybody bother with a God like this one, who seems so infrequently to do the best that is within his power?

Despair   Things are not going very well. A protesting theodicy does not say that God's love controls the universe, nor does it hold that there is any good sense in claims that find this world to be the best one possible. Thus, it must reckon with despair.

To despair is to lose or give up hope. For our purposes two dimensions of that experience are of special significance. First, this theodicy of protest despairs over the hope that history is evolving toward a Kingdom of God on earth. That claim does not deny that there is progress, which one writer defines as "a condition that is better by far than what it replaces after accounting for any side effects."[10] What it affirms, however, is that all progress is cunning, and so one can agree when Rubenstein states: "The Holocaust bears witness to *the advance of civilization*."[11] Far from assuming that things will get better and better if only we work well enough together, this outlook supposes that human life is always under siege. All gains are precarious, periodic, and problematic. Life is one damned problem after another. Many of them are killing.

And yet the human prospect is not hopeless, nor is it without reasons for joy and thanksgiving. In fact, that prospect can be enhanced to the degree that the widespread experience of despair is turned on itself to yield a spirit of dissent. The logic of this reversal makes a straightforward appeal, namely, that once we realize how strong the good reasons for despair really are, then short of abdicating to waste there is little left to do but to turn and fight. Such responses have no utopian illusions. They stand instead with this conviction: Unjustifiable waste is everlasting, but it deserves no more victories.

Second, our theodicy of protest despairs over the hope that there will be any future good "so great as to render acceptable, in retrospect, the whole human experience, with all its wickedness and suffering as well as all its sanctity and happiness."[12] Put another way: No matter what happens, God is going to be much less than perfectly justified. But wait, someone may say, even if it is true that we cannot now fathom how God could possibly salvage this mess in a way that justifies him perfectly, surely that task can be fulfilled. Indeed, the very claim that with God all things are possible would seem to demand such an option. People can believe in that optimistic outcome if they wish, but dissenters demur and the reason is simply history itself. The irretrievable waste of the past robs God of a perfect alibi. Only if he obliterates truth by wiping out the memory of victims can a protesting "Why?" be stilled forever. So long as that question can sound, the whole human experience stands as less than acceptable.

And yet the human prospect is not hopeless, nor is it without reasons for joy and thanksgiving. Life can be less unacceptable. We know that to be true because from time to time there are works of love that people do. Those realities, linked with despair that finds love not enough, may lead us to affirm life by refusing to give despair the final say. In those experiences, one may discover that the issue of whether God is without any justification depends on what he does with the future, his and ours.

May Your Blessings Be with Us

Power Dissenting moods are at the foundation of my approach to theodicy. But those moods also seek to turn dissent into a religious response that can make more sense out of life, not less, without abandoning honesty in facing life's harshest facts. To fill out that response, particularly with regard to its views about what God might be like, requires first a further assessment of power.

This theodicy of protest affirms the existence of an omnipotent God.[13] That is, God is bound only by his will. Nothing except it determines what he shall do or become. All possibilities are within God's reach, and so he could have created very differently. Likewise, his relation to our world could take many forms even now. The one he establishes may have its reasons, but it is contingent nonetheless.

Why make these affirmations? My answer resides in choices made from experience. In a word, I find that the world cannot account for itself. It demands a creator. My understanding of what that creator might be comes to me through the tradition carried forward in Jewish and Christian scripture. Much, but not all, of that tradition continues to ring true in my life, and thus I work to reconcile those aspects with notes of dissonance. The struggle, more than the result, unfolds here.

If God is sovereign, bound only by his will, then apparently he chooses to be the creator and master of this universe. Although he could intervene dramatically at any point in present history, he elects to let freedom work out its own course as it lives in individuals and communities. Thus, God's "plan" for history is virtually no plan at all. It can release the worst as well as the best that is in us, and therefore the presence of this God may feel like the absence of all Gods.

God could predetermine the future; he declines so as to make freedom real. But if the future is in the making, the past is not, at least not enough. Having committed himself to what took place, God can respond to that choice, but his own omnipotence also binds him. Choosing as he wills, he cannot take back the wasted past completely. Therefore, no good that God can do will totally fill the void.

Everything hinges on the proposition that God possesses—but fails to use well enough—the power to intervene decisively at any moment to make history's course less wasteful. Thus, in spite and because of his sovereignty, this God is everlastingly guilty, and the degrees run from gross negligence to murder. Perhaps we should feel sorry for a God so soiled. Not so, says Berish, one of the characters in Elie Wiesel's *The Trial of God:* "If I am given the choice of feeling sorry for Him or for human beings, I choose the latter anytime. He is big enough, strong enough to take care of Himself; man is not."[14]

God's guilt could be reduced to the extent that he lacks power.

But to the extent that God lacks power, he may also be ineffectual. Short of no God at all, what people have to ask religiously, therefore, is whether we should settle for an innocent but ineffectual God or whether we should run the risks of relating to a God who is really master of the universe but much less than perfectly good by any standards that we can comprehend. Are there any good reasons why such risks should be accepted?

Suffering History refutes more than it confirms God's providential care. And yet there are moments, personal and collective, that hint of something more. Promise lives, for example, in the messianic hopes of Judaism and Christianity. Although interpretations of those hopes are pluralistic and often at odds, a core in both affirms that God can and will intervene to heal and restore. Persons who hunger and thirst after righteousness cannot be filled by those claims alone, but to share in their hope is better than nothing. However, to do so without abandoning the world's victims, confrontations with suffering are required.

A Jewish confrontation with suffering occurs in the continued delay of the Messiah's arrival. Whether that arrival is equated with the collective transformation of Jewish and human spirit, achieved by men and women themselves, or whether it is regarded as God's intervention in the midst of human recalcitrance, the waste keeps piling up. The messianic promise is not easy to accept. It may, in fact, be impossible to believe except as one embraces it as an expression of defiance over what has been permitted. Suffering brought on by such acts of commitment may be redemptive, but if so, those same experiences testify that most suffering is not.

At least once, most Christians say, the Messiah came in Jesus of Nazareth. His life, death, and resurrection may make all the difference in the world for those who accept him, but such promise also enjoins face-to-face encounters with suffering. One of those encounters is prompted by a question: Was God really serious about making all things new in Christ when Calvary could lead to the crematoria of Auschwitz?

If God suffered in Christ—as a blood sacrifice to appease his own wrath over human sin, as a sign of grace to show that nothing can separate the world from his love, as atonement for his own injustice toward men, women, and children, for whatever reason—good sense remains in question. God suffers with humanity, according to Christian claims. But the mass of agony does not have to be, and if God is only a suffering God, then we do indeed need a God to help us. The very idea of a suffering God provokes one to insist: What is going on here?

God's promises call for protests. And yet the same realities that make one dissent against the promises can also be the facts that impel us to struggle toward them—unless, of course, we are willing to let suffering rage with impunity or to resign ourselves to death as the end-in-itself. To see how that tension might be real, consider God's servant Job.

Trust   "Though he slay me, yet will I trust in him" (Job 13:15).[15] Job's ancient declaration is crucial for a theodicy of protest. Indeed, his entire story is at the heart of the matter. Some interpretations highlight Job's "repentance" for daring to question God, stressing how he seemed to receive back his fortune as well. But if one concentrates on the statement quoted above, the situation is different and also more honest.

At this point Job argues. Yes, things are wrong, but the wrong is not his doing, nor is it obviously owing to the other victims, whose loss has plunged Job into a defiant grief. Or, at the very least, there is a serious disproportion between crime and punishment. It cannot and must not be accepted. And yet Job's argument is no rejection of God. Rather, it trusts that God will vindicate him.

Job's trust is bold, even extreme. It entails God's confession that he has treated Job unfairly, yes brutally, for according to the story it was only by God's choice that Job was all but destroyed on the pretense of testing his faithfulness. Job was faithful all right, almost with a vengeance. But did he win or lose? God thundered back with his non-answer, challenging Job with a who-do-you-think-you-are.

Then came Job's repentance. Elie Wiesel suggests, however,

that Job's humility was no simple resignation. Wiesel reads it instead as resistance and rebellion masked in hasty abdication. Ultimately God cannot be defeated, which is both our hope and our despair, but in confessing—when God, with greater reason to do so, did not—Job "continued to interrogate God."[16] A protesting theodicy takes heart from that reading, not least because it implies that Job did not give up. Whatever the form of his protest and so long as it lasted, he could still be saying, "Though he slay me, yet will I trust in him."

Hope   Carl Jung's *Answer to Job* states that "God is not only to be loved, but also to be feared."[17] These days it is religiously unfashionable to talk about fearing God. His love is more in vogue, and religious observance tends to drown out all sense of awe and judgment in gluts of celebration. A theodicy of protest both *acknowledges* and *yearns* for the love of God. It does the former because life is a created gift, one that is basically good and able to become even better. To that assumption it adds risk-filled acceptance of the biblical promises that there shall yet be life more abundant. The yearning moves from that same base, but it is rooted even more in the apprehension that there is too little love to be seen. Men and women do not love as well as they can, but neither does God, and therefore Elie Wiesel is right again: "To have hope in God is to have hope against God."[18]

Such a God has no simple nature. He is tugged and pulled by multiple desires, but he is not at their mercy. They are controlled by his own acts of will. This God is no bumbler. He knows what he is doing, and that reality is the problem. Our protests do him no harm. Indeed, his license gives us a mandate to say what we feel, and we must . . . so long as we speak for the sake of human well-being. When dissent is raised in that spirit, its rebellious care may grip God's heart.

Still, the fact remains: The net result of God's choices is that the world is more wild and wasteful than any good reason that we can imagine would require it to be. Thus, to be for such a God requires some sense of being against him as well. To defend the good as we know it best—especially to carry out God's own commandments that we should serve those in need, heal the sick, feed the hungry, forestall violence—we must do battle against forces that are loose in the world because God permits them.

Job, says Elie Wiesel, "did not suffer in vain; thanks to him, we know that it is given to man to transform divine injustice into human justice and compassion."[19] Neither individually nor collectively can human beings fulfill that task completely. The odds set by God are too high. Nonetheless, it remains possible to be for God by being against God, and the way that we do so best is by giving life in care and compassion for others. Then there is reason for hope on earth and perhaps beyond.

Answers   Most theodicies have a fatal flaw: They legitimate evil. They do so by saying too much or too little as they answer questions posed by waste. The first tendency is illustrated in theories that would make all suffering deserved. The second is found in attempts to insure totally happy endings by appealing to God's unfathomable wisdom and goodness, even though we have not the vaguest notion of how such endings could possibly be. There is a sense, then, in which this theodicy of protest is *antitheodicy*. It has no desire to legitimatize waste. It must be wary of answers or of the lack of them—including its own.

It is no legitimation of evil to acknowledge its existence. This theodicy does so without blinking, and that quality is one of its greatest assets. A possible trap, on the other hand, may lie in its insistence that God is guilty and even without apology for apparent refusal to change his worldly ways in the foreseeable future. Without caution that outlook could become a form of scapegoating, one that places a premium on blaming God, leaving the impression as it does so that there is really not very much that human beings can do.

We do face great odds. Still, there is much that we can do. Indeed we shall have to act or there will be too little action on humanity's behalf. The world—too much, no doubt—is in our hands. For if God listens and answers, it is usually in silence. If he is judge or ally, it is less by intervention that metes out justice in total equity and more by letting events fall as they may to reveal the corrupt absurdity, as well as the grandeur, of what we do together. The future is more open than it ought to be. We have all that we can do and then some, and if we fail to act well, the waste will only increase.

" 'My God, my God, why have you deserted me?' " (Matt. 27:46)[20] Jesus' question is contemporary. It evokes others: Can we learn not to blame God as a way of covering over our responsibilities? Can we learn to be boldly honest with God and with ourselves as a means to deepen compassion? A theodicy of protest must keep raising those questions for itself. It must also keep struggling to answer them affirmatively. Coupled with those emphases, its vision of an omnipotent God, whose nature is a self-controlled mixture that gives us freedom and that may yet reduce evil's waste, is an option that can set human souls on fire for good.

Lord, You Have Been Our Refuge Age after Age

As William James summed up *The Varieties of Religious Experience*, he observed that "no two of us have identical difficulties, nor should we be expected to work out identical solutions." A few sentences later he went on to say, "The divine can mean no single quality, it must mean a group of qualities, by being champions of which in alternation, different men may all find worthy missions."[21] Such wisdom informs all sound theodicies. Human religious needs are diverse. No single response can encompass them all or nourish every spirit. Thus, every good theodicy will be, in part, an anti-theodicy. It will disclaim the full adequacy of its own outlook and that of every other as well.

Imperfect as it is, the theodicy explored here does originate in felt needs. Two are fundamental: first, a sense that human affairs are far worse than any good reason can justify or than our powers alone can alter; and second, a yearning that refuses to settle for despair that the first feeling generates. A God encountered in Jewish and Christian experience makes possible an option that keeps hope from dying, without making the dreary facts unreal.

But this God offers little tranquillity because he defers rescue. He allows us—and thereby participates in—our own undoing.

Life is outrageous. Hardly anyone will deny that conclusion outright. Tragedy, pain, injustice, premature death—all of these and more waste us away. No explanation seems quite able to still our anger, hostility, and sadness. A theodicy of protest believes not only that such emotions are profoundly real, but also that they are in many cases justified. Any religious perspective that fails to give them expression diminishes the human spirit. Whether unintentionally or by design, the Christian emphasis on God's love has had a repressive effect in this regard. It strains to make everything fit the care of a Father who is love itself. For some persons that strain is too much. There may be others for whom an open admission of that fact would bring healthy release. Although the faith of us Christians would not be rendered easier, it would be quickened by quarreling with the claim that "God is love" (I John 4:8),[22] even as we refuse to let it go.

Annie Dillard's poetic book, *Holy the Firm*, is a meditation prompted by the crash of a small airplane. Miraculously, no one was killed. But Julie, a seven-year-old flying with her father, has had her face burnt beyond recognition.

There is a small church in the Puget Sound area where Annie Dillard lives. She believes that its minister, a Congregationalist, knows God. "Once," she writes, "in the middle of the long pastoral prayer of intercession for the whole world—for the gift of wisdom to its leaders, for hope and mercy to the grieving and pained, succor to the oppressed, and God's grace to all—in the middle of this he stopped, and burst out, 'Lord, we bring you these same petitions every week.' After a shocked pause, he continued reading the prayer." For his protest, Annie Dillard adds, "I like him very much."[23]

These vignettes suggest that a theodicy of protest has a place in Christian life. Indeed, it should take that life back to some of its most important origins. For instance, the subheadings in this essay are phrases from Psalm 90.[24] Like many others, that psalm is full of lamentations and awesome questions. It can even be read to include dissenting cries over what God had done and left undone. And yet all of these moods are also lifted up not as rejections of faith and hope, but because God is encountered as one whose good promises can be real. Such outlooks are not restricted to the psalms. We have seen them in Job. Anyone who studies the life of Moses or Abraham, Jeremiah or Ezekiel, will find them there, too.

Of course, Christians may ask whether these Jewish expressions have not been superseded by the New Testament, which apparently plays down such themes, if they are present at all. A second reading, however, reveals notes that may not stand out at first glance. Jesus brings signs of what good can be. He urges people to give their lives for others, and at least some people try. But the world does not yield, then or now, and Jesus himself ends up crucified, God-forsaken. So goes one part of the Christian story, balanced by another that stresses resurrection and victory to come in spite of losses now. Promises, glimpses, *and* failure, waste—taken together, as they must be, those realities make the New Testament a source of protesting faith as well. If that is the case, then Christian churches can enhance the disclosure of those feelings by reaffirming Jewish voices that set them out forthrightly. By doing so, Christian preaching may offer less cheap grace and inspire more the fear of God that provokes righteous rebellion. In a similar spirit, prayer, like that of Annie Dillard's preacher, will aim at peace of mind and more at seeking God's strange ways in the disruption of our plans.

William James distinguished between outlooks that are healthy-minded and sick-souled. The former find that, at worst, evil is instrumental; disagreement drives the latter. The late twentieth century is a time for sick souls. If there are those who can look evil in the eye and still be healthy-minded . . . well, that possibility may be a sign of hope in itself. But healthy minds are not for everybody. The theodicy outlined here is one for sick souls who know that their sickness cannot—must not—be cured, and who likewise refuse to acquiesce because to do so would accomplish nothing.

Long ago a Jewish family was expelled from Spain. Plagued at every turn, they could find no refuge, except that sleep turned into death for them, one by one. At last only the father was left, and he spoke to God:

Master of the Universe, I know what You want—I understand what You are doing. You want despair to overwhelm me. You want me to cease believing in You, to cease praying to You, to cease invoking Your name to glorify and sanctify it. Well, I tell You: No, no—a thousand times no! You shall not succeed! In spite of me and in spite of You, I shall shout the Kaddish, which is a song of faith, for You and against You. This song You shall not still, God of Israel![25]

That Jewish story summarizes well one strand of a protesting theodicy. An ageless dialogue sounds out another. God's creation is at stake. It is far from perfect, and thus . . .

Could you have done better?
Yes, I think so.
You could have done better? Then what are you waiting for? You don't have a minute to waste, go ahead, start working![26]

A theodicy of protest is for those who need it. Like the victims of waste in our own day, who knows how many they may be?

Notes

1. See, for example, Frederick Sontag and John K. Roth, *The American Religious Experience* (New York: Harper & Row, 1972), and also our jointly authored sequel, *God and America's Future* (Wilmington: Consortium Books, 1977). Related themes are discussed in my *American Dreams: Meditations on Life in the United States* (San Francisco: Chandler & Sharp, 1976) and in my article, "William James and Contemporary Religious Thought: The Problem of Evil," in *The Philosophy of William James*, Walter Robert Corti, ed. (Hamburg: Felix Meiner Verlag, 1976).

2. The impact of Elie Wiesel on my religious thought is traced best in my book *A Consuming Fire: Encounters with Elie Wiesel and the Holocaust* (Atlanta: John Knox Press, 1979).

3. G. F. W. Hegel, *Reason in History*, Robert S. Hartman, trans. (Indianapolis: The Bobbs-Merrill Co., 1953), p. 27.

4. I am indebted to my colleague Stephen T. Davis for suggesting this concept of "cost-effectiveness" in relation to God.

5. Albert Camus, *The Rebel*, Anthony Bower, trans. (New York: Vintage Books, 1956), p. 297.

6. I quote from an article by Paul Dean, "Coming to the Aid of the Boat People," which appeared in the *Los Angeles Times* on July 23, 1979. See section IV, pp. 1, 4, and 5.

7. Richard L. Rubenstein, *The Cunning of History* (New York: Harper Colophon Books, 1978), p. 67.

8. William Styron, *Sophie's Choice* (New York: Random House, 1979), p. 392.

9. *Ibid.*, 483.

10. Ben J. Wattenberg, *The Real America* (Garden City: Doubleday & Company, 1974), p. 9.

11. *The Cunning of History*, p. 91 (Rubenstein's emphasis).

12. John Hick, *Evil and the God of Love*, rev. ed. (New York: Harper & Row, 1978), p. 386.

13. Over the years, my views on God's power and his relation to evil have been strongly influenced by the work of Frederick Sontag. See especially his books *The God of Evil* (New York: Harper & Row, 1970), *God, Why Did You Do That?* (Philadelphia: The Westminster Press, 1970); and *What Can God Do?* (Nashville: Abingdon, 1979).

14. Elie Wiesel, *The Trial of God*, Marion Wiesel, trans. (New York: Random House, 1979), p. 133.

15. Quoted from the King James Version.

16. Elie Wiesel, *Messengers of God*, Marion Wiesel, trans. (New York: Random House, 1976), p. 235.

17. C. G. Jung, *Answer to Job*, R. F. C. Hull, trans. (Princeton: Princeton University Press, 1973), p. 99.

18. Elie Wiesel, *The Oath*, Marion Wiesel, trans. (New York: Random House, 1973), p. 78.

19. *Messengers of God*, p. 235.

20. Quoted from the Jerusalem Bible. See also Ps. 22:1.

21. The sentences quoted in this paragraph can be found in *The Varieties of Religious Experience* (Garden City: Doubleday Image Books, 1978), p. 470.

22. Quoted from the Revised Standard Version.

23. Annie Dillard, *Holy the Firm* (New York: Bantam Books, 1979), pp. 58–59.

24. In selecting these phrases, I have drawn from the Revised Standard Version, the Jerusalem Bible, and Today's English Version.

25. Elie Wiesel, *A Jew Today*, Marion Wiesel, trans. (New York: Random House, 1978), p. 136.

26. *Messengers of God*, pp. 35–36.

7

A Visit to Belzec

•

WILLIAM HEYEN

I

This is Belzec,
in the East of Poland,
in the Lublin region
where the fumes of Sobibor,
Maidenek, and Treblinka still
stain the air:
smell the bodies
in the factories' smoke,
smell the sweet gas
in the clover and grass.
This is Belzec
where the death compound's gate
proclaims in Hebrew,
"Welcome to the Jewish State."
This is Belzec.
This is *SS* humor.
Curse them forever
in their black Valhalla.

II

*"At 7:20 a.m. a train arrived from Lemberg with 45 wagons
holding more than 6,000 people. Of these, 1,450 were already
dead on arrival. Behind the small barbed-wire windows, children,
young ones, frightened to death, women and men. As the train
drew in, 200 Ukrainians detailed for the task tore open the doors
and, laying about them with their leather whips, drove the Jews
out of the cars. Instructions boomed from a loudspeaker, order-
ing them to remove all clothing, artificial limbs, and spectacles. . . .*

*"They asked what was going to happen to them. . . . Most of
them knew the truth. The odor told them what their fate was to
be. They walked up a small flight of steps and into the death
chambers, most of them without a word, thrust forward by those
behind them."*

III

Reader, you have walked
into the smoke-streaked mirror
of my dream, but I can't,
or won't remember.
Did my jackboots gleam?
Did I fill out quotas?
Was it before, or after?
Did I close those doors,
or did I die?
I can still feel
iron and cold water on my fingers.
I remember running
along the bank of a river,
under trees with full summer
stars in their branches,
the sky lit up with flares
and the slight murderous arcs of tracers,

the night air wet
with the surgary odors of leaves.
Dogs barked.
Were they mine?
Were they yours?
Was I running from,
or after?

IV

"Inside the chambers SS *men were crushing the people together.
'Fill them up well,'* [Hauptsturmführer *Christian*] *Wirth had
ordered, '700 or 800 of them to every 270 square feet.' Now the
doors were closed. . . .*

*"The bodies were tossed out, blue, wet with sweat and urine, the
legs soiled with feces and menstrual blood. A couple of dozen
workers checked the mouths of the dead, which they tore open
with iron hooks. Other workers inspected anus and genital organs
in search of money, diamonds, gold, dentists moved around
hammering out gold teeth, bridges and crowns. . . ."*

V

Reader, all words are a dream.
You have wandered into mine.
Now, as workers rummage among the corpses,
we will leave for our affairs.

This happened only once, but happened:
one Belzec morning, a boy in deathline
composed a poem, and spoke it.
The words seemed true, and saved him.
The guard's mouth fell open to wonder.

Reader, we have walked together
into the smoke-streaked
terror of Belzec,

and have walked away.
                    Now wind,
and the dawn sun,
                    lift our meeting
to where they lift the human haze
                    above that region's pines.

8

Simple Truths

•

WILLIAM HEYEN

When a man has grown a body,
a body to carry with him
through nature for as long as he can,
when this body is taken from him
by other men and women who happen to be,
this time, in uniform,
then it is clear he has experienced
an act of barbarism,

and when a man has a wife,
a wife to love for as long as he lives,
when this wife is marked with a yellow star
and driven into a chamber she will never leave alive,
then this is murder,
so much is clear,

and when a woman has hair,
when her hair is shorn and her scalp bleeds,
when a woman has children,

Reprinted with permission of the publisher from *The Swastika Poems* (New York: Vanguard Press, Inc.), copyright © 1977, William Heyen.

children to love for as long as she lives,
when the children are taken from her,
when a man and his wife and their children
are put to death in a chamber of gas,
or with pistols at close range, or are starved,
or beaten, or injected by the thousands,
or ripped apart, by the thousands, by the millions,

it is clear that where we are
is Europe, in our century, during the years
from nineteen-hundred and thirty-five
to nineteen-hundred and forty-five
after the death of Jesus, who spoke of a different order,
but whose father, who is our father,
if he is our father,
if we must speak of him as father,
watched, and witnessed, and knew.

and when we remember,
when we touch the skin of our own bodies,
when we open our eyes into dream
or within the morning shine of sunlight
and remember what was taken
from these men, from these women,
from these children gassed and starved
and beaten and thrown against walls
and made to walk the valley
of knives and icepicks and otherwise
exterminated in ways appearing to us almost
beyond even the maniacal human imagination,
then it is clear that this is the German Reich,
during approximately ten years of our lord's time,

and when we read a book of these things,
when we hear the names of the camps,
when we see the films of the bulldozed dead

or the film of one boy struck on the head
with a club in the hands
of a German doctor who will wait
some days for the boy's skull to knit, and will enter
the time in his ledger, and then
take up the club to strike the boy again,
and wait some weeks for the boy's skull to knit,
and enter the time in his ledger again,
and strike the boy again,
and so on, until the boy, who,
at the end of the film of his life
can hardly stagger forward toward the doctor,
does die, and the doctor
enters exactly the time of the boy's death in his ledger,

when we read these things or see them,
then it is clear to us that this
happened, and within the lord's allowance, this
work of his minions, his poor
vicious dumb German victims twisted
into the swastika shapes of trees struck by lightning,
on this his earth, if he is our father,
if we must speak of him in this way,
this presence above us, within us, this
mover, this first cause, this spirit, this
curse, this bloodstream and brain-current, this
unfathomable oceanic ignorance of ourselves, this
automatic electric Aryan swerve, this

fortune that you and I were not the victims, this
luck that you and I were not the murderers, this
sense that you and I are clean and understand, this
stupidity that gives him breath, gives him life
as we kill them all, as we killed them all.

9

The Holocaust as a Problem
in Moral Choice

•

ROBERT McAFEE BROWN

I APPROACH THIS PROBLEM with a mixture of eagerness and healthy dread. Eagerness because the occasion is an important one and I am deeply honored to have been asked to share in it; dread because the assignment outstrips my ability to deal with it, or indeed the ability of any theologian, however well-versed or eminent, to unravel the mystery of this most monstrous of all events in the annals of human evil; but healthy dread, as well, since an audience that has successively been exposed to Elie Wiesel, Lucy Dawidowicz and Dorothy Rabinowitz will already have gained enough insight to be generous toward the failings of anyone cast in the difficult position of following them.

How Can One Dare to Speak?

How does one approach even the outer precincts of "The Holocaust as a Problem in Moral Choice"? How, particularly, does a Christian find an explanation when he remembers that Christians were among the chief participants, almost invariably

Reprinted with permission from *Dimensions of the Holocaust* (Evanston, Ill.: Northwestern University Press), copyright © 1977, Northwestern University.

on the wrong side? I have tried to expose myself to some of the literature and some of the persons for whom the Holocaust has been the normative event of our time and have tried to enter into that experience in ways that on any human level I would have preferred to avoid. Yet, of course, both as a non-Jew and as a non-inhabitant of the camps, I cannot really "enter into" that experience at all. I can therefore hardly claim the right to speak about it. To some it may even seem a blasphemy that I dare to try.

This is a dilemma that has faced even those most personally involved in the Holocaust: how can one speak about the unspeakable? After having written half a dozen novels on the Holocaust, Elie Wiesel wrote a book called *The Oath*, in which he examined the notion that it might have been better to remain silent in the face of such evil than attempt to speak at all. The issue was a genuine one for him; if, after writing half a dozen novels, nothing seemed to have changed in human perceptions about the Holocaust, perhaps silence might have been the more powerful witness. *The Oath* chronicles his realization that if, by the telling of the story of countless deaths, one life can be saved, the story must be told, no matter how painful. If a single life can be saved, one must speak, even if in so doing one breaks (as did the narrator in *The Oath*) a sacred oath made half a century before.

That conclusion indicates why we must dare to speak of events our words will seem to trivialize if not distort. We must do so not only so that the dead are not forgotten; not only as a reminder that we, too, might have been able to play the role of SS guards and feel no inner laceration of the spirit; we must also do so as a way of seeking to ensure that such events can never happen again. For we must face the painful reality that there is that in our nature that could allow it to happen again, that could even will its repetition. And if retelling the story can alert us to such possibilities, and increase our resolve that they must be avoided, the retelling, however painful, must take place.

A Variety of Responses

I have discovered that there are many kinds of responses to the Holocaust among both Jews and Christians. For Richard Rubenstein, the reality of Auschwitz has destroyed the reality of God. For him, no other conclusion is possible. God, if God existed after Auschwitz, could only be a moral monster. For Emil Fackenheim, on the other hand, to engage in such a denial of God in the face of Auschwitz would be, as he says in *God's Presence in History*, to grant Hitler a posthumous victory: setting out in his lifetime to destroy the Jews, Hitler would finally have succeeded beyond his lifetime in destroying Judaism. For Elie Wiesel, to whom I shall shortly turn, the greatest problem posed by the Holocaust seems to be the silence of God. One may not have expected much from man; one surely could have expected more from God. Why did God not speak or act? Why did God seemingly remain indifferent? How can one do other than contend with a God so apparently callous?

There are also varieties of Christian responses to the Holocaust. These have been longer in coming and are only now beginning to receive significant articulation. Some Christians are not even willing to confront the issue; it is absent from their deliberation in ways that are harder and harder to understand. Others are so devastated by their discovery of Christian complicity in the event that they are immobilized by guilt. Still others react defensively, seeking to exonerate themselves and their Christian heritage from any responsibility, usually by blaming it on others or letting a few brave Christians go bail for the massive numbers of indifferent and complicit. A few go so far as to assert that there has been an in-built anti-Semitism in historical Christianity that must be purged and replaced by a radical theological reconstruction.

Two Overall Problems

In all these responses, and others that could be noted if space permitted, there are at least two widely-shared problems. The first of these is the problem of *responsibility*. Who is to be held accountable? How widely must the net of accountability be spread? It includes Hitler. It includes Eichmann. Does it include the guards in the camps, the "good Germans" who only "followed orders"? Does it include those who knew what was going on and chose to remain silent? Does it include those who feared what was going on and took special pains not to find out? Does it include the Allied high command who, when told what was going on in Auschwitz, still would not give the order to bomb the railroad tracks leading to the death camp? Does it include the churches and the leaders of the churches who were silent even when many facts were known? This question of responsibility is a particularly burning one for non-Jews, though Wiesel and others have demonstrated that in this period there were even some Jews who preferred not to get involved—a fact I cite as a tribute to Jewish honesty rather than as a means of assuaging Christian consciences.

The second problem is one that all of us share—Jews and Christians alike—even though we approach it in different ways. This is the crisis of *belief* that the Holocaust forces on us. For who, whether Jew or Christian, can believe in a God in whose world such things take place? The perennial mystery of evil, the source of our great vulnerability as believers, reaches unique expression in the Holocaust. No theodicy can encompass this event so that its wounds are closed or its scars healed. It forever precludes easy faith in God or in humanity. Both are placed under judgment, and a verdict of acquittal may not be lightly rendered, if at all, to either party. (To this theme of the crisis of belief I will return toward the end of the present essay.)

The Discipline of Listening

How, then, are we to approach the Holocaust as "a problem of moral choice"? My first task as a Christian must be to listen, and to ask, "Who has the authority to command my ear?" Not the one who says it did not happen. Not the one who says it happened long ago, and we now have more pressing problems. Not the one who says it was only a temporary deviation from an otherwise reliable human norm. Not the one who simply theorizes. No, the one to whom I must first listen is the one who was there, the survivor, the one who knows it happened because he bears forever the scars, both physical and psychic, of the ordeal. In my case, listening to one particular survivor has been particularly important. He has been perhaps the most important single theological influence on me in the last four or five years, even though he makes no claim to be a theologian and prefers to call himself a teller of tales. He is Elie Wiesel. He has been wrestling with the moral dilemma of the Holocaust for a third of a century— he was deported to Auschwitz in 1944. He writes as a Jew and he insists that the more he speaks of his own particularity, out of his Jewishness, the more he speaks universally to non-Jews as well. I can testify to that. He speaks to me.

His words are written out of fire and blood, the fire of the crematoria and the blood of the victims. So they destroy. Just as fire and blood are symbols of destruction, words nurtured by them produce destruction. They destroy illusions, complacency, indifference. But in both the Jewish and Christian traditions, fire and blood have creative possibilities as well. For fire can purge and blood can cleanse; they are symbols of new beginnings as well. So also with Wiesel's words. When their surgery has been accomplished—even while it is being accomplished—they become instruments of healing, reaching out over deep chasms of pain, not to anesthetize or to hide but to transform. Elie Wielsel's pilgrimage through his own "valley of the shadow of death" and beyond, through his series of wrestlings with the question of what we do in the face of the greatest moral obscenity of history —constitutes for me both a searing and a healing experience. As one who has first been called upon to listen, I propose to share some reflections on that listening, as I have had to walk, imaginatively, the path that for Wiesel was not imagination but ugly reality.

Wiesel's Responses to Monstrous Moral Evil

How does one respond, then, in the face of monstrous moral evil? We can distinguish at least five stages in Wiesel's pilgrimage.

The first response is the response not of a choice inwardly made but of a decision outwardly imposed. In the face of monstrous evil it may be that we are simply cast in the role of *victims*. This role is described in Wiesel's first book, *Night*, the autobiographical account of a boy of fifteen, loaded with friends and family onto cattle cars, experiencing the tortures of thirst and hunger and madness, the splitting up of families at the entrance to the camps, and the subsequent dehumanization to which all the "survivors" were subjected. Wiesel had been a pious Hasidic Jew, and on the very first night his Hasidic faith was destroyed. After being parted from his mother and sister forever, he walked into the camp with his father and discovered a large ditch from which giant flames were leaping. Wiesel writes, "They were burning something. A lorry drew up and delivered its load—little children. Babies!" (*Night*, p. 42). He knows that this is a nightmare, that it is not to be believed, that the terrible dream will come to an end. And it is indeed a nightmare, but it is in fact true, and Elie Wiesel will never wake up to find that its truth has been negated. And so, on that night, his childhood faith was destroyed: "Never shall I forget those flames which consumed my faith forever." (*Night*, p. 44) When morning came, he writes, "A dark flame had entered into my soul and devoured it." And the evening and the morning were the first day. Only the first day.

The rest of the journal italicizes the powerless and helpless role of a victim, the unwilling recipient of actions over which he has no control, in this case given unbearable poignancy because they are being etched in the life of a fifteen-year-old boy.

When the war ends, and he is finally released, Wiesel spends the first weeks of his liberation in the hospital at the point of death because, as he writes with crushing honesty, when the prisoners were released, all they could think about was food—and so got stomach poisoning.

One day I was able to get up, after gathering all my strength. I wanted to see myself in the mirror hanging on the opposite wall. I had not seen myself since the ghetto. From the depths of the mirror, a corpse gazed back at me. (*Night*, p. 127)

One may unwillingly be cast in the role of victim. If there are any choices, it would seem preferable to be the *executioner* rather than the victim, and that role is explored in Wiesel's second book, a powerful short novel, *Dawn*. The narrator, Elisha, has "survived" the concentration camps at the end of the war, and while living in Paris is urged by Gad, a leader of Palestinian guerrilla forces, to go to Palestine to work for the establishment of the state of Israel.

Gad pleads all night long with Elisha. No longer, he argues, can Jews simply be the passive victims of historical fate. They must seize their fate in their own hands. He argues convincingly that the only thing to do is to go to Palestine with the guerrilla forces and engage in whatever terrorist activities are necessary to drive out the British and ensure the establishment of a Jewish state. And as dawn is rising in Paris, described as "a pale, prematurely weary light, the color of stagnant water," Gad looks out and says, "Here is the dawn. In our land it is very different. Here the dawn is gray; in Palestine it is red like fire." (*Dawn*, p. 31) Elisha accepts.

They go to Palestine. Elisha is trained, participates in a raid and then, still very young, is chosen to shoot a hostage, John Dawson, who has been seized in reprisal for the seizure of one of the Palestinian leaders. The execution is to take place at dawn. Here is a reversal of roles; as Elisha goes down into the cell under the ground to do the deed, he can almost feel the Nazi swastika on his arm, as though he were now part of the SS troops he had abhorred. He would like to be able to hate John Dawson, because that might give moral meaning to the act, but he cannot whip up a frenzy. When the time comes that he must calculatingly pull the trigger, the shot goes through John Dawson's skull and Elisha comments, "That's it. It's done. I've killed. I've killed . . ." And then he says not "I've killed John Dawson," but rather, "I've killed Elisha." (*Dawn*, p. 126.) Although the victim has become an executioner, the execution turns out to be a self-execution. Murder is a form of suicide.

When Elisha goes upstairs to the Palestinian dawn, the dawn is not the dawn that God had promised, a dawn "red like fire." Instead, "The night left behind it a grayish light the color of stagnant water." It is still the dawn of Paris, not the dawn of the new country and the new hope.

So if it will not solve anything to accept the role of victim, neither will it solve anything to switch roles and become an executioner.

In a third book, which in the original French was called *Le Jour* (Day) but in English is called *The Accident*, we have another young survivor of the Holocaust, this time named Eliezer, Wiesel's own name, who is still trapped in a past he cannot escape. The "accident" is his being run over by a taxi, although he sees in retrospect that it was an accident only in the most euphemistic sense, since he realized that he had willed not to step out of the taxi's way, and had welcomed the possibility of death as a possible escape from the past. He has seen himself only as a "messenger from the dead," among the living. He feels that he brings only death to those whom he confronts. He cannot find a way to escape from the past and affirm the present. He cannot bring himself to engage in a genuine act of love or sharing or commitment.

He has an artist friend, Guyula, who desperately tries to persuade him that this must be done—that he must choose the living rather than the dead, and ruthlessly, if necessary, stamp out the past. As Eliezer is recuperating in the hospital after the accident, Guyula paints his portrait. When the portrait is shown to Eliezer, it is clear that Guyula has ferreted out Eliezer's secret, his will to die. He pleads with Eliezer to love Kathleen and to let her love him; and then, to dramatize the need for a real break with the past, he lights a match to the portrait and burns it.

But it doesn't quite work. For when Guyula goes out, he leaves the ashes. The past is still there. The past is only destructive.

There seems no way to stamp it out and begin again, free of its destructive grip.

Each of these first three books, then, leads into a cul-de-sac. It is only in the fourth book, *The Town Beyond the Wall*, that a new set of possibilities emerges. In this work, perhaps the most fruitful of all of Wiesel's writings, there are three further probings of the question. One of the options, madness, is creatively ambiguous; another, the option of spectator, must be utterly rejected; while the third, the option of participant, provides the beginnings of an extraordinary breakthrough.

On the flyleaf of *The Town Beyond the Wall* is a statement by one of Dostoevski's characters, "I have a plan—to go mad." And *madness* is explored as another way to deal with monstrous moral evil. Mad people are found in all of Wiesel's novels, often as the purveyors of the only true wisdom to be found within the works themselves. On close examination there seem to be two kinds of madness under discussion. (For this distinction, and many other insights within the present essay, I am indebted to a number of articles by Byron L. Sherwin.) There is what could be called "clinical madness," which describes those who simply give up, throw in the towel, and insulate themselves from the rest of the world, refusing to relate at all, living finally in total isolation. That, of course, is another cul-de-sac, a way without promise or hope.

But there is another kind of madness portrayed by Wiesel, what some have called "moral madness." This is the madness of those who said, in effect, "If this world of the Holocaust is to be described as a world of sanity, give me madness any day." When Wiesel himself went to the Eichmann trial in Jerusalem after the war, he was staggered with the ease with which it was possible to certify to the court that Eichmann was "sane." Wiesel wrote, in his *One Generation After:*

It occurred to me that if he were sane, I should choose madness. It was he or I. For me, there could be no common ground with him. We could not inhabit the same universe or be governed by the same laws. (p. 6)

By the same logic, who in the world of the 1930's and the 1940's was sane and who was mad? Were those who were burning babies the ones who were sane, or were those who, for whatever reason, refused to sanction or be part of such actions, the ones who were truly sane?

Mosche, the "madman," was so described because he told people that Jews were being cremated, when everybody knew that such things don't happen in the twentieth century. Wiesel suggests, in other words, that the attitude which the world calls madness may in fact be the true sanity, seeing things as they really are, refusing to accept the values and patterns and standards that were regnant in Europe at that time. Such persons may have had a higher degree of sanity than those around them who called them mad.

So the response of madness, while ambiguous, is an ongoing response that needs increasing attention as a possible moral stance in the face of monstrous evil. For we too, in our era, have burned babies in the name of the American way of life—the napalm of the U.S. Air Force in southeast Asia is simply a more sophisticated weapon than the gasoline of the funeral pyres of Auschwitz.

Another role, one which Michael, the protagonist of *The Town Beyond the Wall*, rejects unambiguously, is the role of *spectator*. After the war, Michael returns to his home town of Szerencsevaros not quite sure why he does so but knowing that he must make his peace with the past in that place from which he had been deported by the Nazis a few years earlier. (Here is a significant advance beyond *The Accident*. Instead of trying to destroy the past, as Guyula had urged, Michael must find what salvation he can by confronting the past and meeting it head on.) Not until he revisits the town square, the scene of the earlier deportation, does the reason for his need to return become clear. Suddenly it clicks. He remembers that there was a face in one of the windows, an impassive face that watched the deportation with no sense of engagement, no sense of involvement. The face of a spectator. And Michael reflects:

This, this was the thing I had wanted to understand ever since the war. Nothing else. How a human being can remain indifferent. The executioners I understood; also the victims, though with more difficulty. For the others, all the others, those who were neither for nor against, those who sprawled in passive patience, those who told themselves, "The storm will blow over and everything will be normal again," those who thought themselves above the battle, those who were permanently and merely spectators—all those were closed to me, incomprehensible. (p. 159)

The spectator still lives in Szerencsevaros. Michael talks to him and can discover no sense of passion or concern even after the event. And he makes an awesome discovery about himself. He discovers that he cannot hate the spectator, for, as he says, "Hatred implies humanity." All he can feel is contempt, a contempt which implies not humanity but something less than humanity, something decadent. It is noteworthy that the spectator realizes this and seeks desperately to be hated, because hatred will at least be an acknowledgment of his humanity and personhood. But Michael refuses to give him even that satisfaction.

For Wiesel, remaining a spectator is the most morally reprehensible response of all. The one who simply opts out, the one who will take no part, the one who will be neither for nor against, is not only inhuman, but is in reality *against*, for the spectator by his lack of involvement casts his vote for those who are doing the dirty work.

Where beyond these roles can one go? Wiesel develops a creative alternative in the latter part of *The Town Beyond the Wall*. It is a role that cannot be described by a single word like "victim," "executioner," "madman" or "spectator." But it is a role that can at least be pointed to by such words as "reciprocity," "identification," "sharing," perhaps even "love." Let us call it the role of *participant*, of one who decides, even in the face of terrible risk, to make an act of identification with another, to side with the victim.

This role is powerfully illustr.ted in two relationships in *The*

Town Beyond the Wall. The first is the relationship between Michael and Pedro, a man with whom Michael begins to be able to relate as they build up a sense of mutual trust for one another —a quality that Michael, as a survivor of the death camps, had never since been able to feel toward another person. Pedro and Michael begin to discover that they can share, and that in sharing, their own identities become bound up with one another. As they are parting, Pedro says to Michael of their previous conversation, "I won't forget last night. From now on you can say, 'I am Pedro,' and I, 'I am Michael.'" (*The Town Beyond the Wall*, p. 131) Pedro can henceforth be identified only in relation to Michael, and Michael only in relation to Pedro. It is this sense of reciprocity, of participation, that frees Michael to be able to look at and engage in the human venture once again. He is soon called upon to test its reality.

Michael carries this precious truth with him into the prison cell in which he shortly finds himself incarcerated with a prisoner who has gone mad, totally cut off from the world, incapable of initiating any response whatsoever. Michael realizes that relationship must be established, or in a short time both of them will be mad. In an imaginary conversation, Pedro says to him, "Re-create the universe. Restore that boy's sanity. Cure him. He'll save you." (*The Town Beyond the Wall*, p. 182) This is the creative possibility that Pedro has offered to Michael in a compressed juxtaposition of five words: "Cure him. He'll save you." The mad prisoner needs Michael. Michael needs the mad prisoner. They must find one another, enter into relationship with one another. And so Michael sets out to break through the recesses of madness to discover a point at which relationship can begin. For, as he says, "One of us will win and if it isn't me we're both lost!" (*The Town Beyond the Wall*, p. 185.) By various devices Michael begins to elicit little flickers of response from the other, enough so that he can say to the one who is as yet uncomprehending:

One day the ice will break . . . You'll tell me your name and you'll ask me 'Who are you?' and I'll answer, 'I'm Pedro.' And that will be a proof that man survives, that he passes himself along. Later, in another prison, someone will ask your name and you'll say, 'I'm Michael.' And then you will know the taste of the most genuine of victories. (*The Town Beyond the Wall*, pp. 188–189)

And as the book ends, Wiesel writes of the prison counterpart to Michael, "The other bore the biblical name of Eliezer, which means *God has granted my prayer.*" (*The Town Beyond the Wall*, p. 189) It is highly significant that Wiesel gives to "the other" his own name—a clear affirmation that for Wiesel himself it is in relationship with another, in participation in the lot of the victim or potential victim, that a meaning can begin to be found that draws one out of the shell of isolation and depersonalized existence represented by the roles of victim, executioner and spectator.

At the end of this book night is receding and dawn is breaking, not the false dawn that greeted Elisha after he shot John Dawson, but the true dawn, full of fresh promise for a new day.

A way to summarize the extraordinary progression that has taken place in these books is to compare their endings. At the conclusion of *Night*, Wiesel looks into a mirror and sees himself as a corpse. At the end of *Dawn* Elisha looks out a window and likewise sees only a reflection of himself. He knows what this means, for he has been told by an old man ("mad," naturally) that if he looked in a window and saw a face, he could know that it was night—not dawn, not day, but night. At the end of *The Accident* Eliezer is looking only at a portrait of himself.

In all of those situations, the protagonist is still locked into himself, *seeing only himself*. But at the end of *The Town Beyond the Wall* he is looking into *the face of another*, and in that reciprocity, in that sharing, it is clear that creativity and healing have truly begun. Let us further note, as a transition to what follows, that at the end of the next book, *The Gates of the Forest*, the protagonist is in Williamsburg as part of a group that has formed a minyan for a service. He has found his way back to the midst of the Hasidic community. As the book ends, Gavriel is saying kaddish for his dead friend, giving expression to a relationship that extends beyond himself, beyond even another human being, to the God to whom the prayer is being offered.

Is There Still a Role for God?

I have tried to suggest that within the arena of the re-creation of human relationship and trust, Wiesel sees the possibility of rebuilding a life that has been destroyed by the Holocaust, and that in such sharing the reality of God begins once again to intrude.

But we must not jump to easy formulas or answers. It still remains difficult to talk about the Holocaust, difficult to talk about God, and even more difficult to talk about these together, without seeming to blaspheme. How can this ever be done?

Let us recall that for Wiesel it is the questions that count, not the answers. He is rightly suspicious of those who offer answers. He recalls a question to one of the participants in the Eichmann trial, in which the participant was asked if he could now discern a meaning in Auschwitz. The reply came, "I hope I never do. To understand Auschwitz would be even worse than not to understand it." Such a response is important. If we have a view of God into which Auschwitz somehow "fits," if we can conceive of a universe congruent with Auschwitz, then such a God must be a moral monster and such a universe a nightmare beyond imagination.

Nevertheless, for Wiesel and for many others the issue will not go away. He must *contest* with God, concerning the moral outrage that somehow seems to be within the divine plan. How can one affirm a God whose "divine plan" could include such barbarity? For Wiesel, the true "contemporary" is not the modern skeptic, but the ancient Job, the one who dared to ask questions of God, even though Wiesel feels that Job gave in a little too quickly at the end.

There is another way to approach the relation of God to the Holocaust. We must note that when Wiesel is writing about the relationship between person and person, he is also writing about the relationship between persons and God. Each relationship sheds light upon the other. The Hasidic tale with which he concludes *The Town Beyond the Wall* shows how this double dimension suffuses his writing:

> Legend tells us that one day man spoke to God in this wise:
> "Let us change about. You be man, and I will be God. For only one second."
> God smiled gently and asked him, "Aren't you afraid?"
> "No. Are you?"
> "Yes, I am," God said.
> Nevertheless he granted man's desire. He became a man, and the man took his place and immediately availed himself of his omnipotence: he refused to revert to his previous state. So neither God nor man was ever again what he seemed to be.
> Years passed, centuries, perhaps eternities. And suddenly the drama quickened. The past for one, and the present for the other, were too heavy to be borne.
> As the liberation of the one was bound to the liberation of the other, they renewed the ancient dialogue whose echoes come to us in the night, charged with hatred, with remorse, and most of all, with infinite yearning. (*The Town Beyond the Wall*, p. 190)

What happens (in Buber's phrase) "between man and man," also happens between man and God. And the qualities of the one relationship are likewise true of the other. In both relationships there is hatred. In both relationships there is remorse. In both relationships, also, there is infinite yearning.

Menachem, the believing Jew who was for a while in Michael's prison cell in Szerencsevaros, is surely echoing Wiesel's own yearning question when he asks, "Why does God insist that we come to him by the hardest road?" (*The Town Beyond the Wall*, p. 146) Wiesel (who lived through Auschwitz) once had an exchange with Richard Rubenstein (who did not, but for whom Auschwitz meant the death of God and the consequent difficulty of living in a world where belief in God is no longer possible). Wiesel said:

I will tell you, Dick, that you don't understand those in the camps when you say that it is more difficult to live today in a world without God. NO! If you want difficulties, choose to live with *God* . . . The real tragedy, the real drama, is the drama of the believer. (Littell and Locke, eds., *The German Church Struggle and the Holocaust*, p. 274)

So if it is true that when Wiesel is writing about man he is writing about God, and when he is writing about God he is writing about man, we may retrace the human pilgrimage we took a few moments ago, and make the fascinating discovery that the roles Wiesel attributes to human beings in responding to monstrous evil are similar to the roles human beings have frequently attributed to God.

It is clear, for example, that many today believe with Rubenstein that in the face of the reality of the Holocaust, God has become a *victim*. A survey of the Holocaust and post-Holocaust world leads them to proclaim that "God is dead." The phrase, to be sure, was initiated long before the Holocaust, but the Holocaust has put the final seal upon the verdict; a God worthy of the name has not survived. God is victim.

There are others who, whether they intended it or not, come perilously close to describing God as *executioner*, God as the one who is finally the author of evil. This is a difficult conclusion for orthodox Christian theology to avoid, at least to the degree that logic inhabits orthodox formulations, for any theology that postulates belief in an omnipotent God has a difficult time evading the conclusion that an all-powerful God is ultimately responsible for evil. Such a God seems either to have willed, or decreed, or at the very least, "permitted" it.

There are some who would say that God is *mad*, a diabolical creator, or at least (in the other notion of madness we examined) a God who, like some of those who are humanly denominated as mad, has a totally different set of priorities and criteria for action. Wiesel, indeed, has written a play called *Zalman, or The Madness of God*, in which he sets forth the notion of a response to a God who makes demands so different from those of the world that those who respond will find themselves in grave difficulty with the world. Perhaps God and the world are simply incommensurate. That could be a consolation. It could also be a new source of despair.

The notion of God as *spectator* has frequently characterized human thinking about God; whatever else we affirm about God, we find that God seems to be aloof and removed from where we are. Either God can do nothing about evil in the world, or refuses to do anything about it. In either case, God becomes a spectator to evil. This, I think, is what Wiesel is wrestling with when he talks about the silence of God in the face of cries for meaning. And just as the human role of spectator seems the most morally culpable, so also would the divine role of spectator seem to be the most damaging charge we could lay against God—that the God who knew what was going on did nothing.

There remains the possibility of describing God as *participant* in the struggle with evil. This seems to me a possibility toward which Wiesel's thought has been moving. In the account of the reciprocity between Michael and Pedro, and between Michael and the silent prisoner, in *The Town Beyond the Wall*, we sense that in that give and take, that sharing, that risk-in-love, whatever has been meant by the word "God" is broodingly and hauntingly present. The theme is further pursued by Wiesel, not only in *The Gates of The Forest* and *A Beggar in Jerusalem*, but also in a yet later writing, *Ani Maamin*, which employs an even more direct use of Messianic imagery as a way of stating a demand that God share, at least, in the plight of creation. While we cannot pursue the themes of this remarkable poem in detail, we must note certain things that Wiesel emphasizes.

Ani Maamin is the libretto for a cantata Wiesel wrote that was set to music by Darius Milhaud shortly before his death. The words come from Maimonides' statement of faith, "Ani maamin beviat ha-mashiah"—"I believe in the coming of the Messiah." How, Wiesel asks, can a Jew still sing that song? Was it not lost in the camps? How is it that those who have hoped for a Messiah, who have hoped for a divine vindication in history, can continue to believe, when such belief has received no vindication? Could one *still* hope for a vindication? What does it take to bring the Messiah, if God really cares?

With such questions in mind, Wiesel retells the old Midrashic tale of Abraham, Isaac and Jacob going down from heaven to earth to find out what was going on, and reporting back to the divine throne. In Wiesel's version of the story, the terrestrial visitation occurs during the time of the Holocaust. The patriarchs report back to God. But no matter how loudly they talk, no matter how painfully they describe the horror, there is nothing but silence from the divine throne. Nothing but silence.

So the Messianic question for Wiesel becomes the question: *The world is so evil, why does the Messiah not come?* What does it take to bring him? Are not six million dead enough? And even if he came after six million deaths, would that not already be too late? That is the Jewish form of the question. But let us note that there is a Christian form of the question which is just the reverse. If the Jewish form of the question is, "The world is so evil, why does the Messiah not come?" the Christian form of the question is surely: *The Messiah has come, why is the world so evil?* In a presumably redeemed world, redemption is not so evident. Perhaps a time is coming when, at this point of their greatest division, namely their conflicting interpretations of the Messianic claim, Jews and Christians can begin to acknowledge that they are, among all the religions of the world, at least dealing with the same problem. Both acknowledge that a spectator God would indeed be a moral obscenity; that, somehow, to talk of love must mean to talk about participation and sharing.

And the extraordinary thing that happens at the end of Wiesel's drama is this: when the patriarchs have exhausted their patience and elect to return to the children of earth with a report of divine indifference, each tells the story of a Jew who continued to believe—who continued to believe *in spite of* everything, against all odds, with no conceivable reason to do so. And *this*, so the narrator informs us, breaks through the divine impassivity. The cumulative impact of the three stories reduces God to tears, tears of love. And as Abraham, Isaac and Jacob turn to go to earth, we are told:

They leave heaven and do not, cannot, see that they are no longer alone: God accompanies them, weeping, smiling, whispering: *Nitzhuni banai*, my children have defeated me, they deserve my gratitude. (*Ani Maamin*, p. 105)

This is no *deus ex machina* victory that ties everything together. Wiesel immediately writes, "The Word of God continues to be heard. *So does the silence of his dead children*." (*Ani Maamin*, p. 105, italics added) But it is a powerful evocation of the theme of participant as a role we can be audacious enough to ascribe to God as well.

How, Finally, Do We "Respond"?

We have looked at some of Wiesel's responses to monstrous evil: some may have no choice but to be victims; others, seeing evil's immensity, may capitulate and become evil's enablers, opting for the role of executioners; some may choose suicide or madness as attempts to cope with the problem; others may elect the ultimate cop-out of being spectators, or even the worse cop-out of pretending that the evil didn't really happen. Finally, some may insist that however feeble the effort may seem, it is crucial to side with those who are victims or potential victims and to do so in actions of participation, identification, and sharing, believing that only thus can there be created a counterforce whose very power, whose very unexpected power, may lie in its seeming fragility. Those who do so may or may not acknowledge that whatever terms they use, they will be wrestling with God, posing questions and remaining unsatisfied with answers, particularly answers that seem to satisfy and relieve them of further responsibility.

Woven into all those responses is a further response, mentioned early in these pages and so patent that we may almost have overlooked it. For we can also respond to monstrous evil by *chronicling it*, reporting it, reminding all listeners that whatever else they forget they may not forget *that* evil, lest they make its repetition possible.

Can one, however, chronicle a unique event—an event incommensurate with all other events—in such a way that it speaks to

those in other situations? Some would argue that the very uniqueness of the Holocaust renders inappropriate any attempt to relate
it to other events, lest it seem to be scaled down to just another
instance of moral perversity.

I disagree. I want to test the reason for my disagreement, so
that if I am wrong I can be further instructed. Start with the
patent truth that we can never "justify" the Holocaust or, indeed,
any instance of evil. We must always remain outraged, and resist
the drift toward complacency that time and distance so easily
induce. But continue with a recognition that we not only have
an opportunity, but an obligation, to make use of the Holocaust
for some kind of creative end. We point to good and positive
events of the past as events that cast light on the rest of experience: Moses before Pharaoh saying, "Let my people go!" The
Exodus and the giving of the Law, the prophet of the Exile
singing "Comfort, comfort my people, says your God." Perhaps
we need to point also to evil and dark events of the past. If we
passionately exhort people to emulate great events, perhaps we
must also passionately exhort people to repudiate dark events, to
put them so far off that they can never be repeated.

It may be that the fires of Auschwitz are powerful enough to
illumine otherwise dark corners of our moral landscape, making
us aware of present acts of human demonry we would not otherwise see. Those fires have served a sensitizing purpose for Jews
in relation to subsequent Jewish persecution in Russia, in relation
to threats against the survival of Israel, in relation to anti-Semitic
remarks that have recently emanated from the Pentagon. I think
they can serve that purpose for the rest of us as well.

I have recently returned from a visit to Chile, Argentina and
other Latin American countries. On the surface all seems well—
just as on the surface all seemed well in Germany in 1933. But
in the light of the fires of Auschwitz it was clear to me that all
was *not* well in Chile and Argentina—just as all was not well in
Germany in 1933. Arrests, "disappearances," confiscation, torture,
all the marks of diabolical cunning, are present just below the
surface, but not below the surface to those who can see. I think

we are finally challenged by the Holocaust to the daring and frightening notion that an obscenity can be used as a way of forestalling other obscenities. If we can so affirm, then there is hope that the Holocaust, unredeemably evil in itself, could be a grotesque beacon, in the light of which we could gird ourselves against its repetition toward any people, in any time, in any place. *And I believe that unless we can use it as such a beacon, the Nazis have finally won.*

Wiesel and other Jews look to Israel as they make this point, but they look elsewhere as well—to Vietnam, to Chile, to the Sohel, to Bangladesh, to any place where people are suffering. I do not believe there exists a people who wants to say, "Only our pain is important." I believe there exists a people who not only wants to say, but does say, "Because of the magnitude of the pain we have suffered, we know that there is no pain anywhere that can be ignored. We know that pain everywhere must be combatted."

There is great wisdom in some advice offered by Azriel in *The Oath:* "So you hope to defeat evil? Fine. Begin by helping your fellow man. Triumph over death? Excellent. Begin by saving your brother." (*The Oath*, p. 14) For, as the narrator later says to us all, "Every truth that shuts you in, that does not lead to others, is inhuman." (*The Oath*, p. 73)

Can one, then, out of ashes and bitterness, affirm more than ashes and bitterness? Wiesel himself is proof that one can. He has earned the right to be heard. In the passage with which I conclude (from Littell and Locke, op. cit., pp. 276–77), Wiesel speaks to Jews, but as always, in such a way as to include the rest of us as well:

When Rabbi Ishmael, one of the ten martyrs of the faith in Roman times, was led to his death, a heavenly voice was heard, saying, "Ishmael, Ishmael, should you shed one tear I shall return the universe to its primary chaos." And the Midrash says that Rabbi Ishmael was a gentleman and did not cry. And I couldn't understand that for quite a while. Why didn't he cry? The hell with it! If this is the price to pay, who needs it? Who wants this kind of world? Who wants to live in it? Yet there are many reasons why he didn't cry.

One, he was a martyr. Two, he obeyed. Three, the last and most poetic ultimate reason why he didn't cry was because he wanted to teach us a lesson in Judaism . . . Even while dying, he wanted to teach us a lesson: Yes, I could destroy the world and the world deserves to be destroyed. But to be a Jew is to have all the reasons in the world to destroy and *not to destroy!* To be a Jew is to have all the reasons in the world to hate the Germans and *not to hate them!* To be a Jew is to have all the reasons in the world to mistrust the church and *not to hate it!* To be a Jew is to have all the reasons in the world not to have faith in language, in singing, in prayers, and in God, but *to go on telling the tale, to go on carrying on the dialogue,* and to have my own silent prayers and quarrels with God.

Amen.

10

Anti-Zionism
and the Christian Psyche

•

EDWARD H. FLANNERY

THE CONDITION OF JEWISH-CHRISTIAN relations can be learned from happenings in the world as well as from formal conversations between Christians and Jews. Events of contemporary history are, in effect, perhaps the best clarifiers of the past and gauges of the future of these relations and can thus contribute to an understanding of the nature, causes, and prospects of our present misunderstandings.

This paper proposes to discuss two such events—the Nazi holocaust and the emergence of the State of Israel—both rich sources for insights into these misunderstandings. They are, in a sense, incommensurate events, indeed polar opposites. It is possible to see them as positive and negative limits of Jewish post-biblical history. This very polarity is what constitutes their interest to us, because despite their opposition, these events have elicited the same reaction in many Christians. The reaction was, by and large, one of indifference, even of irritation and hostility.

It is the thesis of this paper that this similarity of reaction to totally disparate, even contrasting, events is symptomatic of the

Reprinted with permission from *Journal of Ecumenical Studies*, Spring 1969, copyright © 1969, Temple University.

presence of determinative unconscious forces, specifically, of an unrecognized antipathy against the Jewish people. Our intent is to indicate, all too briefly, a few facts to support this thesis and to outline elements of an explanation. We shall consider each event separately.

First, the holocaust. During World War II more than six million Jews were systematically murdered by Hitler and his allies. The genocide, methodically and secretly begun in 1941, came to light only gradually, but was certainly known by the Allied governments, the Vatican, and other church officials by the end of 1943 at the latest. Calls for protest and intervention were made from various sources, but with little result. After the war, well before Hochhuth's dramatization of the matter, charges of apathy and silence were made, principally against Pope Pius XII. Since then research has placed many of the Allied governments, including that of the United States, under the charge.

The complexity of this serious issue must be respected, and facile, armchair judgments of hindsight avoided. Yet, in the final analysis, some degree of the charge must be validated. Great or small, the apathy or silence was excessive. The fact remains that in the twentieth century of Christian civilization a genocide of six million innocent people was perpetrated in countries with many centuries of Christian traditions, and by hands that were in many cases Christian. This fact in itself stands, however vaguely, as an indictment of the Christian conscience. The absence of reaction by those not directly implicated in the genocide only aggravates this broader indictment.

A word here may be said about two points that have been controverted among scholars.

Was Hitler's genocide the final flower of a millennial Christian anti-Semitism, as some have said? Or was it a development that was as anti-Christian as it was anti-Jewish, as others say? For our purpose the debate can be eschewed if we accept the conclusion —an inescapable one—that Christian civilization and culture prepared the way at least in a secondary manner for the Nazi genocide. Non-Christian, post-Christian, and anti-Christian architects of modern secularist anti-Semitism found their target ready-made as they formulated their racist theories and policies. The degraded state of the Jews, brought about by centuries of opprobrium and oppression, gave support to the invidious comparisons with which the racists built their theories. And in their evil design, they were able to draw moral support from traditional Christian views of Jews and Judaism.

A second controversy relates to Hochhuth's charge against Pius XII. Again, for our purpose, it is not necessary to decide the issue. The centralization of the charge on the pope has unfortunately deflected attention from the scope of a silence that affected many churches, governments, and people. More recent research has shown that apathy toward the Jewish plight was a pervasive thing. The question of collective guilt, or participation in Hitler's crime, has been raised as a result. Many moralists reject the concept and insist on the individuality of moral guilt. One may ask, nonetheless, whether there is not a certain psychological complicity in an action (in this case a silence or an indifference in the face of Hitler's crime) that constitutes a diluted form of assent. Be this as it may, our interest here is not so much in the morality of the matter as in its psychology. Our interest is in the dearth of appropriate reaction to the crime. It would appear that over and beyond the confusion caused by the war, the uncertainties about what was going on and what should best be done, the reaction should have been much greater.

There are other data that tend to support a suspicion of complicity. Since the war, further indifferences have been detectable: quibbling about the number of Jews killed; tendencies to excuse Hitler's accomplices in the genocide, for example, excessive concern for the jurisdictional status of Eichmann's trial; a certain banality about the genocide manifested by the desire to hear no more about it; and so forth—many indications that the so-called silence during the war was not a pure misunderstanding.

If the holocaust was unique in human annals, so was the emergence of the State of Israel. The creation within fifty years of a strong, vibrant, and viable nation and state in the face of insuperable difficulties places a strain on the powers of rational explanation; and many will see this extraordinary development in frankly supernatural terms. The Israeli state emerged in response to age-old aspirations toward a return to Zion implanted in the Jewish heart by the sacred pages of Scripture common to Christian and Jew, and came at a moment in history when the Jewish people were under a threat of extinction, when the doors of Christian nations were for the most part closed to them. The nation and State of Israel was built in the face of formidable obstacles. Millennial aspirations were not enough. Settlement in an inhospitable terrain; struggles for international juridical validation; blood, sweat, tears, and huge monetary outlays that tested to the limits Jewish ingenuity and resources—all these were necessary. The survival of the state, moreover, had to be won at the cost of three wars within twenty years, each of which could have put it definitively out of existence. From each war Israel emerged stronger than before.

The reaction of Christians to this Israeli epic has been mixed. A minor portion of it has been unreservedly favorable; another, hostile; whereas a large middle section has been questioning and cool to the new state and its successes. (We do not take into account Arab reactions here, Christian or other, which constitute an aspect of the question that requires special treatment.) At the risk of oversimplifying, we may encapsulate the spectrum of Christian neutral and unfavorable reactions in the term "anti-Zionism," more specifically "Christian anti-Zionism." This anti-Zionism deserves more attention than it has received; it has much to reveal of the Christian consciousness.

For brevity's sake, we may limit our attention to Christian reaction to the Arab-Israeli War of June, 1967. It was on that occasion that the threat of destroying Israel was at its peak, and that the charge was made, mostly by Jewish opinion, to the effect that the churches were guilty of another silence anent a genocidal threat against Israel. Again the charge of silence was, in our estimation, as in the case of Pope Pius XII, too narrow. The silence was not only of the churches as institutions but of Christian opinion as a whole. The official churches merely reflected a more general apathy, which we have designated by the name Christian anti-Zionism. It is not our purpose here to discuss this question in detail, but merely to affirm that an excessive silence or lack of concern did exist.

It is true that in June, 1967, most Christians responded with admiration for Israel's remarkable victory. But the admiration was short-lived. As Israel strove to bolster its position of defence in order to guarantee its future security before withdrawing to former borderlines, this opinion ceased to see her as a stouthearted David facing a gigantic aggressor and inclined to regard her as an aggressive and expansionist Goliath. It riveted its attention on questions of borderlines, refugees, "overreaction" by Israel to Arab terrorism, anniversary parades, and the like, ignoring meanwhile the persistent threat from the Arab countries to eliminate Israel.

The rationale of this position is usually justified on the grounds of anti-Zionist stance. Critics of Israel and its triumphs repeatedly remind us that they are neither anti-Jewish nor anti-Semitic, but simply anti-Zionist. This distinction is generally linked with another between Judaism as a nation or state and Judaism as a religion. The anti-Zionists simply assert: Judaism is only a religion; the Israeli state is nothing but the creature of Zionist politics. It is curious to see here Christians crashing into the difficult subject of what Judaism and Jews are, and adopting a now almost wholly abandoned classical Reform Judaism concept of Judaism in order finally to tell both Christian and Jew categorically just what Judaism and Jews are. Zionism is, in this way, assumed to be a purely secular and political development in the margin of Judaism. These critics are quick to remind us, too, that many Jews are anti-Zionist, in spite of the fact that an extremely small number today really are.

For a Jew—or an Arab—to be anti-Zionist is one thing; for a non-Arab Christian to be such is another; and his espousal of this stance demands an explanation. This writer is not one of those who hold that every anti-Zionist is an anti-Semite, but his experience tends to show that most are to some degree thus tainted. The pertinent question is, Why should a Christian be an anti-

Zionist at all? I am not, of course, referring to disagreement with Israeli policies or practices, the matter of refugees, of Arab rights and aspirations, but rather to rejecting Zionism as a concept *tout court*, as so many Christians do. Many reasons have been offered in support of the anti-Israeli position, of which we mention but a few. The State of Israel is, we are told, an injustice against Arabs; it is a purely secular phenomenon; it entails a double loyalty on the part of Jews; support of Israel is not in the national interest; it places Christian interest in Arab lands in jeopardy; and so forth. It is a contention of this paper that these reasons are neither sufficient nor fully relevant; nor are they fully explanatory of the anti-Zionism of Christians, of their coldness or hostility to the State of Israel. This latter, we believe, is rooted in deeper soil than that of political and sociological considerations.

Anti-Zionism, we propose, is frequently built on an emotional substructure that is usually well disguised—and almost always denied. And here we rejoin our discussion of the holocaust. We have indicated the polar opposition of the holocaust and the new State of Israel in the existence of the Jews. One is its nadir; the other, its zenith: Israel prostrate and Israel triumphant. Both have evoked a similar response from many Christians, an apathy or indifference which edges toward hostility. It is a phenomenon, we said, that requires investigation. One might expect the average person to be profoundly moved with horror at Hitler's attempt at the Jewish genocide, and with great sympathy toward the efforts of the most oppressed people in Christian history to obtain for themselves a homeland and a haven for their dispersed. One might expect a still greater degree of horror and sympathy from a Christian, for reasons that we shall see. Why, then, apathy and indifference? Why a *Christian* anti-Zionism?

Some of the reasons given in support of anti-Zionism have been mentioned; and there are, of course, many more, indeed, too many—so many, in fact, that one is allowed to inquire whether their very multiplicity does not conceal a motivation that is both unavowed and unrecognized. It is the burden of this paper to suggest that this is the case. This direction, of course, will take us from the level of historical events, whereon we began, to that of psychological analysis. Is such a turn justified? It would seem so. The psychological study of anti-Semitism, toward which our inquiry has led us, is not new. The psychological and historical sciences have, in effect, vied with each other to render the final account of the anti-Semitic animus. A James Parkes or a Jules Isaac will seek its total causality in history (and theology). Otto Fenichel, psychoanalyst, states: "Anti-Semitism is more a conflict within a person than between persons,"[1] thus placing the subject entirely within the dominion of psychology.

The recourse to psychological explanation, further, is not arbitrary. Identical conscious reactions (apathy-hostility) to two highly disparate stimuli (the holocaust and the State of Israel) warrant it. The effect evoked was, in other words, inappropriate, hence, not from rational sources. The inappropriate similarity of effect indicates a common and hidden source that the justifying reasons given (rationalizations) do not evince. An unconscious source of motivation thus becomes a distinct possibility. The inappropriateness of the effect attending these events tends to render the reaction suspect, but, of course, does not in itself demonstrate the existence of a latent (or repressed) hostility. The suspicion takes on credibility only when viewed in the light of other data independently available from historical, psychological, and theological research. These data can be ranged in four main categories:

1. The Pathological

Pathological anti-Semitism is evident in Christian history even to the nonalienist, and studies of it have attracted professional attention in recent years.[2] Analysis has detected anti-Semitic trends in certain "authoritarian personalities," among anxiety-ridden and paranoidally inclined persons. Found in its purest culture among the clinically abnormal, it is nonetheless a syndrome that can be found to shade off toward the normal personality. One investigator has observed that in some patients anti-Semitism survives an otherwise successfully terminated analysis.[3] Although it is not legitimate to build a psychology of the normal on a purely pathological model, neither is it acceptable to posit a complete break between the normal and the abnormal. It is important, furthermore, to note the presence of pathological anti-Semitism in society as a source of infection that can contaminate the normal in times of stress. It would, in fine, be foolhardy to discount all pathology (and unconsciousness) in the attitudes of large numbers of otherwise normal members of society with respect to Jews and Judaism.

2. The Sociological

Few students of depth psychology today would minimize the influence of the cultural and social upon the interpsychic processes, and it is in this direction that we must also look for an understanding of the prevalence of the anti-Semitic syndrome.[4] It is here no longer a question of the deepest instinctual strata of the mind (Freud's primary process) but of the ego system that is closer to reality but unconsciousness nonetheless (Freud's preconscious). This system is fed by social institutions and mores, and not always in a wholly conscious way. Our Western culture, Christian and post-Christian, has incorporated into itself over the centuries an anti-Jewish element that has left its mark on these institutions and mores. What once came mostly from the church comes today for the greater part from the secular realm, from the street into the church. As religious anti-Semitism declines, a secular brand, more subtle and more dangerous, lives on with a life of its own. Without his realizing it, the average individual in our society takes on in his formative, and later, years, both a religious and a secular bias against Jews, but which his morality and ideals condemn and force him to repress. Pressed into his unconscious, this bias may join there with whatever sources of pathology he has within him.

3. The Theological

Until recent years Western culture has, we have said, included theological presuppositions which left their imprint on our ways of thinking about Jews and Judaism, and which may be summarized in the "deicide charge." This notion of Jews as a people accursed and dispersed by God in expiation for the crucifixion waxed among the fathers of the church and became fairly universally accepted by the later Middle Ages, enduring until the present time. Among several of the fathers the charge included the belief that Jews could never again acquire their homeland or Temple, a belief that accompanied the deicide charge in its course through the centuries.[5] These views, though never a formally imposed teaching of the church, comprised a species of religious sociology of Christianity that exerted a most baleful influence on Jewish-Christian relations and left its mark not only on Jews but also on the Christian mentality to this day. Today, however, as the Christian consciousness becomes more aware of the total implications of the Christian outlook, these views have gone underground and persist rather as unconscious or semiconscious traces of the erstwhile belief. One need not decide here whether the vehicle of such traces is found in the form of a "collective unconscious" that is actually hereditary (Jung), or it is merely passed on by more or less explicit assumptions of the formative years of Christian training, to be forgotten, or repressed (Freud's preconscious). The effect is the same. A certain vague uneasiness attends the idea of Jews restored to Palestine, and to Jerusalem in particular. This uneasiness *may* serve as the subliminal foundation for a Christian anti-Zionism and as the dynamics for the various "reasons" supplied for disfavoring the State of Israel, its policies, and its activities.

4. A Theologico-Psychodynamic Theory

An attempt has been made by scholars, principally psychoanalytic, to explain Christian anti-Semitism as an unconscious, displaced hatred of Christ or Christianity—a Christophobia. Perhaps the first to suggest this was Freud himself, who wrote, "Hatred for Judaism is at bottom hatred for Christianity."[6] Since Freud many others, including Jewish and Christian psychologists and theologians, have elaborated this theory, which combines in a single explanation the data of both depth psychology and history.[7] The theory, briefly, explicates how the unregenerate depths of the Christian soul resent the burden placed upon it by Christian standards and, unable to vent this resentment on its true object, Christ, transfer it to a surrogate, one with whom Christ may be partially but not totally identified, namely, his own people. Some confirmation of this theory may be taken from the observation that Christian rigorists are, as a rule, the worst of anti-Semites. Rigorists, in other words, are those who bear their Christianity more heavily than others and are accordingly more resentful. To extend the theory to the larger number of Christians it must be reformulated thus: To the measure that any Christian finds his Christianity burdensome, to that measure will he tend to be anti-Semitic.

Serious consideration should be given this possibility that much of the antipathy or apathy toward Jews in their distress is fed on the deepest levels from a dissatisfaction with the Christian faith. It is easy to see by virtue of this theory how anti-Semitism can taper from a frank hatred of Jews toward mere coolness or neutrality toward them—or toward anti-Zionism. The gradation of alienation among Christians ranges, of course, from total commitment to total loss of faith, with every shade of rebellion and loss in between. It may be well to warn at this point against any inclination to accept this theory as the sole and sufficient understanding of anti-Semitic motivation in all cases or in any one case. Anti-Semitic etiology is complex and derives from every level of human experience. The question rather is whether other causes are secondary and are sustained at their roots by this Christophobic force. Another note of caution is to warn against regarding the theory as inimical to educative efforts against anti-Semitism. Even if anti-Semitism at its deepest layers is Christophobic, and therefore inaccessible for most, anti-Semitism can nonetheless be effectively attacked on all levels of its existence by retraining and education. Even Freudian analysis makes room for correcting the phobia by showing the patient that the object he has chosen is symbolic and mistaken—in this case, the Jews.

What conclusions are to be drawn from the foregoing analysis? There are several:

1. That there is a strong probability that many Christians harbor a deeply repressed death wish for the Jewish people;

2. that this wish is nourished both from our social atmosphere, secular and religious, and from aggressive forces within ourselves;

3. that, thanks to our ideals and our guilts, the wish is consciously manifested only through a process of attenuation, through rationalizations which disguise its presence and its source;

4. that the apathy manifested during and after the holocaust is explicable on this basis;

5. that one of the chief repositories of this unconscious anti-Semitism is often cloaked in a commitment to anti-Zionism;

6. that consideration should be given to the possibility that at its deepest root Christian anti-Semitism is a hatred of Christianity.

Caution is required in applying these conclusions. Since they deal with unconscious motivation, they remain within the realm of probability rather than of immediate and binding evidence in any particular case. At best, perhaps, they place our negative opinions and observations respecting Jews under suspicion. They suggest, further, that purely objective analyses in *rebus Judaicis* should be tested for underlying negative emotional attitudes.

These conclusions are not such as will appeal to the rationalistic-minded, to those who reject as "imputing motives" all procedures that refuse to accept a person's "reasons" on their face value, or to those objectivists who give short shrift to the probings of the psychology of the unconscious. This latter science has sufficiently proved its validity today, however, and not only entitles but encourages us to test all our motives and our *rationalia* by its standards. The high probability that there exists a widespread, low-toned, and unconscious anti-Semitism in the Christian community urges us to suspect even the least of our disagreements with Jews and to employ every instrument that may aid us to sound their depths. Anti-Semitism and its attenuations are no doubt a part of the pathology of our times, as the holocaust and the reactions to it amply show. The instruments of mental pathology are not, therefore, to be spurned in analyses of contemporary problems that touch on Jewish-Christian relations. The dialogue between Christians and Jews in particular, difficult enough in itself, should not be expected to thrive on a foundation of unconscious antipathies that are allowed to go unscrutinized and unchallenged.

It is Christian theology, not merely Christian guilt, that commits the Christians to a special love of Jews and Judaism. For they [Jews] "have the adoption as sons, and the glory and the covenants and the legislation and the worship and the promises" (Rom. 9:4), and "the gifts and calling of God are without repentance" (ch. 11:29). Our common patrimony makes Jews "most dear" to Christians (v. 28). Between this part of Christian theology and the actual Christian mentality, long under the influence of the deicidal tradition, there remains a sharp conflict. It is in the interest of Christian truth and love as well as of Jewish-Christian friendship that the conflict must be resolved.

We conclude where we began: it is the Christian above all who is expected to react most strongly to attacks on Jews. It is especially the Christian who is expected to rejoice at the upturn in the fortune of Jews that Zionism, or any other agency, has brought about in our own time. The distance we appear to stand from this horror and rejoicing is the measurement of that estrangement which separates us on the deepest level of our souls.

Notes

1. Otto Fenichel, "Elements of a Psychoanalytic Theory of Anti-Semitism," in *Anti-Semitism: A Social Disease*, Ernst Simmel, ed. (New York: International Universities Press, 1946), p. 11.

2. See *Studies in Prejudice*, 5 vols., ed. Max Horkheimer and Samuel Flowerman (New York: Harper & Row, 1949–1950); *Anti-Semitism: A Social Disease*, ed. Ernst Simmel, *supra*; Rudolph M. Lowenstein, *Christians and Jews: A Psychoanalytic Study* (New York: Delta Books, 1963).

3. See Morris L. Haimowitz, *The Development and Change of Ethnic Hostility* (Chicago: University of Chicago, Ph.D. Thesis, 1951).

4. It will be noted that the discussion at this point has moved from apathy toward Jewish difficulties to anti-Semitism. The transition is in function of the thesis which this paper purports to substantiate: that conscious opposition to Jews can often be reduced on a deeper level to anti-Semitism. If the presence of an unconscious anti-Semitism can be proved, the first step has been taken toward questioning the more conscious attitudes.

5. See E. Flannery, "Theological Aspects of the State of Israel," in *The Bridge*, Vol. III (New York: Pantheon Books, 1958–1959), p. 301.

6. S. Freud, *Moses and Monotheism* (New York: Vintage Books, 1955), pp. 116–117.

7. See E. Flannery, "Anti-Semitism—A Spiritual Disease," in *Thought*, XLI, 160 (Spring, 1966).

11

Holocaust

•

BERNARD LEE, S.M.

It has become increasingly clear that "patch" theology is not enough to make being fully Christian and fully contemporary congenial enterprises. Congenial does not necessarily mean comfortable, but it does imply a lack of deep, logical contradiction. Sometimes the whole fabric of an understanding must be replaced, not patched. That happens when the basic presuppositions of a system (and not just applications of them) are replaced by other presuppositions. And I would agree with Whitehead that one system does not replace another by refutation. Old systems are simply (but not easily) and slowly abandoned. Nowhere in religious thought is this more evident now than in our thinking about God.

One thing that recommends process theology to Christian thought is that it is a contemporary system of thought which has grappled seriously and creatively with our understanding of God. Process thought offers some new understandings on the God question which add consonance between our understanding of God and our understanding of our world, without violating the basic mystery of either God or world.

Previously published as "The Helplessness of God," *Encounter* 38, no. 4 (Fall 1977). Copyright © 1977, Christian Theological Seminary, 100 W. 42 Street, Indianapolis, IN 46208, reprinted with permission.

I have in mind particularly the classical understandings of "omnipotence" and "omniscience," which in many ways are organically related concepts, and both of which are problematic if we wish to meet the modern critique of God in respect to matters of freedom and evil. In the classical understanding, God created the universe *ex nihilo*, and bears the full responsibility for the whole character of it. In a process understanding, every created event is a co-production of God and the world. Whitehead insists that God is with the world, not before the world. Secondly, in the classical understanding, God does not instigate evil (though he does in Job!), but *permits* it. It is clearly the sense, however, that God *could* intervene with an exercise of omnipotence, but does not. Process thought would be more inclined (as in Charles Hartshorne) to insist that the power of God in the world is adequate to the long run needs of the world, but (as in Whitehead) that the power of God *only* persuades and never coerces—not by choice but by character.

Our basic understandings of God have immense implications for Christology, for in some way or another Jesus as the Christ is the "Sacrament" of God. By that I mean that "something about" Jesus is also truly "something about" God, and that God's "something about" is in Jesus precisely through Jesus' participation in the Father.

In regard to Christology I feel some affinity with Jürgen Moltmann's *The Crucified God*—but with some important differences. I think it is more accurate to understand Jesus as the Sacrament of a God who indeed suffers rather than to speak of the crucified God. Moltmann, like Paul Tillich, is influenced by Schelling in his pursuit of a theological dialectic. Moltmann cites Hippocrates, that *contraria contrariis curantur;* and similarly from Schelling, that every being can be revealed only in its opposite. (Hippocrates, of course, means the kind of contrasting opposites at work in applying cold packs for high fever. A *contrarium* makes a disclosure about its opposite by way of contrast.) In the experience of abandonment, therefore, one has a sense of the meaning of God's care. My point, however, is that there is something *real* in the character of God (not a *contrarium*, therefore) which makes it valid to speak positively about a helplessness in God. That something real is God's respect for human freedom— a respect necessitated by the character of human freedom. There is a helplessness in God that is a corollary of the character of freedom in creation. (In the final analysis, the behavior of even a single electron is not fully predictable. That kind of spontaneity is an analogue, in non-living events, of human freedom. It represents the power to break through inherited givens into something different.)

Further, as I will develop, there are circumstances in which the impasse which a person encounters is the result of having responded precisely to God's call—and one *is* abandoned, for God *cannot* extricate that person from his Gethsemane. I think this is not Moltmann's position finally, for I do not think this is a matter of a *contrarium*.

I want to point out that I consistently use "abandon" in the passive voice. I am not saying that God actively abandons. He does not decide to abandon. But we do become stranded, left alone in crucifixions from which God *cannot* extricate us. The abandonment is real, active or passive voice notwithstanding.

I am also conscious of trying to respond to the modern critique of religion: Feuerbach, Marx, Freud, Sartre, etc. I thought of titling this paper: "Dear Mr. Sartre" and asking whether he would still have to be a necessary atheist if God and human freedom are as I describe them here. Yet I feel my position is not a matter of concocting a God who meets the requirements. I hope it is a matter of using a contemporary hermeneutic for interpreting our experience as well as the religious experience of others (i.e., the Biblical experience).

I also feel the pressure of taking most seriously the Jewish holocaust experience. I do this knowing that in some basic ways I stand outside of the inside of that experience. Yet it is part of my history too, for I am of this century. I have never in my life experienced silences comparable to the two stunned silences I experienced in Dachau and at the Yad Vashem in Jerusalem.

And finally, though I operate mostly within the school of

process theology, I have felt that in some ways the God of Alfred North Whitehead and of Charles Hartshorne is too aseptic. Whitehead speaks of experiencing God the Enemy as one of the three stages of religion, but I do not think he hints at what may be the case that would let a person so speak. It is perhaps Carl Jung in his *Answer to Job* who speaks most powerfully about God the Enemy (though metaphorically and not metaphysically). Although I am not, therefore, developing a specifically Whiteheadian conviction about God, I do believe that "the helplessness of God" is consistent with the character of Whitehead's thought (not that such is the touchstone in the first place).

In his last moments on the cross, as life waned, Jesus said to his Father: "My God, my God, why have you forsaken me?" He called his Father a forsaker.

Some commentators say that Jesus was citing the twenty-second psalm. If he was, I want to suggest that he was using someone else's words, but that the forsakenness was his own.

Other commentators have suggested that perhaps Jesus, in his humanity alone, felt forsaken. That explanation presumes a certain Christological model. And the explanation may perhaps be the case. But if that is the case, I want to suggest that the feeling of having been forsaken was an adequate response to the *fact* of having been forsaken.

These reflections stem in part from some of the most provocative of Whitehead's comments about religious experience. (Few philosophies are as thoroughgoingly relational as Whitehead's "philosophy of organism," so it is all the more striking to hear him speak about solitariness.)

Religion is what the individual does with his own solitariness. It runs through three stages, if it evolves to its final satisfaction. It is the transition from God the void to God the enemy, and from God the enemy to God the companion. . . . The great religious conceptions which haunt the imaginations of civilized mankind are scenes of solitariness: Prometheus chained to his rock, Mahomet brooding in the desert, the meditations of the Buddha, the solitary Man of the Cross. It belongs to the depth of the religious spirit to have felt forsaken, even by God (*Religion in the Making*, pp. 16, 19).

I would like to explore the character of forsakenness and to suggest that there is some real helplessness in God. Further, I want to hold that God's helplessness, at some junctures of historical event, undergirds not just feeling forsaken, but being forsaken by him.

I see no alternative to this position if we take seriously the inviolability and irreducibility of human freedom. Let me draw some analogies from our own experiences of helplessness.

If you know me well and love me well, you may have a very clear intuition into some possibilities for me which would call me to be more than I already am. You may invite me to become more, challenge me, cajole me, lure me, tease me to be more. You may pressure me. But you can never capture my subjectivity and coerce my decision. Force that would attempt to violate freedom, though it could not, would not be an act of love in the first place.

Probably all of us have had the experience of helplessness in regard to someone we dearly love. Truly so, or mistakenly so, we may feel that we know what is good for someone we love, someone who is "doing bad things" to himself or herself. We try everything that we can, and finally stand by in sheer helplessness. For what we cannot do is violate the sanctuary of personal freedom. Our helplessness is fully real before the mystery of another person's freedom.

God's relationship with us is quite like that.

In all the events of our lives we have certain "stuff" out of which we fashion our reality. That "stuff" includes our own past history; it includes a whole universe of experience; it includes new possibilities offered us that we might become more (and this is a work of God). But the outcome of all that "stuff," the outcome which *is* our personal identity, emerges from the decisions we make. *We* decide what we will do with what we are given. In the celebrated phrase of Harry Truman, our decisions are where the buck stops. There stands nothing behind that. We are conditioned by our inheritance. We are pressured by our circumstances. Our freedom is never total, but it is always radical. The decisions we make *are* ourselves. We are not separate from our decisions. We are not makers of our decisions so much as our decisions are makers of us. At the moment of decision we are simply alone, terribly alone. That is the moment of solitariness, aweful solitariness, when *we* decide what *we* will do with what God offers us and calls us to. In the deepest sense, religion is what we do with that moment of irreducible solitariness where God and the human personality intersect.

If freedom is genuine, and my presumption is that it is (Burris F. Skinner notwithstanding), then not even God can violate the total subjectivity of the moment of solitariness when decision is made. That is clearly the sense of Whitehead's insistence that God's action in the world is always by means of persuasion, and never by means of coercion.

Every event is a co-production of God and the world and itself. There is something which God offers (possibility), something which the world offers (all past events, most important of which is my own past), and finally there is what I do with what I have been given. My real freedom means that while God and the rest of the world have made this present moment possible, they must finally stand by, watching for my decision, and hoping for a response that is faithful to the best of my ownmost possibilities for the present situation. But that moment of watching is a helpless moment because of the impenetrability of my solitariness, which is the impregnable fortress of my freedom.

I feel great sympathy with Sartre's necessary atheism. The experience of freedom is so real, and the evolutionary way that things have come to be is so convincing, that a God who is absolutely omnipotent, and who determines the natures of all things, is simply untenable. If there is a God who knows the future in perfect detail, then somehow, somewhere, there is already the pattern—and history is our illusion. The problem is not with the reality of freedom. Nor with the non-illusory character of history. Nor with the character of God. The problem is with the classical understanding of God.

I feel an equal sympathy with Rabbi Richard Rubenstein in his book, *After Auschwitz*. If God *could have* prevented the attempted genocide and slaughter of six million Jews and *did not*, then he has forfeited his right to be called the Lord of History. I think the lesson is that if God *did not*, it was because God *could not*. He did all he could. But then he had to stand outside that sanctuary of human freedom and helplessly watch the desecration of the temple.

There seems to be no choice but to surrender the notion of the omnipotence of God. It is a comfortable symbol. It may even be a security blanket. But it is not consonant with the logic of experience. Nor is the sacrifice of omnipotence, in favor of the sometime helplessness of God, as large a sacrifice as it may seem, the more clearly we see that the earlier notion reflects the logic of a Greek world view more than the Biblical record of religious experience. And it may finally be possible to say something that rings true to both logic and experience about freedom and about evil. Calling evil a negation might have got God off the hook, but it also milked the snake of its poison. And maybe God is on the hook after all, and maybe Jesus on the Cross is a symbol of God on the hook. At least this is the way I think God must be conceived if we are to give a unified account of his character.

I would like to pursue further some sense of our experience of freedom, and its consequences. I have spoken of the limitations of our ability to influence the outcome of each other's lives. We may persuade, but can never coerce the freedom that resides at the heart of another's subjectivity. Nor can God. Our freedom leaves him genuinely helpless at some points, for no matter what he offers and how alluring the offer might be, we may still say No, and often we do say No.

Let me reflect on how we sometimes get each other into painful impasses, all with the best of intention. Suppose that I know you well and love you with a strong love. I divine some of your ownmost possibilities for your own growth into more than you are now. I sense those possibilities for you in the large context of the world in which you live. Your personal history is organically inter-related with the rest of human history. For you are relational to the core. So I must also try to divine history's ownmost possibilities for its own growth, as I divine your potential for the same. You and history, your responses need each other. They nourish each other. They are nourished by each other. Granted that you and the world respond adequately to the possibilities offered to you both, your mutual outcomes will be happy ones.

But there is always the possibility that you may respond fully, and the world may respond poorly, so poorly that you become an anomaly at best, a thorn in the side of the world at worst. When I called you to be more I knew that even if you responded to that call, the world might not. I called you *and* the world to something, with no assurance that either of you would say Yes. And I could not coerce a Yes from you. So in a given situation you have said Yes to the possibility to which I called you, but the part of history that is your working context said No to those possibilities which could make it better. Those possibilities which the world refused are nevertheless necessary for your environment, given the Yes which you have uttered. You have said your Yes, but now you are deprived of the support system of your environment. You cannot go back to where you were before, because your love and fidelity have grown, and one does not go back on that. But you and the world threaten each other badly. That is not what I had in mind when I called you to be more. It is not what I want for you now. The rejection you feel from the world around you occurs precisely because you said Yes to my persuasion. You are at an impasse. In a real sense I got you there. And in an equally real sense, there is nothing I can do for you. My persuasion didn't work in parts of your world. I am helpless to get you out of the suffering into which I have led you. Because of my helplessness, you are indeed forsaken. There is nothing I can do, I who got you into this in the first place.

I think we must understand God to be in a parallel situation if we are to give a unified account of his character. The Yes which Jesus spoke to the Father was unremitting. Yet it was at best an intermittent Yes which history at that time mustered. It was often a No. The situation emerges in which Jesus and that part of history which was his more immediate context were in serious conflict. Jesus was in a mess. There was nothing the Father could do. The Father was impotent to extract the Son from the passion of the world. The Son says, "If it is possible, let this cup pass." It is not possible. The Father does not choose a cross. It is just not possible to avoid it. The cross is the price of the perfect Yes of Jesus and the imperfect Yes and sometime No of the world of Jesus. Jesus is indeed forsaken. He had been led to this point. God brought him here. But now God can do nothing. Jesus is forsaken. Human freedom is that radical.

We know something of the experience of Jesus because he cried, "My God, my God, why have you forsaken me?" Perhaps we can guess at the experience of God in response to his own helplessness. He did all he could do, and was turned down by the world that should have received his son, but received him not. At this point in God's experience it seems reasonable to suppose that "My God, my God, why have you forsaken me?" in the mouth of Jesus is a fully adequate sacrament of the utterance of God, "My world, my world, why have you forsaken me in my son?" God and humanity stood accusing each other, and each was right!

I think the holocaust experience is not unlike this. The cohesiveness and strong identity of the Jewish people is a response to God's caring. But it is that very response, the strong identity of that people, that elicits a response from part of history which incites the dynamics of holocaust. Elie Wiesel's words in his book *Night* are a modern way of questioning God about abandonment:

This day I had ceased to believe. I was no longer capable of lamentation. On the contrary, I felt very strong. I was the accuser, God the accused. My eyes were open and I was alone—terribly alone in a world without God and without man. Without love or mercy. I had ceased to be anything but ashes, yet I felt myself stronger than the almighty, to whom my life had been tied for so long (*Night*, p. 79).

And in another place:

The injustice perpetrated in an unknown land concerns me. He who is not the victim is with the executioners. This was the meaning of the holocaust: it implicated not only Abraham or his son, but their God as well (*The Gates of the Forest*, p. 168).

Another way of putting the matter would be to suggest that God is not free of the ambiguity that we too face as a necessary consequence of the radical character of human freedom and the intricacy of inter-dependent webs of relationality. There is always the element of unpredictability. If I call you to some better possibility, I do not know for certain whether you will say Yes. Nor do I know whether the milieu necessary for making the best sense out of your Yes will eventuate even if you do say Yes.

There may have been several Marys who said, "This is absurd," before one finally said, "Behold the handmaid of the Lord. Let it be done as he says." There is always the element of calculation, and the validity of the evaluation is at the caprice of the radical freedom of human agency. The whole historical enterprise is shot through and through with contingency. Constant readjustment must reckon with whatever configuration of reality emerges from the welter of contingent and ambiguous possibilities.

Elie Wiesel, also in his book *Night*, says:

How I sympathized with Job. I did not deny God's existence, but I doubted his absolute justice (*Night*, pp. 55–56).

There is no way of making sense out of the forsakenness experienced in the face of evil, and hold to the omnipotence of God at the same time. We understand suffering we bring upon ourselves by our selfish and uncircumspect decisions. But Job was responding in remarkably selfless and circumspect ways.

Carl Jung has suggested in his book, *Answer to Job*, that in situations like that of Job we encounter what can only be called the divine darkness. Jung is concerned, and I am concerned, "with the way in which modern man with a Christian education and background comes to terms with the divine darkness which is unveiled in the Book of Job, and what effect it has upon him" (p. 22). If God is omnipotent, as we have understood him, then Jung wonders why God did not deal with Satan directly. "It would seem much simpler," Jung muses, "if Yahweh would, for once, call this 'practical joker' severely to account, get rid of his pernicious influence, and thus eliminate the root of all evil. He would then not need the elaborate arrangement of a special Incarnation with all the unforeseeable consequences which this entails" (p. 82). If God did not simply control Satan, the metaphor for evil, it was because he could not. Spontaneity and freedom are in the character of reality, and that puts reality partially out of God's control. Sometimes he is helpless. His calculations, as he offers the world its possibilities, are made squarely in the face of ambiguity: it could go this way, it could go that way. Ambiguity is not absent from the divine experience.

Against the background of these reflections, I would like now to sketch the theological elements that I think must be components of any unified account of the character of God. I believe that these are components of the experience of Jesus, who is the primordial sacrament of God. And I believe that contained within such a theology are components for an authentic contemporary spirituality.

1. I do not see how we can continue to hold that God knows the entire future in exact detail. He knows what is actual as actual, and knows that wholly. He knows what is possible as possible, and knows that wholly. Greek understandings, which have influenced Christian theology so deeply, understood perfection in a way that demanded that God could not undergo real change. Getting new knowledge means real change. So God had to know it all in one fell swoop. Or his knowledge was thought to be efficiently causative of its objects—equally problematic. But these positions, I believe, result from demands imposed by the Greek world view, and not demands imposed by the character of God or by the Biblical experience.

A process theological interpretation removes the metaphysical confusion between the actual and the possible. If the whole pattern of actuality were known in advance, the situation metaphysically would have to be one of complete determinism. We would merely think we were free and history would be *our* illusion.

God fully knows the whole actuality of the universe. He knows fully the whole pattern of possibility. And he makes available to the universe the possibilities that best (an ambiguous and contingent best) persuade it in the direction of its own self-transcendence towards God.

Aware of the long theological tradition about God's perfect knowledge of the future, even in Church pronouncements, I simply stress here the need for a huge amount of form-criticism on our accumulated credal and dogmatic propositions, the more we become aware of how much those propositions are historically and culturally shaped. That historical and cultural relativity pertains to many areas of thought in addition to the one presently under discussion.

2. This second point is a corollary of the previous one. I think we must hold that God really experiences history *for the first time* as it unfolds. He knows it as it becomes real. God's knowledge is conditioned by the character of history as it creates itself in conjunction with him. There is becoming, therefore, in the experience of God which gives God's concreteness some of the particular individuality which it bears. Reality is pervasively relational and God is its chief exemplification.

But once again, to posit real becoming in God is an absurdity in the Greek world view where the ability to change is an indication of imperfect being. Such is not apt to be the case for the contemporary human being who more and more understands process to be normative—to be the very condition of being concretely real, and that includes God. Human experience contributes to the experience of God, to his sometime enrichment and to his sometime impoverishment.

3. I think we must acknowledge that the outcome of every event is a co-production of God and the world, and each can do only so much. This is but another way of asserting that identity is an emergent from the full texture of all relationships. To be me I need even that possibility, and God offers it. I need my own past and I need much history, and they are there for me. But what I do with them, in the solitariness of my decision, is my business

alone. I may do my business admirably and with distinction, as Jesus did. The absence of discrepancy between what God offered Jesus and what Jesus achieved let the Logos of God for humanity become transparent in Jesus. But I may also do my business dismally, and God is helpless before the radical character of my freedom. Many of the people who made up the world to which Jesus was called did their business dismally while Jesus did his admirably. It got him on a cross and there was no way out. Jesus was forsaken. And he was the Sacrament of God who was equally forsaken by the circumstances that mounted his Son on a tree. At that moment there was nothing more that could be done. It was right to utter the word "Forsaken."

4. The fourth item of this recapitulation is that I believe we must acknowledge that God too has to contend with the ambiguous character of the world's unfolding. His calculation is from a totality of vision and a privileged circumspection of which our vision and circumspection are but the dimmest likeness. But it is still calculation. In the twinkling of an eye human decisions and revisions can and do make the best calculations go awry. Not always. But sometimes and often. And sometimes largely. God's own decisions about the best possibilities he can offer the world, therefore, partake of the character of ambiguity.

The ambiguity is not precisely about what is best at *this* instant —that would be quite clear. The ambiguity is precisely about the next moment and the next after that which will determine whether that last moment continues to be best fitted for the world in which it finds itself. Other free decisions that create configuration in a person's world of relationships are the source of the ambiguity about each present moment's best option. I do not see how God escapes that. And more especially, I do not see how the situation implies any imperfection in the providence of God. The blame is put where it belongs, if indeed blame is the word we need. It is "the sin of the world."

5. Because of the steady presence of evil in the world, the most perfect response to God's offerings to an individual is often likely to distance him from the world which is his context. That distance,

not infrequently, gets a person in trouble with his world, stemming from the fact that he is more Godly than his world, and stands as a reproach to it. So the world crucifies him. Or at best, the chosen one of God is often a lonely runner.

The lonely Man on the Cross is the constant New Testament witness. The experience of Jeremiah is perhaps a classical Old Testament witness:

You duped me, O Lord, and I let myself be duped; you were too strong for me and you triumphed. All the day I am an object of laughter; everyone mocks me. Whenever I speak, I must cry out, violence and outrage is my message; the word of the Lord has brought me derision and reproach all the day. I say to myself, I will not mention him, I will speak his name no more. But then it becomes like fire burning in my heart, imprisoned in my bones; I grow weary holding it in, I cannot endure it (Jeremiah 20:7–9).

In either case, crucified or lonely, the chosen one of God knows what it means to be forsaken, even by God.

These reflections have to do with a theology and spirituality of the cross. What stands here is an incomplete reflection, needing the complement of a congenial Paschal theology and spirituality (a theology and spirituality for the Easter event), for which the process-relational hermeneutic is well equipped. That I think remains as homework to be done in the process school of theology.

At least this much needs to be said: if the forsakenness of any given moment is real, it is not the final word. That moment perishes that another may live, and yet another word may be spoken. Or to put it differently, helplessness to prevent wreckage that occurs *this* moment of vision may yet include the power of revision to bring life out of death. The sin of the world does not have the final say, someone else does. That is the proclamation of the New Testament.

I am aware that many of my reflections depart, even radically at times, from certain convictions of classical theology. Then as now there is always the danger of doing nothing more than fashioning gods to our own image and likeness. But in a sense we have no other choice. We take the best persuasions that we can cull from our experience, and try to forge out of them the best possible rendering of the character of God.

If there is a single moral buried in this theology, it is the immense responsibility that humanity bears for the outcome of history. There is the real possibility that human history could fail utterly, that is, that it could end itself as human history (which might still leave the rest of the cosmos with a second and third chance). This is not my prediction. But we need to take seriously that we are co-responsible with God for creation: we are history's co-producers.

It is almost trite (and that is tragic) to talk about the possibility that time is running out on history. But I shall, because our sciences and our technological productivities appear to be outstripping our wisdom to manage them. As people increase in sheer number, as ecological balances become increasingly tenuous, as our weapons of death multiply in destructive savagery—the more likely it is that our human lives will suffer deeply. In terms of powers for living and dying, we live on a scale unimaginably larger than all generations and civilizations before us. The possibilities for new forsakenness are overwhelming.

The new theology and spirituality needed are not simply rehashes of the many versions of secularization theory—that theology put *all* of the responsibility on man, and knew little or nothing of transcendence. Its predecessor had the omnipotence of God tucked away for a last resort security blanket. I am suggesting a spirituality of the partial power of God and the partial power of humanity, a theology of the partial (but real!) helplessness of God and the partial (and obvious!) helplessness of human agency. Such a spirituality and theology are desperately needed if humankind and God are ever to soften their cries of "Forsaken!" to each other.

12

The Holocaust:
A Technological Triumph

•

W. ROBERT McCLELLAND, S.T.D.

"Unless the Lord builds the house, those who build it labor in vain."
Psalm 127:1

DURING THE THIRTY YEARS THAT FOLLOWED World War II, there has been an embarrassed, even guilty, silence regarding the Holocaust—the killing of six million Jews in Germany. It is only recently that the dam has broken and a flood of Holocaust literature has come rolling off the presses. Largely by Jewish authors, it seeks to wrestle with the meaning, the incomprehensible, absurd, insane meaning of that event. Elie Wiesel, one of the most provocative of the writers, tells in his book *Night* of seeing a young boy hanged. His body was so emaciated that it did not weigh enough to help him to die. For more than half an hour he continued to sway, struggling between life and death. Wiesel, at a loss to comprehend the meaning of the event, closes that episode with just seven words: "That night the soup tasted of corpses."

In the same book we read of a cattle car experience. The writer witnesses a son murder his own father in order to steal bread

Previously unpublished sermon.

from the old man's mouth. The killer, in turn, is beaten to death by others. Again, the incomprehensibility of it. Wiesel concludes by saying, "I was 15 years old."

Another survivor, younger than Wiesel, says that she was eleven years old before she realized that you could die of natural causes. Eleven years old before she realized that people died one at a time, rather than in groups! And so the literature comes, trying to comprehend the enormity of the evil.

Yet we can make no sense of the Holocaust by dwelling on its horror. Rather, if we are to learn anything from the Holocaust, we must ask, "What lessons does it teach us?" "How are we to understand our present situation in the light of that event?" Certainly, as Christians, we must approach the Holocaust with deep humility and without preconceptions or ready definitions. We cannot come as Jews, nor can we come as those who suffered. As Wiesel once said, "The victims are our problem; the killers are a Christian problem." And so on this Labor Day Sunday, this national holiday when we celebrate American business and industry, the technological envy of the world, I want to look at technology from the perspective of the Holocaust.

Consider first of all that the Holocaust was possible only in a technological world. The killing of six million Jews could not have happened during the time of Alexander the Great. Not because Alexander the Great was any less demonic than Hitler; not because Alexander the Great was more benevolent. Alexander the Great couldn't have killed six million Jews because he never thought of it. And the reason he never thought of it was because the technology of his time did not make such a thought conceivable. How many people can you kill with a sword? Say fifty an hour. That would be a pretty good rate, but after an hour your arms gets tired and the rate begins to drop off. If you have an army killing fifty an hour with swords, who then keeps the people in subjection while your army is busy killing? No, to conceive of liquidating an entire portion of the human race is possible only if given the technology. Gas kills en masse and with little effort on the part of the executioner. Thousands could be killed in an hour. Bulldozers to dig mass graves made it possible to conceive of disposal of so many bodies. Modern technology is what made it possible to conceive of the extermination as "The Final Solution."

That raises another dimension. Technology presents itself to the world as a Savior. Technology offers hope for solving the problems of the world. When we talk about the Holocaust as the persecution of the Jews, we obscure the chilling fact that for Hitler and for Germany, the extermination of the Jews was not *persecution;* it was the final *solution* to a problem. The problems of Nazi Germany were overpopulation and a declining economy. Thus, first by mass enslavement and later by extermination, Hitler hoped to solve the problems, and he ordered his solution.

Now let us be clear on what is being said. I am not suggesting that technology is evil. What I am saying is that technology makes conceivable solutions that can be demonic. Take, for example, the technology of war. All of the superpowers conceive of war as a last resort for solving problems. When everything else fails, we go to war. But war offers a reasonable hope of solving the problem only if we have the military technology. Goebbels, one of Hitler's most trusted servants, wrote in his diary: "The war made possible for us the solution of a whole series of problems that could never have been solved in normal times." Some historians suspect that Franklin Roosevelt knew in advance of the attack on Pearl Harbor. He allowed it to happen because he knew that the attack would galvanize sagging American morale and because the war effort could be counted upon to provide peak employment and prosperity for this nation. War for Franklin Roosevelt was a solution to a domestic problem. Terrorists look upon the technology of war, especially its explosive devices, as solutions to their problems. Terror is news and news publicizes the cause for which the terrorist is concerned. We are terribly naive if we think it will be long before we will be the victims of nuclear blackmail by irresponsible terrorist groups. It is only a question of time, because the technology offers solutions to their problems.

From a somewhat different perspective it can be seen that the Holocaust is the inevitable result when technological thinking triumphs over wisdom. I take it that the art of living in a technological age is to make use of technology without being dehumanized by it. The Nazis knew that. The Nazis knew that they could be dehumanized by their technology and they took great pains *not* to be dehumanized by it. Heinrich Himmler, for example, said, "To eliminate the Jews and still to remain decently human is the hardest and the highest challenge we have to face." That they were successful in using technology to solve their problem and yet remain human is a fact of history. For the Nazis loved their wives as you and I do; they kissed them good-bye in the morning when they went to work; they greeted them joyously and happily when they came home at night. They were good fathers of their children, tucking them into bed at night, some of them even saying prayers with their children. Nora Levin, in her definitive history of the Holocaust, says:

In Hitler-Germany, a highly developed people devised the rationale and methodology for exterminating six million human beings—over a million of them children—and for converting them into fat for soap, hair for mattresses and bone for fertilizer. For the Nazis, Jews became part of the non-human universe—the objects of functional exploitation, undifferentiated from other non-human matter in nature, and requiring the same detachment. This new formulation enabled mass murderers to think of themselves as technicians following orders and to call mass murder "special treatment."

How, how could such a highly developed society, so advanced technologically, maintain a sense of dignity and respect about itself without losing its humanity? The answer is that Germany developed technological thinking at the expense of wisdom.

Technological thinking is manipulative thinking. It thinks in terms of controlling, manipulating, and using. By nature it is impersonal and objective, and by nature it is aggressive. Technological thinking is contrasted with *contemplative* thinking, which is passive by nature, open, and receptive, waiting upon, rather than aggressively asserting, molding and using. Contemplative thinking is given to wonder and awe. It is amazement at the mystery in both the human and the divine.

Western civilization has put a premium on technological thinking and has devalued contemplative thinking because contemplative thinking does not produce. There is little financial value to be associated with contemplative thinking. Our education and our economy are tooled to produce technological thinkers. Franklin Littell, one of the few Christian theologians who has wrestled with the question of the Holocaust for Christian theology, warns us of the consequences of emphasizing technological thinking at the expense of contemplative thinking. He says:

The application of mathematical formulae and models, the very "objectivity" and detachment which have contributed so much in the hard sciences, have led to Auschwitz, Babi Yar, the massacre in the Katyn forest, and the atrocity at My Lai. A common misstatement of the problem is that "science" is neutral and crimes are committed when science escapes the control of humanities. The real problem is that a single pattern of thinking has become normative in sociology as well as chemistry, in political science as well as engineering, in theology as well as nuclear physics. A prideful contempt for the human person, his present condition and his past experience, stains the thoughts and visions of "modern man." Each age has been "the modern age" in turn, of course, but only in the last two centuries has the contempt for history and the lessons of past human experience become obsessive.

Those are strong words, but when you put the spectacles of the Holocaust on, you begin to see the straws in the wind announcing the hurricane. In the news of late, for example, has been the decline of the SAT (Scholastic Aptitude Test) scores of our nation's students. The verbal scores have been particularly obvious. There is great concern over the inability of our graduates to spell and use the language properly. But that is only the tip of the iceberg. Language—and our ability to use it—is the vehicle by which we convey meanings. When we can no longer use language adequately, we can no longer convey meanings adequately and we are cut off from the roots that give us a sense of responsibility and accountability. What is at stake is our identity as members of the human community when we emphasize technological thinking on the one hand at the expense of contemplative thinking on the other.

The Church has been worried about this for years. The Church has been concerned about the fact that we are basically biblically illiterate. The Bible is our source of identity; it is the vehicle by which we maintain a sense of responsibility, but most of us don't read the Bible. Why? Because we're too *busy!* Busy-ness is typical of a technologically aggressive society, such as Western civilization. It is not typical of a contemplative society, such as the Eastern cultures represent.

Franklin Littell continues:

The role of technology—in its aversion to the mysterious and open— has sealed off that dimension of human experience. From the elementary school, the young person is taught to think in the symmetry of the closed, the traditional mathematical model, and by the time he has finished with the university, he may be a skilled technician—but he is rarely a wise man. . . . He can build bridges, guide missiles, or install pacemakers with equal competence for the Soviets, the Chilean junta, the Iraqi national socialists, or the Canadian federal republic.

It was no great problem for Werner von Braun to transfer his technological skills from the Nazis to the Americans.

Quoting Littell again: "If such a person were a man of wisdom, he would be troubled in some alliances—or perhaps even impeded in maintaining them." We graduate people in the American educational system of whom it can be said, "His work is good; energetic; shows initiative. He has a great capacity for independent action, particularly in organization. He is known as a specialist in his field." I suppose some of us would even envy a recommendation like that. If those qualifications could be put on our dossier, that would be a consummation devoutly to be wished. They would look good to an employer. Those were precisely the words of the dossier of Adolf Eichmann. The Holocaust is the apocalyptic symbol of where Western civilization is headed if its social and educational values remain intact.

Consider finally then that the Holocaust makes it clear that technology is no cure for human sin. It may offer hope; it may present itself as a savior, and we may believe in it, but it is a false hope. It is a false Messiah. The Holocaust makes it abundantly clear that technology cannot cure human sin. Technology cannot solve the world's problems. It may change the world's problems; it may alter their shape, but it cannot solve them. DDT was used to kill the corn bore so that we could produce more food to feed the world's starving, but DDT polluted the streams and the fish began to die. Penicillin and the antibiotics were the wonder drugs of medical technology. Now we discover that pneumonia, along with other diseases, is developing a resistance to and tolerance of the wonder drugs.

In our society there is a lot of romantic thinking about the capabilities of technology. In that very popular book, *Zen and the Art of Motorcycle Maintenance*, the author argues that technology is "not exploitation of nature, but a fusion of nature and the human spirit into a new kind of equation that transcends both." What bothers me about that is his word "transcends"; his naive assumption that the fusion of nature and the human spirit will *transcend*. The Holocaust ought to make it abundantly clear that it can *descend* as well. Sin is not a popular word, but the Holocaust reminds us of the ever-present reality of it in an age in which we want so desperately to believe in ourselves . . . in an age in which we can explore the creation of new life forms and explore the celestial bodies in our solar system, we want to believe that all things are possible to us and for us. It is easy to become intoxicated with our own capabilities and to assume the optimistic best about our intentions and our efforts. But the Holocaust stands as that somber objective reminder that sin is an ever-present and terribly important dimension to human nature, *that we dare not ever forget it*, especially as our technological capabilities increase and the stakes become so high. As the psychologist Bruno Bettelheim said—himself a prisoner in Dachau—"If all men are good, then there never was an Auschwitz." *But there was an Auschwitz, and we cannot forget it!*

In point of fact, Hitler did not act alone. We cannot dump all of the guilt upon one man as if he were Satan personified. The whole German nation, almost without exception, was willing to go along silently if not actively cooperating in "the final solution." And so, too, were the Allies. Richard Rubenstein shares one incident:

When informed by Joel Brand, a Hungarian Jewish emissary, that there was a possibility of saving one million Hungarian Jews from extermination at Auschwitz through Adolf Eichmann's infamous "blood for trucks" deal, Lord Moyne (the British High Commissioner in Egypt in 1944) replied, "What shall I do with those million Jews? Where shall I put them?" Lord Moyne and his government understood that Hitler's "final solution" was the most convenient way of solving the problem of disposing of one group of surplus people for themselves as well as for the Germans. The British government was by no means averse to the "final solution" as long as the Germans did most of the dirty work.

And Christians are guilty. Dietrich Bonhoeffer was certainly one of the very few exceptions to that in the German Christian Church. Pope Pius XII looked the other way. In this country the American Christians knew what was going on, but there were only two voices that spoke out: Reinhold Niebuhr and the editor of the Roman Catholic journal, *Commonweal*. One has to conclude from any objective analysis that Hitler alone was not to blame and that, indeed, Paul's assessment of human nature is correct: "There is none righteous, no, not one." Unless we keep that fact in mind, that there is none righteous, and that sin is ever-present, we are apt to embrace blindly the totally false promises of those who offer technological solutions to save us.

There is a chilling story told by Shirley Jackson entitled "The Lottery." She tells about a town that holds an unusual lottery every year. Tradition demands that the game be played and that everyone in the town draw lots. There is only one loser; everybody else wins. When the lottery is over, the loser is stoned to death in the town's square by the winners.

The story offers an interesting analogy to the situation in which we find ourselves. The hazards of today's technological world are encountered in the form of a gigantic production, marketing, consumption lottery game. The stakes are the benefits we reap from the goods that technology produces, and the risks are those of polluting our culture or people through guns, tobacco, alcohol, and drugs; pesticides; automobiles and motorcycles; dangerous work places; and chemically contaminated foodstuffs and detergents. The game, of course, is played by a small group of people, usually a corporation, offering to the public the promise of something very good, albeit with a risk. But the risk is small and only a few will lose. Most will win, and so the Most buy in because the Most never think that they could be the loser. Besides, there are economic values to the promise that technology offers; hence, Leonard Woodcock last year argued against strict pollution standards for auto emission controls because it would mean the losing of jobs in the auto industry. Consumers join in because they are resentful of the increased prices they will have to pay for cars with the controls. Few believe they will be the loser. Few think pollution will affect them. And so we play the lottery game.

The same can be said of alcohol. The consumption of beer and wine is on the increase. So is the increase of alcoholism. According to the National Council of Alcohol and Alcoholism, one out of ten who takes the first drink now becomes an alcoholic. The National Council of Alcohol and Alcoholism, which was the governmental agency that used to speak of drinking "in moderation," has dropped that term because it now believes there is no such thing as responsible drinking, not with that kind of odds. It's a game of Russian Roulette. But still we play because we don't think we'll be the loser. The same thing can be said of hand guns and cigarettes and flame retardants and pesticides, etc., etc.

The Holocaust reminds us that, given the fact of human sinfulness and the possibilities of a technological society, the prospects for the survival of the human race are not bright. But we are called to be a people of hope who live, not by trusting human capabilities or technological promises; we are called to live by the absurd promise of a God who says, "I will return." Let us pray.

Oh God, we live in a world in which there are so many things we would like to forget or ignore, but we do so only at our own peril and the peril of those whom we love and those future generations for whom we are already now responsible. The lessons of history are not gentle, nor are they reassuring. Indeed, our hope of learning and of changing is born only of faith, which derives not from the evidence but from your promise in Christ. It is in His name that we pray and offer ourselves, our lives, our energy, our gifts, and our money. For Christ's sake. Amen.

13

Holocaust Day: 1975

●

JACK S. BOOZER

As WE COME TOGETHER today for a special reason, we ought to be aware of two things happening in this community which manifest concerns similar to those we bring to this occasion. One is the centenary celebration of Albert Schweitzer's birth, which includes an emphasis on "reverence for life." The other is the commemoration of the life and work of Martin Luther King, Jr., which recalls to us the song "We shall overcome," which means not that one people will overcome another, but that together we shall overcome every arbitrary obstacle to the dignity and fulfillment of human life.

I am deeply honored to be entrusted today with one part of this commemoration of persons who died or were scarred for life by the most monstrous deeds of evil in human history. You understand, I am sure, that in what I say I am not claiming to speak from within Judaism, from among those who were killed or brought so close to death that their bodies and spirits were seared by the flames of the gas chambers. But I do claim to speak for the Christian family and for the human family who were there indirectly if not directly, all too silently allowing the doing of what was done, and in ways even now incomprehensible, drawn into

Previously unpublished.

deep indebtedness to the Jews for their testimony toward the salvation of us all.

Two passages have obsessed me in recent days, the first from the Bible, the second from the Baal Shem Tov.

Psalm 137:1–6, from the Jerusalem Bible:

Beside the streams of Babylon
we sat and wept
at the memory of Zion,
leaving our harps
hanging on the poplars there.

For we had been asked
to sing to our captors,
to entertain those who had carried us off:
"Sing," they said,
"some hymns of Zion."

How could we sing
one of Yahweh's hymns
in a pagan country?
Jerusalem, if I forget you,
may my right hand wither!

May I never speak again
if I forget you!
If I do not count Jerusalem
the greatest of my joys!

And from the Baal Shem Tov:

"Forgetfulness prolongs the exile; remembrance is the secret of redemption."

Remembrance is the key to the meaning of this day, not only for the Jews, but for the Christians of the Western world; indeed, for the whole of Western culture. If that claim sounds exaggerated, let me suggest that the catastrophic meaning of Auschwitz and the series of events it represents have caused some to suggest a revision in our manner of counting time, and that henceforth there is only time B.H., before the Holocaust, and A.H., after the Holocaust. There is some merit in the suggestion. Something absolutely unprecedented happened in the Holocaust, something unprecedented but unfortunately repeatable. Because the event is repeatable in our present and our future and in our land as well as in any land, it is desperately important that the entire human family "remember," comprehend, experience in sober awareness the full meaning of the Holocaust. For there is no possible step forward that rests on a solid foundation without going back to that pivotal event in which one claim for humanness died and another claim for humanness lived. If we cannot recover the clarity of a vision of the human, of dignity and sanctity, of justice and holiness, to which all principalities and powers are subject, then the future of project humanity is very much in doubt. Strange to say, for Western humanity *there is no sure future* unless we can remember the past, most particularly the Holocaust.

But why, you may ask, is the Holocaust all that important? Because the Holocaust demonstrated the radical evil of which persons, human beings, are capable, that people can destroy the humanity of others while they are still alive; and it showed the relative ineffectiveness of any means to stop that evil when the evil is combined with the totalitarian powers of government. Hannah Arendt and Elie Wiesel give different kinds of testimony to the same point.

In her brilliant study of totalitarianism, Arendt speaks of "total domination" by the Nazis. The effect of this is a calculated program in the death camps to destroy not just the ideas and faith of people, but to *destroy their humanity*.

She traces three steps in the process: (1) the destruction of the *juridical person* by removing any external law or right to which he could appeal for justice. The person in the camp was neither guilty nor innocent; he was merely there and subject to the whim of the leader. There was no common law to which any inmate could appeal. (2) The second step in the destruction of the inmate's humanity was the eradication of the *moral person* in man. The death camps made martyrdom impossible for the first time in history by making all the decisions of conscience absolutely equivocal and questionable. What does conscience do when a mother is required to choose which two of her three children will die? Or when Elie Wiesel does not know whether putting his sick father in a hospital will mean healing or deliberate killing? The camps intended to make an individual anonymous, belonging to no one and to no moral order, and with no one belonging to him. (3) The final step in destroying humanity was to remove the *individuality of a person*. The camps succeeded in this by shaving all the hair off the body, dressing all in the same kind of clothes, bringing all to a state of sameness in malnutrition through diet, work, and disease. There was no privacy for any function of life. With the destruction of individuality, there was also the destruction of spontaneity and all of the resources for self-maintenance and resistance that spontaneity provides. In destroying the juridical person, the moral person and the individual person, the SS created a system of "total terror," because they knew that "the system which succeeds in destroying its victim before he mounts the scaffold . . . is incomparably the best for keeping a whole people in slavery" (p. 153).

Here these words of Arendt:

Until now the totalitarian belief that everything is possible seems to have proved only that everything can be destroyed. Yet, in their effort to prove that everything is possible, totalitarian regimes have discovered without knowing it that there are crimes which men can neither punish nor forgive. When the impossible was made possible it became the unpunishable, unforgivable absolute evil which could no longer be understood and explained by the evil motives of self-interest, greed, covetousness, resentment, lust for power, and cowardice; and which therefore anger could not revenge, love could not forgive. Just as the victims in the death factories or the holes of oblivion are no longer "human" in the eyes of their executioner, so this newest species of criminals is beyond the pale even of solidarity in human sinfulness. (Arendt, *The Origins of Totalitarianism*, p. 157)

Wiesel gives poignant testimony to the same process.

These absent no longer touched even the surface of our memories. We still spoke of them . . . but we had little concern for their fate. We were incapable of thinking of anything at all. Our senses were blunted; everything was blurred as in a fog. It was no longer possible to grasp anything. The instincts of self-preservation, of self-defense, of pride, had all deserted us. In our ultimate moment of lucidity it seemed to me that we were damned souls wandering in the half-world, souls condemned to wander through space till the generations of man came to an end, seeking their redemption, seeking oblivion— without hope of finding it. . . .

Within a few seconds, we had ceased to be men. . . .

I, too, had become a completely different person. The student of the Talmud, the child that I was, had been consumed in the flames. There remained only a shape that looked like me. A dark flame had entered into my soul and devoured it. (*Night*, pp. 46–47)

The evil of the Holocaust cannot be understood, cannot be punished, and cannot be forgiven; it can only be remembered. *And what is it to remember?*

—To know this evil, the destruction of the human, is now possible. It has happened and it may happen again. The capability of this evil is in us all.

—To honor and to hold tenderly those children and men and women who were killed.

—To give thanks for those who maintained their human dignity when Hitler and the SS had lost theirs.

—To realize that if we do not resist the first and second attacks on *anyone's* right and dignity as a person, it may be impossible to resist later without the risk of one's life.

—To recognize that had Hitler succeeded in genocide against the Jews, he would have applied genocide against others. Hence, what the Jews did to resist Hitler, what you now do to remember the Holocaust and to survive as a people, you do not only for yourselves but for the whole human family and to the glory of the God of Abraham, Isaac, and Jacob and of the whole creation.

Reflecting on the Nazi period after the war, Elie Wiesel said: "It was neither German nor Jew who ruled the Ghetto . . . it was illusion" (*Night*, p. 21). In our public life today we are very near to being ruled by illusion, superficiality, naiveté, wishful thinking, oversimplification, and glibness. The future holds no promise under such a rule. That is why what you do here today is so crucially important. There is an extremely uncertain future for the Jew and for all of us together if we forget the Holocaust. The way forward for the Jew and for us all is the way backward, back to the Holocaust to recover there in tenderness, in clarity, and in certainty our guilty, bruised, sensitive, vulnerable, striving, suffering, believing, and hopeful humanity, and what the Holy One of Israel calls us to be and to do in these days of anguish and opportunity.

Without being presumptuous and, I hope, without being patronizing, I speak for a large company in saying: I offer thanks for you, that you remain Jews, that you remember the Holocaust without despair, that you marry and have children, and that you instruct your children in Jewish faith. If you, having suffered these offenses, can still survive and believe and hope, you are surely children of encouragement to all who have eyes to see, ears to hear, and souls to feel. If you will accept me, I join you in the covenant task to "battle evil and to perfect the world," to hold the line together against the violations of the Jews, the God of our Fathers, of Israel, and of every human being.

Forgetfulness does prolong the exile; remembrance is the secret of redemption. Hence the words of the psalmist have particular meaning now:

> Jerusalem, if I forget you,
> may my right hand wither!
>
> May I never speak again,
> if I forget you!
> If I do not count Jerusalem
> the greatest of my joys!

14

Auschwitz and the Nurturing
of Conscience

•

ROBERT E. WILLIS

IT HAS BEEN ARGUED recently that it is not possible to ground Jewish theology legitimately in the Holocaust.[1] Whatever the significance of that event might be for Jewish life and thought, it is asserted, it cannot, in itself, provide the basis for a revitalized faith. Jacob Neusner, for example, is particularly blunt in rejecting that possibility:

One who did not believe in God before he knew about the Holocaust is not going to be persuaded to believe in Him on its account. One who believed in the classical perception of God presented by Judaic theologians is not going to be forced to change his perception on its account. . . . Jews find in the Holocaust no new definition of Jewish identity because we need none. Nothing has changed. The tradition endures.[2]

Thus, Neusner categorically sets aside the efforts of Emil Fackenheim and Richard Rubenstein, among others, to see in the Holocaust an utterly unique event requiring a new departure for Jewish theology. Rubenstein's suggestive metaphor of the Holocaust as a time bomb ticking within the Jewish community[3] is

Reprinted with permission from *Religion in Life*, Winter 1975, copyright © 1975, Abingdon Press.

neutralized when placed within the salvific contours of the tradition, and Fackenheim's urging of a new and commanding word
from Auschwitz—that Jews continue to exist as Jews, lest Hitler
be handed a posthumous victory[4]—is silenced by the sustaining
power of the original 613.

Whether or not Neusner is ultimately proved correct in his
view of the insignificance of Auschwitz for the Jewish story and
its accompanying metaphors, and of the enduring sufficiency of
tradition, no such appeal will suffice when the focus shifts to the
implications of that event for the Christian story. What then
becomes clear is that the tradition that has informed and shaped
the sensibility of the Christian community through time has itself
contributed to the development of anti-Judaic and anti-Semitic
attitudes and actions. Rosemary Ruether has attempted to describe
the form of that contribution in her suggestion that "anti-Judaism
in Christian theology stands as the left hand of Christology."[5]
Moreover, she continues,

the stance of church leadership toward the results of theological anti-
Judaism has been one which might be described as "the right hand not
knowing what the left hand is doing," and that continues to be the
attitude of the Christian church toward the history of anti-semitism
in Christian history up to our own time, despite the Holocaust.[6]

Ruether's analysis of the ambiguity present within the Christian
tradition raises what is surely the most difficult and agonizing
question of all: the degree to which the church is to be held accountable for the Holocaust. Did Christian theology—the developing (and developed) explication of the Christian story, which
began with the New Testament writings—prepare the way, wit-
tingly or unwittingly, for that horror? For A. Roy Eckardt, at
least, the answer is unequivocal:

The Holocaust remains merely the final act of a uniquely unique
drama. It is simply the hour that succeeds the drawing up of all the
doctrinal formulations. It is the attaining of the "right time" (*kairos*)
following upon all those *practice sessions* of crusade, inquisition, and
the like. The Holocaust is *no more than* this consummation. Yet in

that very simplicity, in that very absence of originality, there is contained all the insane complexity. Only in these latter years could we fully and finally ready ourselves for the eschatological deed (*Endlösung*). Only the final destruction was left to be carried out. . . . The Nazis were nothings. They could only provide concrete, practical implementation of the dominant theological and moral conclusions of the Church, with the aid of technological devices not previously available to Christendom.[7]

And, with regard to the impact wrought by the Holocaust on the subsequent thinking of the church, Eckardt finds no basis for optimism. "Very largely," he asserts, "the churches continue to live in the midst of the *Endlösung*."

It is impossible to conceive a more massive or absolute indictment of the Christian conscience and the story framework within which it is set. Indeed, if it is really the case that the Holocaust—the acting out of the "final solution"—can be seen as no more than the necessary expression of what was present implicitly in that story from the beginning, then it is hard to see what hope remains for any sort of fundamental reorientation or reshaping of it. The only possible conclusion would have to be that the Christian tradition, despite its ostensibly positive intent, and the contributions it may have made to human well-being, is in its very essence evil, the final embodiment of the Antichrist. Moreover, both the claims advanced on behalf of the capacity of the Christian conscience to respond in a morally fitting way, and the presumed ability of the Christian community to give it appropriate shape and direction, would have to be rejected.

Understandably, one shrinks from embracing so stark a conclusion. Not even Richard Rubenstein, in his analysis of the fateful relationship that has existed between Judaism and Christianity, found it necessary (or possible) to see in the death camps a *necessary*, and therefore unavoidable, consequence of the Christian outlook.[8]

Even so, we must not move too quickly to neutralize Eckardt's judgment, for it represents a profound *cri de coeur*, a resounding *mea culpa* spoken on behalf of the Christian community as a whole. At the very least, it serves as a dramatic reminder of the burden of guilt and responsibility which must be shouldered for the contribution which the church's theology did, in fact, make to the *Endlösung* of the Nazis. The fact that that event cannot fairly be seen as a direct entailment of the Christian story does not lessen the evil consequences it helped to produce.

It seems clear, at any rate, that the response of the Christian community to the moral crisis represented by the Nazis and their policies was at best ambiguous, and at worst the most explicit embodiment to date of the limited power of the Christian story to shape conscience and behavior in a morally appropriate fashion. Indeed, what emerges from that piece of history is a precise indication of the ambiguity and the complexity of the relationship between moral agency (in both its corporate and individual forms) and the story, or stories, by which it is shaped and directed.[9] To put it differently, we can say that it exposes dramatically the gap between the ideal and the actuality of the church, a gap which gains specific embodiment in the tension between what, from a moral point of view, is required and what in fact is done.

What is required now is the effort of attempting to expand the content and the dynamics of the Christian conscience through an absorption of the lessons conveyed to it by Auschwitz. To put it differently, the church must allow its conscience and those of its members to be nurtured by the Holocaust to a new embodiment of the relationship between story and moral agency. The urgent need for such an exploration has been expressed forthrightly by Friedrich Heer: "For the Church to assume her share of permanent co-responsibility for the whole Jewish community presupposes an illumination of the Christian conscience which is only just beginning. To put it into practice, a complete revision of Christian theology is needed."[10]

It has been proposed—by Stanley Hauerwas and Michael Novak, among others—that a theory of the moral life which seeks to do justice to the intentionality of moral agency must take seriously the particular story that has come to be embodied in the life of the self. It is only in relation to the complex story that is lived by the self, and the ways in which that informs and shapes the overall direction of its life, that moral assessment and action can occur.

To stress the relationship between story, intentionality, and action is not to reject the place of principles and rules in the moral life. It is, rather, to focus attention on what may be called the aesthetic component of morality—that larger and richer background which comprises its ethos, and which enables the specific actions of the self to be displayed as part of an ongoing character pattern rather than merely a discrete series of actions. As Hauerwas puts it:

Our moral lives are not simply made up of the addition of our separate responses to particular situations. Rather we exhibit an orientation that gives our life a theme through which the variety of what we do and do not do can be scored. To be agents at all requires a directionality that involves the development of character and virtue. Our character is the result of our sustained attention to the world that gives a coherence to our intentionality.[11]

The story that we come to embody and make our own is not, however, self-generated. The formation of character and the shaping of intentionality occur within a social context, or, more accurately, within the several communities—family, nation, church—with which we have to do. The moral biography of the self is thus to be understood in relation to the stories, symbols, and metaphors generated by those communities, and appropriated as one's own.

It goes without saying that the process of appropriation will be complex rather than simple, for although there may well be points at which the various stories presented will mesh, there will also certainly be others where conflict and tension will arise—the claims of the family against those of the nation, those of nation and family against those of the religious community, and so forth.

It is in relation to this welter of potentially conflicting claims, loyalties, and obligations that the self must attempt to forge a coherent and durable pattern of moral response. That necessity points to the cruciality of a story which both transcends our undertakings and grounds us in them, providing an outlook whereby we are enabled to resist the tendency to identify completely (and immorally) with partial stories, and the roles and demands they present to us.

For the Christian moral self, such a transcending story is unfolded within the Christian community, which provides a setting within which moral awareness can be nurtured to a potential, albeit always provisional, embodiment of maturity.[12] It is within such a setting that the moral self *in its wholeness* can be specified in terms of the category of conscience. "Conscience" then serves as a shorthand designation for the complex of factors that impinge on the moral identity of the self, and points to the possibility of actions that exemplify continuity between character (virtue) and obligation. As James Nelson has remarked: "If we think of conscience with its several interrelated and social dimensions, then it is obvious that we are pointing not only to one particular element or faculty but to the entire moral self in all its richness and complexity."[13]

The understanding of conscience suggested above has certain obvious affinities with the views of such thinkers as Lehmann, Tillich, H. R. Niebuhr, and Bonhoeffer. In each, though not in precisely the same way, there is a concern to view the moral identity of the self—the totality of which I have designated by the term "conscience"—in relation to the social reality of the Christian community, and the meaning-complex of symbol, metaphor, and story by means of which it carries on the process of reflection, self-criticism, and action. The theonomous or transmoral image of the self as moral agent that emerges here points to the transcendent ground of the moral life in the sovereignty of God (or God-in-Christ), and to that final level of accountability which must be exhibited faithfully throughout its duration.

One way of expressing the force of that accountability is to say that the understanding of the moral agency of the self that is projected within the Christian story entails the concept of deputyship. James Gustafson has indicated in a precise way the connection that holds therein between conviction and accountability.

Our convictions are that God, made known through his deeds in Israel's perceptions of them, and in the face of Jesus Christ as the apostles have depicted it to us, is the sovereign Lord of all things. To be deputized by him is to be particularly responsible to him for the things over which he is Lord. No person, no event can be arbitrarily left out of our concern. And certainly the particular events and persons in our particular spheres of life give location to our deputyship. To fulfill this is to think carefully about God's will and way, to be perceptive with reference to our world, to be sensitized and directed by our faith and conviction, and to shape our intentions and actions with clarity. It is also to acknowledge that we are *only* deputies, and subject to the limitations and perversions of agency. God remains sovereign, and we live in hope as well as in solemn moral obligation.[14]

The nurturing context provided by the Christian community and its story is thus possessed, in principle, of the power to affect the dispositions and characters of its members. Within that setting, the universal and the personal dimensions of moral responsibility and accountability can be maintained and brought to the level of conscious reflection and enactment. Therein we find a perspective inclusive enough to relativize, without submerging, our lesser, though unavoidable, loyalties, so that our tendency to settle into some form of either moral polytheism or moral henotheism is transformed.

It is obvious, however, that we are dealing here with an ideal view. The requirements of deputyship are beset, as Gustafson notes, by our "limitations and perversions," and by our persistent tendency to fall into self-deception with respect to the implications of Christian moral identity and the way in which it ought to penetrate the various roles we inhabit, and define the limits of their claims upon us.

Nor is the possibility of self-deception an eradicable element in our lives. Despite the nurturing efficacy of the religious community, it remains a potent force in the very being of the moral agent. As David Burrell and Stanley Hauerwas have noted, "To be is to be rooted in self-deception." Given that fact, it becomes clear that "the moral task involves a constant vigilance: to note those areas where the tendency has taken root. This task is made more difficult by the illusions of the past which we have unsuspectingly inherited."[15]

Coming to an awareness of those aspects of our lives which contain the seeds of self-deception involves more than mere self-examination. It must encompass, as well, an insight into the ways in which the basic story by which persons are nurtured within the Christian community has itself contributed to the development of a deficient conscience, so that the venture of deputyship becomes fundamentally distorted.

That point applies with especial force to Auschwitz, for, as Burrell and Hauerwas have noted,

the complicity of Christians with Auschwitz did not begin with their failure to object to the first slightly anti-semitic laws and actions. It rather began when Christians assumed that they could be the heirs and carriers of the symbols of the faith without sacrifice and suffering. It began when the very language of revelation became an expression of status rather than an instrument for bringing our lives gradually under the sway of "the love that moves the sun and the stars." Persons had come to call themselves Christians and yet live as though they could avoid suffering and death. So Christians allowed their language to idle without turning the engines of the soul, and in response, their lives were seized by powers that they no longer had the ability to know, much less to combat.[16]

The perversion of language into a story exposed to the risk of being interpreted as an indication and guarantee of status—the triumphalist posture contained, implicitly if not explicitly, within much Christian theology—brings again into view the other side of that image. A story which evokes the motif of triumph requires the counter-motif of defeat and rejection. In short, it requires what became an increasingly prevalent component of Christian theology after A.D. 70: the assertion of the covenant unfaithfulness of Judaism and the Jewish people, and their subsequent rejection and replacement by Christianity.

What seemed a development with the power to counteract that pattern, the rejection by the church of Marcion's position in the second century, in fact proved to be an ironic certification of it. Marcion was judged heretical by the emerging orthodox consensus, the Jewish scriptures were affirmed as part of the Christian canon, but Judaism, viewed subsequently, was granted no continuing validity or worth. The only avenue of escape from the crime of deicide and a perverted story lay in conversion. The refusal to turn down that road provided additional proof, if any were needed, of Jewish hardness of heart, and made possible the emergence of a conscience within the church which could entertain, with only an occasional loss of equanimity, the spectacle of Jewish persecution and suffering.

Nor have the anticipation of the eventual conversion of the Jewish community, and the withering away of Judaism which it presupposes, yet been laid to rest, as Franklin Littell has noted: "Both during the conflict and in church gatherings after the war, even the best and most courageous churchmen continued to define the Jew's place in history for him, refusing to recognize Judaism as a religion in its own right, stressing a provisional tolerance based on expectation of the Jew's coming conversion to Christ."[17]

And the most recent effort on the part of the Vatican, announced in January of this year, to develop a more cordial atmosphere for Jewish and Christian relations, remains captive, despite its positive aspects, to that model. Marc Tannenbaum's comment is apt: "The assertion of a conversionary intention within the framework of guidelines for the improvement of Catholic-Jewish relations cannot but cast doubts about the motivations of the entire program."[18]

If, after Auschwitz, it is still possible for Christians to cling to the pretension that their story undergrids a responsibility for the conversion of Jews, then it is questionable whether we can learn anything from the events of history. For unless the consciences of those who profess to live out the Christian story can be reawakened by a consideration of these events—and the Holocaust in particular—then it would appear that there is a fated quality to the outlook the Christian story engenders which prohibits significant revision. If that is the case, however, we are doomed to achieve not only an ambiguous, but a perverted and evil embodiment of the deputyship entailed by that story. The range of responsible, conscientious caring is foreshortened to exclude fellow humans who happen to be Jews, and the silence of Pius XII becomes, as Arthur Cochrane suggests, the symbol of collective disobedience and failure.[19]

We are faced, at this point, with the alternative posed earlier by Paul Lehmann: either to dispose of the conscience altogether, or to transform it. Lehmann's solution was to present a vision of the theonomous conscience, grounded in the life of the *koinonia*, and responsive to the humanizing action of God in the world. In that setting, faith (i.e., response to the story) provides the basis for human actions in conformity with the directionality of the divine movement toward humanization, in an atmosphere set free from the demands of prescriptive legalism and from strict dependence on the guidance afforded by moral principles and rules. However, Lehmann's prospectus for a refashioned conscience does not avoid the danger of "forgetting the difference between the ideal church and the real church," as Alan Davies has pointed out.[20]

The possibility of overcoming that difference is, at best, limited. If self-deception is part of the given nature of human existence, then it follows that *any* story elaborated by a community and embodied in the lives of its members will suffer from partial insight and wisdom, and will run the risk of producing evil effects as well as good. Given that fact, it is perhaps understandable that historians like J. H. Plumb have tended to view the category of story in strongly pessimistic terms, arguing that it serves *only* the process of self-aggrandizement, thereby leading inevitably to oversimplification and distortion. The only reasonable course of action, then, is to reject story entirely, and to replace it with history, which (as Plumb sees it) can provide a true and impartial recounting of the facts.[21]

In view of the relationship that exists between story and conscience in the religious community, however, such a move would be both inadmissible and disastrous to the enterprise of moral agency. Whatever its distorting capacities—and they are both real and persistent—it is hard to see what sense could be attached to the concept of Christian moral action (or any other, for that matter) apart from the storied context within which it is set. It is doubtless true that "a person who habitually thinks in terms of parable and fable, most of all a fable of the highly organized sort which we call a religion, has a difficulty about altering an individual moral judgment, which is not experienced by the follower of principles."[22] That difficulty applies *a fortiori* to the sorts of moral assessments Christians have been led to make about Judaism and the Jewish people under the tutelage of their dominant story. What is required, then, is that the pattern laid down within it become "open to moral claims from without," so that it is empowered to "admit its own inadequacy."[23]

The approach taken by H. Richard Niebuhr provides a useful way of coming to grips with the problem. In *The Meaning of Revelation*, he underscores the importance of the inner history of the Christian community (its own story), and indicates also the significance, potentially, of outer, external views of it for limiting the tendency toward self-deception and for heightening moral awareness:

Every external history of ourselves, communicated to us, becomes an event in inner history. . . . The church has had to respond to them. Though it knew that such stories were not *the* truth about it, it willingly or unwillingly, sooner or later, recognized *a* truth about it in each one. In so far as it apprehended these events in its history, these descriptions and criticisms of itself, with the aid of faith in the God of Jesus Christ it discerned God's judgment in them and made them occasions for active repentance. Such external histories have helped to keep the church from exalting itself as though its inner life rather than the God of that inner life were the center of its attention and the ground of its faith. They have reminded the church of the earthen nature of the vessel in which the treasure of faith existed. In this practical way external history has not been incompatible with inner life but directly contributory to it.[24]

There is a difference, of course, between what Niebuhr means by outer history and the event of Auschwitz. It is a difference, however, which serves to heighten the tragedy of that occurrence. For although the Holocaust was not, in any intentional sense, an "external history of ourselves, communicated to us," it ought to become such, for what is presented there is the dreadful irony of a community, long accused of the crime of deicide, embodying totally the image of crucifixion claimed by the church as the most potent symbol of God's love and the meaning of discipleship.

That judgment must be followed immediately by the recognition that the image of the crucifixion can be applied to Auschwitz only imperfectly, as something *imposed*, not chosen. The possibility of the Christian story and conscience receiving instruction from that event depends on seeing it properly. Only if it is seen for what it was and is—a radical calling into question of the credibility of Christianity—can its significance begin to be unpacked. When it is so seen, however, when Christians allow the horror of Auschwitz to penetrate their consciousnesses steadily and without flinching, then they are enabled to receive a new training in Christianity.

That training must begin with the shock of recognition, the willingness to accept guilt and admit complicity. Does this imply a concept of cellective guilt? I believe that it does, but at the level of shared memory and participation in the ongoing life of a community rather than at the level of interpersonal assessment and judgment of the actions of others. It is obviously true that none of us here were directly involved in the policies that led to the death camps. Nevertheless, the effects of the Christian story through time in creating a potent seedbed for contemporary anti-Semitism, and the actions of those who professed allegiance to it during that crisis, can become, through intentional appropriation, part of my (and our) history as well. Theodore R. Weber has expressed the point well: "The self's memory . . . provides a track on which the guilt of other persons in other ages can run into the present, and the identification of the self with selected or given historical antecedents provides the coupling mechanism by which their guilt becomes my guilt."[25]

The acceptance of one's complicity in Auschwitz provides no basis for assessing the intentions and actions of others. It is an action that each of us must perform for herself or himself, but it is done in the name of, and on behalf of, our participation in the community as a whole. Nevertheless, it is not a merely religious action devoid of moral import. Rather, it is, following Karl Barth's analysis, the *primary* moral deed—repentance, *metanoia*—which must precede and inform all subsequent thinking and doing.

Once that act has been performed, there are further implications that follow from the training in awareness afforded by Auschwitz. To begin with, we are forced to a radical reopening of the question of the relationship between God and evil. It is ironic, in that respect, that the emergence of Christian theologies of the death of God took their departure, not from that event, but rather from various assumptions about the state of contemporary consciousness in a secularized world. That fact, surely, provides a stunning indication of the degree to which Auschwitz has failed to penetrate the minds of Christian thinkers.

Franklin Sherman and A. Roy Eckardt have grappled recently with the problem of belief in God after Auschwitz, with strikingly different proposals.

Sherman's approach is to stress the participation of God in human sufferings and the moral imperative that follows, viz., that women and men are called upon to become active participants in that suffering. Nor is he unaware of the moral ambiguity involved in appealing to that symbol, centering, as it does, in the cross: "It is tragic that this symbol should have become a symbol of division between Jews and Christians, for the reality to which it points is a Jewish reality as well, the reality of suffering and martyrdom." Nevertheless, an emphasis on voluntary suffering, divine and human, can, Sherman believes, cut through the pretentiousness of a triumphalist outlook, and recall us to a remembrance of our shared humanity under God: "A God who suffers is the opposite of a God of triumphalism. We can speak of God after Auschwitz only as the one who calls us to a new unity as beloved brothers—not only between Jews and Christians, but especially between Jews and Christians."[26]

It is clear that Sherman's proposal assumes the continuing validity of traditional covenant theology, now corrected and chastened by an acknowledgment of the ambiguities latent within it and the need for continual repentance for the evils they have produced.

Eckardt, by contrast, maps out a position which stresses God's voluntary *abrogation* of the covenant as the only (morally) proper act of repentance for his complicity in the evil of involuntary suffering to which it has led. That must mean, however, that "the myth of the Jew as 'suffering servant' can surrender its horrible power only as the erstwhile Covenant is given a decent and moral burial."[27] Following Emil Fackenheim, Eckardt argues for a new understanding of Jewish existence in which the primary motif is that of survival rather than suffering, and in which the categories of traditional theology give way to the process of moralization and secularization.

There are problems in both Sherman's and Eckardt's approaches. The former must confront the challenge of making credible, after the Holocaust, *any* appeal on the part of Christians to the efficacy of the cross, and the image of sacrificial, voluntary suffering it presents. At the very least, it is an image which must, for the time being, be embodied in the *life* of the Christian community, rather than merely proclaimed.

The latter must wrestle with the implications for Christians of a Jewish identity set free from the storied framework of the covenant, in view of the continuing reality of secular anti-Semitism. In short, it is possible, in this case, to do the wrong thing for the right reasons. If the first Holocaust occurred, in a sense, under Christian auspices, the possibility of a second under secular sponsorship must be taken seriously. Thus, the judgment that the symbol of covenant can be accorded neither credibility nor place in Christian language about Judaism and Jewish existence must be weighed with care, lest it provide the basis for an indifferent, rather than an informed, conscience.

Perhaps the safest, and most obvious, point to be made at this time is that the Holocaust looms, unavoidably and consumingly, as a mystery for the Christian thinker, and that the first response must be a respectful silence. When the effort is undertaken of bringing that event into conjunction with the God professed to be the center of value within the Christian story, then the process of exorcising those elements within it which contribute to and sustain, however subtly, either a presumed superiority or anti-Semitism, presents itself as the first task for a renewed conscience.

Auschwitz can also be seen as the final exposure of the dangers that attend the privatization of religion, a development that must be judged an important contributing factor to the inability of the church to respond properly to the threat posed by Hitler and his policies. To put it differently, the Holocaust presents a stark reminder of the consequences of making the Christian story one's own without at the same time appropriating a consciousness of its grounding in community and its universally inclusive potency.

There is at present a good deal of interest in various approaches to the spiritual life which stress individual effort, concentration, or meditation; and the task of "getting one's head together" has achieved the status of moral obligation for the young, and, perhaps, for the not-so-young as well. If Peter Berger is correct, we are witnessing the flowering of impulses set in motion at the time of the Reformation.[28]

In short, the privatization of religion emerges, albeit ironically, out of the Protestant emphasis on the sole sovereignty of God's grace and the corresponding need to search diligently in scripture in order to discover the access routes that enable one to experience a sense of contact and relationship with it. The contemporary secular view of the religious life as essentially an affair between the isolated individual and whatever sources of transcendence he or she can discover may well be a perversion of the Protestant outlook, but it is, at any rate, a perversion from which the church is not free.

This side of Auschwitz, there is a pressing need to recover a sense of the importance of the institutionalization of the Christian story, that is, an awareness of the ways in which it shapes persons into a community of nurture, and provides a sense of identity which cuts across their various offices and roles, thereby informing moral agency at every point in their lives.

The consciences of Christians can receive further instruction from Auschwitz when it is seen as the parable par excellence of human vulnerability. As Rubenstein has pointed out, the Holocaust represented the bringing together of the concept of superfluous persons with heightened technological efficiency and power.[29]

Thus, it was not only the question of Jewish survival that was posed at Auschwitz. The death camps point to the question mark hanging over the collective future of us all, for they expose our penchant for falling back on various kinds of "final solutions" to the problems that confront us, with their attendant evils. The process remains the same, whether it takes the form of the continued insanity of believing that the best road to peace is through a continually increasing defense budget and stockpiles of nuclear arms, through bombing the Vietnamese back to the Stone Age, through adopting policies of "benign neglect" toward black people and "termination" toward Native Americans, or through a calculated indifference to the sanctity of the environment and the legitimate needs of others in order to satisfy the consumption level of the United States and other presumably "developed" countries.

Moreover, it is sobering to consider that just now, when death education and the process of dying have found a receptive audience in the schools and churches of our society, we are witnessing a growing tendency to expand the limits of permissible death. Regardless of one's position on the issue of the morality of abortion, it should at least be conceded that it raises profound and complex issues about the meaning and status of developing life, and that those are not even seriously broached, much less engaged, by talk about "fetal tissue," the risk factor in various surgical procedures, and the like.

Equally profound and complex issues are now surfacing as the result of new discoveries and techniques in the biological and medical professions: the appropriateness and limits of experimentation on human beings; the proper range to be allowed to genetic planning and control; the guidelines, surgical and moral, that must be observed in relation to organ transplantation; and the moral appropriateness of employing procedures of direct euthanasia.[30]

To view these developments from the perspective of human vulnerability bodied forth at Auschwitz is not to reduce their complexity or to provide ready-made solutions. What can happen is that the conscience informed by that image will remain more sensitive to the potentially serious threats they pose to our capacity to endure as morally sensitive persons. The lure of technological efficiency that made Auschwitz a reality has not, certainly, departed from our midst.

Nor need one be an alarmist to make that point. That one may be accused of falling into that posture by the simple act of asserting that there are perhaps some actions that ought to be (even if they are not for all) both unthinkable and undo-able, is surely a mark of the times, and of a growing tendency to embrace the notion that some lives are indeed superfluous (provided only that they are not our own), and thus expendable.

Finally, in the light of the restoration of Israel, Auschwitz can instruct the consciences of Christians of a fact which has, often enough, been denied: the ongoing durability and existence of Judaism and the Jewish people. It is tempting to view the relationship between the Holocaust and a restored Israel in terms of the model of crucifixion and resurrection. It is, I am convinced, a model, which should be approached with extreme caution. At the very least, it is not something which Christians are in any sense permitted to say to Jews, for it manages simultaneously both to deepen and to make innocuous the horrors of Auschwitz, by making them a condition for eventual rebirth and liberation. It is additionally offensive, moreover, in that it attempts to make sense of, and perhaps to justify, events which simply cannot be fitted into any tidy conceptual scheme. Elie Wiesel's comment is apt:

Israel, an answer to the holocaust? It is too convenient, too scandalous a solution. First, because it would impose a burden, an unwarranted guilt-feeling, on our children. To pretend that without Auschwitz there would be no Israel is to endow the latter with a share of responsibility for the former. And second, Israel cannot be an answer to the holocaust, because the holocaust, by its very magnitude, by its essence too, negates all answers. For me, therefore, these are two distinct events, both inexplicable, unexplained, mysterious, both staggering to the mind and a challenge to the imagination. We shall never understand how Auschwitz was possible. Nor how Israel, scarcely a few years later, was able to draw from itself the strength and vision to rebuild its home in a world adrift and in ruins.[31]

The challenge posed for the Christian conscience by the restoration of Israel is, quite simply, whether we have the capacity to learn, in however limited a fashion, from the past, or whether we are, as Eckardt asserts, still living in the *Endlösung*, the time of the "final solution." For the simple fact of the matter is that the difficulties occasioned for Christian consciousness by a Judaism and a people who refused to cease existing in conformity with the story informing that consciousness are, if anything, intensified by their continuation—despite the time and effort expended during the Holocaust—as a definite and (potentially) enduring political and geographical reality.

I am not suggesting that Israel as a nation is exempt, or to be exempted, from the sorts of factual, empirical analyses and judgments ordinarily applied to nation states. A recognition of the symbolic import for the Christian conscience of Israel's reappearance among the nations need not, and should not, entail automatic acceptance of every policy decision made by its government. Nor on the other side, should it mean that Israel is to be judged by standards of conduct which are not expected of others. The right of a nation and its people to exist cannot justifiably be tied to the condition that their behavior should exhibit moral superiority to others at every point.

The crucial question, then, is whether Christians can endorse, wholeheartedly and without reservation, the right of the Jewish people to exist *in that particular, definite form.* For the image of the Jew presented by Israel represents the incarnation of a potential and a dream (within the Jewish story) which has simply had no place in the traditional Christian outlook: Jewish identity and existence *despite* Christianity; the land restored and made fruitful *despite* the destruction of the temple; the possibility of hope *beyond* despair; the burden of precariousness *removed*, to a degree, by the freedom to be; and the having of a place within which being can receive form and extension through time.

If that dream and its fulfillment can become a part of the consciousness of the Christian community, then it will be possible to understand from within, as it were, why there is continued anxiety in Israel today over the possibility of a second Holocaust, and why it is possible for someone like Golda Meir to express the unimaginable dread aroused by that vision in terms of a "Masada complex." It is doubtless true, as Robert Alter has argued, that Masada, with its image of mass suicide, comes into sharp conflict with the value placed on life within the Jewish tradition.[32] It is also important, however, to see in that image a symbol of the final rejection of passivity. In short, if there is to be a second destruction of the Jewish people, it will at least occur, this time, by their own hands, not by those of others.

In the end, the degree to which the Christian story and conscience are informed by the reality of Israel will provide a measure of what has been learned from the Holocaust. The moral imperative that ought to result from the latter has been put succinctly by Franklin Sherman: "In a world in which human freedom and human perversity are both very real, we cannot say that it *could* not happen. We say that it *must* not happen."[33]

This article represents at best a beginning in what must become an ongoing process of appropriation and reflection. For the God who summons us to community and obedience in the Christian story is envisioned as the universal center of value whose valuing knows neither partiality nor limit. To make that story one's own while continuing to exclude from consciousness the implications it carries for us as moral agents who bear a special burden and responsibility for Judaism and the Jewish people, and thereby for all persons, signifies only that we have, to our shame, missed the point.

Notes

1. See, e.g., Michael Wyschogrod, "Faith and the Holocaust," *Judaism*, XX, 286–94; and Jacob Neusner, "The Implications of the Holocaust," *Journal of Religion*, LIII (1973), 293–308.

2. Neusner, "The Implications of the Holocaust," p. 308.

3. Richard Rubenstein, *After Auschwitz* (Indianapolis: Bobbs-Merrill, 1966), p. 223.

4. Emil L. Fackenheim, *Quest for Past and Future* (Boston: Beacon Press, 1968), p. 20.

5. Rosemary R. Ruether, "Anti-Semitism in Christian Theology," *Theology Today*, XXX (1974), 365.

6. *Ibid.*, p. 380.

7. A. Roy Eckardt, "Is the Holocaust Unique?" *Worldview*, XVII (1974), 33–34.

8. *Ibid.*, p. 34.

9. Rubenstein, *After Auschwitz*, pp. 20–21.

10. See Stanley Hauerwas, "The Self as Story: Religion and Morality from the Agent's Perspective," *Journal of Religious Ethics*, I (1973), 71–85.

11. Friedrich Heer, "The Catholic Church and the Jews Today," *Midstream*, XVIII (1971), 27.

12. See Paul Lehmann, *Ethics in a Christian Context* (New York: Harper & Row, 1963).

13. James B. Nelson, *Moral Nexus* (Philadelphia: Westminster Press, 1971), p. 38.

14. James M. Gustafson, *The Church as Moral Decision-Maker* (Philadelphia: Pilgrim Press, 1970), p. 108.

15. David Burrell and Stanley Hauerwas, "Self-Deception and Autobiography: Theological Reflections on Speer's *Inside the Third Reich*," *Journal of Religious Ethics*, II (1974), 111.

16. *Ibid.*, p. 100.

17. Franklin H. Littell, "Christendom, Holocaust, and Israel," *Journal of Ecumenical Studies*, X (1973), 487.

18. *St. Paul Pioneer Press*, January 3, 1975.

19. Arthur Cochrane, "Pius XII: A Symbol," in Eric Bentley, ed., *The Storm Over the Deputy* (New York: Grove Press, 1964), pp. 157–62.

20. Alan T. Davies, *Anti-Semitism and the Christian Mind* (New York: Herder and Herder, 1969).

21. J. H. Plumb, *The Death of the Past* (Boston: Houghton Mifflin, 1971).

22. R. W. Hepburn, "Vision and Choice in Morality," in Ian T. Ramsey, ed., *Christian Ethics and Contemporary Philosophy* (New York: Macmillan, 1966), p. 193.

23. *Ibid.*, p. 190.

24. H. Richard Niebuhr, *The Meaning of Revelation* (New York: Macmillan, 1941), pp. 62–63.

25. Theodore R. Weber, "Guilt: Yours, Ours, and Theirs," *Worldview*, XVIII (1975), 21.

26. Franklin S. Sherman, "Speaking of God After Auschwitz," *Worldview*, XVII (1974), 29–30.

27. Eckardt, "Is the Holocaust Unique?" in *ibid.*, p. 34.

28. See Peter L. Berger, *The Sacred Canopy* (Garden City: Doubleday, 1969), part II, "Historical Elements."

29. See Richard Rubenstein, "Religion and the Origins of the Death Camps," in *After Auschwitz*, pp. 1–44.

30. See James B. Nelson, *Human Medicine* (Minneapolis: Augsburg, 1973).

31. Elie Wiesel, *One Generation After* (New York: Bard Books, 1965), pp. 166–67.

32. Robert Alter, "The Masada Complex," *Commentary*, LVI (1973), 19–24.

33. Sherman, "Speaking of God After Auschwitz," p. 30.

15

What Are They Saying About Christian-Jewish Relations?

•

JOHN T. PAWLIKOWSKI

No CHRISTIAN SCHOLAR has spoken more forcefully of the implications of the Nazi holocaust, the murder of six million Jews and millions of other peoples by Nazi Germany, than the church historian Franklin Littell. According to him, the holocaust is something that happened to Christians as well as to Jews. He insists that the holocaust "remains the major event in the recent church—signalizing . . . the rebellion of the baptized against the Lord of History . . . Christianity itself has been 'put to the question'."[1] And from the Jewish side Rabbi Irving Greenberg has spoken of the holocaust as an "orienting event" for both Jews and Christians and as a direct refutation of much of the Enlightenment philosophy that has shaped the thought patterns of Western society.[2] The growing scholarly emphasis on the significance of the holocaust for faith and meaning in the modern world has been brought home on a popular level through the special on the holocaust broadcast by the NBC television network in the Spring of 1978.

As Christians and Jews have struggled with this epochal event, several interpretive problems have arisen. Professor Emil Fackenheim of the University of Toronto, for example, has warned that it is immoral to search for meaning in the holocaust event.[3] From one perspective he makes an important point. To make a positive affirmation about any aspect of the holocaust would be to risk destroying all human sensibility. Yet the evil of Auschwitz cannot be ignored. There is a desperate need to confront the effects of Hitler's attempt at the "Final Solution" on the soul and spirit of the human community. To fail in this task would be to endanger human integrity.

There has also been considerable debate among holocaust interpreters as to whether the holocaust fundamentally falls into the category of "irrational" or "rational." In the final analysis, it would seem that only an understanding of the holocaust as basically a rational event does full justice to the monumental challenge it presents for human self-understanding. To place the holocaust in the category of the irrational would offer some relief for the human spirit. Irrationality has always manifested itself in human experience. As tragic as its consequences can be, the challenge to the overall creative and hopeful image of the human person would not be as great if the irrationality perspective were to be accepted.

The most striking feature of the holocaust now emerging from the detailed studies on the manifold operations of the Nazi enterprise by such scholars as Professor Raul Hilberg[4] is the comprehensive and detailed planning involved in its execution. Every step in the process was highly calculated by some of the best minds in Germany. And the holocaust's roots lay in philosophies developed by thinkers still recognized as giants of liberal Western thought. The ideological parents of the holocaust represent the mainstream of Western culture, not its lunatic fringe.

Within a rationality perspective, what emerges from the holocaust is the attempt to create the highest ideal of humanity, the person truly liberated from all physical, mental and cultural deficiencies. This person was to be the universal ideal for all humanity. To achieve this goal, all the supposed "dregs of humanity"—

the Jews, the Poles, the Gypsies, the physically and mentally incapacitated—had to be eliminated as "polluters" of authentic personhood. The Nazis endeavored to bring into being the "new man" that the philosopher Nietzsche had spoken of so forcefully in the nineteenth century.

The "Final Solution" launched by the Nazis was not aimed exclusively at the elimination of the Jews despite its deep ties to traditional Christian anti-Semitism. As the Israeli historian Uriel Tal[5] staunchly maintains, the "Final Solution" was meant to answer a universal crisis of man. It aimed at a total transformation of values. It wished to free humankind from the shackles of a God concept and its attendant notions of moral responsibility, redemption, sin and revelation. It sought to transfer theological ideas into anthropological and political concepts.

Professor Michael D. Ryan offers further confirmation of this basic thrust of Nazism in his theological analysis of Hitler's *Mein Kamp*. Hitler's "salvation history" was rooted in the myth of the Aryan race and its rise in history through the great cultures of the past and their fall by inter-marriage with the lesser race. The present age of wrong was understood as alienation from one's own racial heritage. Salvation constituted the restoration of that heritage through the national program of biological regeneration. This would result in the new age of the master race, the race of men and women who would create a new culture for the future —one that would last a thousand years. Such was Hitler's eschatology.

According to Professor Ryan, what is especially striking about this Hitlerian "salvation history" is that from beginning to end it clearly confines itself to the limits of time:

It amounted to a resignation to the conditions of finitude, while at the same time asserting total power for itself within those conditions. This is what makes the logic of *Mein Kampf* theological. By asserting total control within the limits of finitude, Hitler deified himself and made himself into the Savior of the German people. It was in this respect that he thought of himself as the child of providence. . . . His world view amounted to the deliberate decision on the part of mass man to live within the limits of finitude without either the moral restraints or the hopes of traditional religion. . . .[6]

The Nazi conception of the holocaust makes the event a chapter in the history of civilization as such, not only a chapter in the history of the Jewish people. It represents the coming together for the first time of the power of modern technology, the skills of bureaucratic organization and the emancipation from traditional values. This combination resulted in the consciousness among the Nazis that they were free, and had the power to reshape humanity according to their own vision without any fear of a higher moral law.

The response to the Nazi period by Christian and Jewish theologians has taken several different directions. Most express the deep conviction that it is no longer possible to speak easily of God in traditional biblical and theological categories after Auschwitz.

On the Jewish side, one of the first thinkers to grapple in a radical fashion with the significance of the holocaust for an understanding of God was Professor Richard Rubenstein. In his volume *After Auschwitz* Rubenstein insists that only paganism can now guard against the transformation of the new power and creativity discovered by contemporary humanity into forms of mass destructiveness. He writes:

I would like to offer my own confession of faith after Auschwitz. I am a pagan. To be a pagan means to find once again one's roots as a child of earth and to see one's own existence as wholly and totally an earthly existence. It means once again to understand that for mankind the true divinities are the gods of earth, not the high gods of the sky; the gods of space and place, not the gods of time; the gods of home and hearth, not the gods of wandering. . . . They (i.e., the Jewish people) have gone home. They have once again found a place of their own on this earth. That is paganism.[7]

While many Jewish scholars would reject Rubenstein's position as overly radical, he remains nonetheless an influential speaker on the holocaust in the Jewish community, and in interreligious meetings as well. To some degree he appears to have modified his position, claiming in recent public meetings that his approach has many parallels to that articulated by Rabbi Irving Greenberg.

Turning to Greenberg we find that in his discussion of the holocaust he examines three possible models for dealing with the God-human person friendship. They are the ones found in the book of Job, the Suffering Servant imagery present in the book of Isaiah and the "controversy with God" approach based on Lamentations 3 which tends to dominate the writings of the holocaust novelist Elie Wiesel. Greenberg finds possibilities in all these models. Yet all need serious critiquing in the light of Auschwitz:

> . . . None of these models can fully articulate the tensions of the relationship to God after the holocaust. And it will take time to develop these models. This suggests that we are entering a period of silence in theology—a silence about God that corresponds to his silence. In this silence, God may be presence and hope, but no longer the simple *Deux ex machina*.[8]

Greenberg goes on to argue that recreating human life is the fundamental religious testimony that needs to be given. In giving this testimony the human community may once again begin to find something of meaning, something of the presence of God. To create a life or to enhance its dignity is to offer the only possible effective counter-testimony to the holocaust:

> To talk of love and of a God who cares in the presence of the burning children is obscene and incredible; to leap in and pull a child out of a pit, to clean its face and heal its body, is to make the most powerful statement—the only statement that counts.[9]

As Greenberg perceives the situation, the reborn State of Israel is for Jews today the fundamental act of life and meaning. To fail to understand this inextricable connection and response is to remain totally in the dark regarding the theological significance of Israel.

A third major spokesperson in contemporary Judaism relative to the theological impact of the holocaust is Professor Emil

Fackenheim of the University of Toronto. For him Auschwitz poses serious religious problems for the Jew, and in significant ways these problems are new despite the continual Jewish awareness of evil in history. Fackenheim acknowledges that Jews may be tempted to contradict traditional Jewish assertions about God's presence in history in their search for God after the holocaust. Yet he feels that such temptations may be due to lack of an in-depth understanding of the Jewish tradition's approach to God. In the end Fackenheim seems to come down on the side of the continued validity of the traditional Jewish notion of God's presence in history despite the trauma of Auschwitz even though the religious Jew must continue to wrestle with this notion.

Fackenheim comes close to Greenberg in maintaining that Jewish survival, particularly Jewish survival in the State of Israel, has become the primary religious duty of Jews in the postholocaust era. How to reconcile the death of so many during the Nazi era with the continued existence of God remains a manysided mystery. He concludes by insisting:

For a Jew after Auschwitz, only one thing is certain. He may not side with the murderers and do what they have left undone. The religious Jew who has heard the Voice of Sinai must continue to listen as he hears the commanding Voice of Auschwitz. And the secularist Jew, who has all along lost Sinai and now hears the Voice of Auschwitz, cannot abuse that Voice as a means to destroy four thousand years of Jewish believing testimony.[10]

Several Christian theologians have also looked at the implications of the holocaust experience for theology within the church. Gregory Baum is convinced that Auschwitz forces us into a new understanding of the relationship between evil and the will of God. In light of the holocaust experience it is no longer possible to assert that God permits evil. Rather God must now be seen as the personal power at work among people, summoning them to uncover and oppose the evil in human life, to redirect history and to transform the human community. For Baum, "the death that destroys is never the will of God. On the contrary God is the never-ending summons to life."[11]

According to Baum the expression "This is God's will" can never again be understood to mean that God wants or even permits terrible calamities or injustices to occur. For the person of faith, however, it can signify a continuing trust that God will help fashion new life out of a death experience such as Auschwitz:

Jewish men and women on the way to the extermination chambers may have said to themselves that this incomprehensible and groundless evil was in some mysterious way God's will—in the sense that they continued to trust in God. But on the lips of an observer such a statement would be a dreadful blasphemy.[12]

For Baum, we must cease explaining God's power over the world as the miraculous action by which he makes things happen as he chooses. Rather the only valid interpretation after the holocaust is to see it as a redemptive action by which God enables people to deal with their problems and by which he calls them to resist evil and discover new ways to overcome it.

Another Christian theological perspective that has emerged in recent years connects Jewish suffering during the holocaust with the suffering endured by Christ. One example of this school of thought can be found in the writings of Professor Franklin Sherman. For him the only legitimate way for Christians to speak about God after Auschwitz is to recognize his participation in the sufferings of people who in turn are called upon to take part in the sufferings of God. Sherman writes:

For Christianity the symbol of the agonizing God is the Cross of Christ. It is tragic that this symbol should have become a symbol of division between Jews and Christians, for the reality to which it points is a Jewish reality as well, the reality of suffering and martyrdom.[13]

He thus sees in the cross the revelation in the first instance of a profoundly Jewish reality. Subsequent interpretations by Christians of the sufferings of Jews must always be conscious of this Jewish reality. The God of the post-Auschwitz age is the God who calls all people into a new unity, not only a unity between

Jews and Christians, but one in which that unity has a very special significance.

A perspective somewhat similar to Sherman's is espoused by the Catholic Israeli writer Fr. Marcel Dubois. He is aware of the difficulties Christians face in trying to locate Auschwitz within a theology of the cross. He is likewise conscious that such an association may appear to Jews as an obscenity given the church's role in the holocaust. Yet he remains convinced that this is the direction Christians must move in interpreting the holocaust:

> . . . In the person of the Suffering Servant there appears to take place an ineffable change. Our vision of Jewish destiny and our understanding of the Holocaust in particular depend on our compassion; the Calvary of the Jewish People, whose summit is the Holocaust, can help us to understand a little better the mystery of the Cross.[14]

Dubois believes that a faith perspective will allow Christians to affirm that Jesus completes Israel in her role as the Suffering Servant and that Israel in turn, through her experience of anguish and solitude, symbolizes, even if unconsciously, the mystery of the passion and the cross. Christians and Jews need to be united today in their affirmation of the fidelity of God despite the experience of massive annihilation and in their certitude of the victory of life over death.

There may be legitimate uneasiness among some Christians about combining the theology of the cross with the holocaust experience or viewing Israel as the precursor of the sufferings of Christ. But insofar as these interpretations stress that Auschwitz forces upon Christians a new understanding of the God-human person relationship, and insofar as they underscore that the holocaust inextricably links the fate of Jews and Christians, they help to build the foundations for a new Christian theology that still awaits full formulation.[15]

Though up till now we have stressed the implications of the holocaust experience for contemporary theological reflection, the church can never set aside the question of her failure in moral responsibility during the Nazi era. While any investigation of the root causes of the holocaust will inevitably uncover a multiplicity of factors, the words of Fr. Edward Flannery are very much to the point:

. . . In the final analysis, some degree of the charge (against the church) must be validated. Great or small, the apathy or silence was excessive. The fact remains that in the twentieth century of Christian civilization a genocide of six million innocent people was perpetrated in countries with many centuries of Christian tradition and by hands that were in many cases Christian. This fact in itself, stands, however vaguely, as an indictment of the Christian conscience. The absence of reaction by those most directly implicated in the genocide only aggravates this broader indictment.[16]

A position that the holocaust was due primarily to forces at work in modern secularism in no way exonerates the complicity of many churchpeople in the Final Solution. The architects of the holocaust found a population well primed for the acceptance of their racist theories as a result of centuries of Christian preaching and teaching about Jews and Judaism. As Flannery puts it:

The degraded state of the Jews, brought about by centuries of opprobrium and oppression, gave support to the invidious comparisons with which the racists built their theories. And in their evil design, they were able to draw moral support from traditional Christian views of Jews and Judaism.[17]

The lessons of the holocaust have not been studied very deeply by Christians at large up till now. There has been a profound fear to probe the significance of this tragedy for Christian self-understanding. Professor Alice Eckardt has documented the Christian reluctance to deal with the holocaust in a survey of Christian and Jewish responses to the holocaust. The vast majority of Christians view the holocaust as primarily a Jewish problem, whereas, in her eyes, in far deeper respects it remains a Christian problem.[18] Her findings concur with the sentiments expressed by Professor Elwyn Smith. Smith asks:

Was not the holocaust a terrible test—which the Church failed? . . . . It may be . . . that the question whether Christianity is to remember the holocaust or dismiss it is a question of the ability and the right of Christianity to survive in a form in any way conformable to Scriptures.[19]

During the last few years a number of pioneering Christian scholars such as Alan Davies, Gordon Zahn, Michael Ryan and Franklin Littell have begun to probe the question in greater depth.[20] This process must continue if the Christian-Jewish dialogue is to experience a genuine growth in the future.

Notes

1. "The Meaning of the Holocaust: A Christian Point of View," address at the University of Michigan, 3 November 1971. Also cf. Franklin Littell, "Christendom, Holocaust and Israel," *"Journal of Ecumenical Studies,"* Vol. 10 (Summer 1973), pp. 483–497 and *The Crucifixion of the Jews.* New York: Harper & Row, 1975.

2. "Cloud of Smoke, Pillar of Fire," in Eva Fleischner (ed.) *Auschwitz: Beginning of a New Era?* New York: KTAV, 1977.

3. Cf. "The People Israel Lives," *"The Christian Century,"* Vol. 87 (6 May 1970), pp. 563–568 and *God's Presence in History.* New York: New York University Press, 1970.

4. *Destruction of the European Jews.* New York: Watts, 1966.

5. "Forms of Pseudo-Religion in the German *Kulturbereich* Prior to the Holocaust," *"Immanuel,"* No. 3 (Winter 1972), pp. 63–72.

6. "Hitler's Challenge to the Churches: A Theological-Political Analysis of *Mein Kampf*," in Franklin A. Littell and Hubert G. Locke (eds.), *The German Church Struggle and the Holocaust.* Detroit: Wayne State University Press, 1973.

7. "Some Perspectives on Religious Faith After Auschwitz," in Littell and Locke (eds.), *The German Church Struggle,* p. 267.

8. "Cloud of Smoke, Pillar of Fire," p. 41.

9. *Ibid.,* pp. 41–42.

10. *God's Presence in History,* p. 89.

11. *Man Becoming: God in Secular Experience.* New York: Herder & Herder, 1971, p. 245.

12. *Ibid.,* pp. 242–244.

13. "Speaking of God After Auschwitz," *"Worldview,"* Vol. 17 (September 1974), p. 29.

14. "Christian Reflections on the Holocaust," *"Sidic,"* Vol. 7, No. 2 (1974), p. 15.

15. For a more detailed discussion of post-holocaust Christian theology, cf. my monograph *The Challenge of the Holocaust for Christian Theology.* New York: ADL, 1978.

16. "Anti-Zionism and the Christian Psyche," pp. 174–175.

17. *Ibid.*

18. "The Holocaust: Christian and Jewish Responses," "*Journal of the American Academy of Religion*," Vol. XLII (September 1974), p. 453.

19. "The Christian Meaning of the Holocaust," "*Journal of Ecumenical Studies*," Vol. 6 (Summer 1969), pp. 421–422.

20. Cf. Alan Davies, *Anti-Semitism and the Christian Mind.* New York: Herder & Herder, 1969; Gordan Zahn, *German Catholics and Hitler's Wars*; Franklin Littell, *The Crucifixion of the Jews*; Franklin Littell and Hubert Locke (eds.), *The German Church Struggle and the Holocaust.*

16

Holocaust Literature: Today's Burning Bush

•

HARRY JAMES CARGAS

HOLOCAUST LITERATURE IS GENERALLY OVERLOOKED as a genre. Yet it is probably the most important new type of literature developed since World War II. It is a record of diaries, essays, dramas and novels which make up the contemporary religious history of Jews. It might not be too much to say that it is the current continuation of the Hebrew scripture.

Auschwitz, Buchenwald, Dachau, Treblinka, Birkenau, Belsen, Mauthausen, Belzec, Majdanek, Ponar, Sobibor: burning bushes from which Yahweh continues to reveal His impossible message. The master of the universe gives new meaning to the sentences by Jakob Boehme, German mystic: "I will tell you what God is. God is fire."

And while the Jew struggles to interpret the meaning of the ovens of Europe for himself, non-Jews are having to face the same question.

Elie Wiesel, the most significant of the novelists in holocaust literature, told me in a television interview that "Auschwitz represented a failure, a defeat for 2,000 years of Christian civilization."

For the Christian this idea is immensely relevant. Buckminster Fuller says that ours is the "age of maximum immorality"—we can see the consequences of our acts, yet we keep on acting as we do. One is fearful that the Christians have not learned from World War II. It will be remembered how defensively Catholics reacted to Rolf Hochhuth's play, *The Deputy*, which condemned Pius XII for not decisively attempting to aid Jewish victims.

Yet it is surprising that the over-all tone of holocaust literature is not condemnatory. It is sometimes moralistic, frequently celebratory of the Jewish spirit, always sad, but almost never vengeful. It is as if every Jewish sufferer consciously made the important distinction of Jewish philosopher Max Brod between noble and ignoble misfortune. The former is unavoidable (death, for example), while that which can be avoided, even eradicated, Brod terms ignoble. War is under this heading.

In her diary writings, Anne Frank did not articulate the sophistication of Brod's philosophical distinction. Yet her tone implies it. Here is suffering, but there is hope. Now is sadness, but then will be joy. With the erasure of ignoble misfortune will come the good days of earth.

Anne Frank's and a myriad of other diaries make up one segment of holocaust literature—personal documents recording the life of the Jews from 1939 on. Critic Irving Halperin has observed that Jews were deeply concerned "that their deaths should not be meaningless." Survivor Eugene Heimler, who wrote *The Night of the Mist*, said it remarkably: there were "messages I had to deliver to the living from the dead. . . . Of their dead, burnt bodies I would be the voice." The diarists who did not survive, but whose writings did, became their own voices from the graves.

Chaim Kaplan's Warsaw diary was discovered after his murder at Treblinka and published as *Scroll of Agony*. A Hebrew scholar, Kaplan wondered how God could treat his people in such a tragic manner—essentially a question that Job asked. But perhaps more important to a secular society is the problem of man's treatment of man. Kaplan wrote that the victim (Jew) was a stranger to his torturers. "Then why this cruel wrath! How is it possible to attack a stranger to me, a man of flesh and blood like myself, to wound him and trample upon him . . . without any reason?"

Thomas Aquinas philosophized seven centuries earlier that we cannot love what we do not know. Kaplan is asking how man can hate man he does not know. Kaplan's laments have the authority of suffering in them that the writings of a Leon Uris cannot achieve. Even John Hersey's *The Wall* dims considerably when placed beside Kaplan's lights.

All holocaust literature which is written by victims is in some real sense diary literature, even the novels. Thus, it is true that holocaust fiction is not to be judged by traditional literary standards. For example, what might appear as an unprepared-for "moment of grace," which we frown upon in ordinary literature, cannot be so easily dismissed in this genre. When Elie Wiesel closes *The Gates of the Forest* on a note of hope, we are privileged to accept this ending because it is the authentic conclusion born of suffering. Or in the same novel, when we read "an act of love may tip the balance," we have to recognize that these words, which might be superficial from the pen of a Scott Fitzgerald, are a profundity arrived at and presented through the authority of suffering. Wiesel is himself a survivor of both Auschwitz and Buchenwald. His mother and sister died in camps, his father was beaten to death before his own eyes when Wiesel was fifteen. His first book is a memoir of these events and is titled *Night*, because it covers the period during which God died for Wiesel. When this man can say "An act of love can tip the balance," we must listen with other than aesthetically oriented ears.

Neither Wiesel nor his co-sufferers claim a privilege in their suffering. T. S. Eliot's Prufrock is ironic when he says, "There will be a time to murder and create." But Eugene Heimler is not ironic in this passage: "I learnt that within me, as in others, the murderer and the humanitarian exist side by side: the weak child with the voracious male. That I am not in any way superior, that I am not different from others, that I am but a link in the great chain, was among the greatest discoveries of my life."

Perhaps the "Jew as link" is a theme that could be expanded. How indeed are we bound? In *The Holocaust Kingdom*, Lena Donat contributes to this idea: "... I know that through mankind flows a stream of eternity greater and more powerful than individual deaths." (Compare Aleksandr Solzhenitsyn in *The Cancer Ward:* "Sometimes I feel so clearly that what is in me isn't all of me. There is something quite unconquerable, something very lofty! Some fragment of the World Spirit.")

The holocaust Jew is more than a link among men, he is a message—not only the bearer of the message, but the message itself.

In *The Plague*, Albert Camus gives us these words: "All I maintain is that on this earth there are pestilences and there are victims, and it's up to us, so far as possible, not to join forces with the pestilences." In Wiesel's *Gates of the Forest* we read: "He who is not among the victims is with the executioners." And in a more recent, nonfiction book, *One Generation After*, Wiesel notes that man is "condemned to choose between the roles of torturer and victim," and that whoever kills, "kills God."

The Jew of the holocaust *is* this message. Holocaust literature is its literary manifestation.

There has been other concentration camp literature but it has not had the quality or the impact of what we here define as holocaust literature. This has arisen particularly in France. For example Robert Antelme could describe the horror of experience in *L' Espèce Humaine*. David Rousset gave readers *a* real world that was indeed separated from *the* real world in *L' Universe Concentrationnaire* and Jean Cayrol even developed a new Christian world concept in a concentration camp existence, while Roger Vailland introduces Communist clichés in several of his novels, particularly *Turn of the Wheel*.

But none of these works have proven influential. Somehow they have failed to give us the kind of literature that the Jew as *Jew* has done.

There might be a falsely simple implication here that through all of his suffering it was relatively easy for the Jew to maintain his identity. One might get that impression if all one read were André Schwarz-Bart's magnificent novel *The Last of the Just.* But the Jew had to struggle against terrible brutality to keep not only his identity, but his very humanity.

Tell Me Another Morning is a novel by Zdena Berger in which the main character, a woman, Tania, is almost obsessed to keep her identity. "The only thing that remains is the I in me," she insists at one point. In all of Elie Wiesel's works he is trying to place his characters in the context of Man. This is especially difficult for the postholocaust generation of Jews who cannot obey the liturgical command to pray at their parents' graves since such graves, such symbols of identity, do not exist.

Nor is it less difficult when the survivors reflect on the words Wiesel wrote in *Judaism* magazine: "Never before have so many Jews been abandoned by so many Jews. The massacre in Europe had almost no bearing on American Jewish life."

And yet, incredibly, there emerges in holocaust literature, a spirit of hope. In a book whose very title signifies a positive value, *From Death-Camp to Existentialism*, Viktor Frankl, who survived Auschwitz writes: "Not only our experiences, but all we have done . . . and all we have suffered, all this is not lost, though it is past; we have brought it into being. Having been is also a kind of being, and perhaps the surest kind."

Earlier Frankl had written on the salvation of man through love. "I understood how a man who has nothing left in this world may know bliss, be it only for a brief moment, in the contemplation of his beloved."

Holocaust literature is the contemporary literature of prophecy. The tragedy may be that Wiesel and Frankl and Schwarz-Bart and Primo Levi and Josef Bor and others will be as ignored as Isaiah and Jeremiah and Hosea and Habakkuk and Ezekiel were during their times.

17

Art and the Inhuman:
A Reflection on the Holocaust

•

THOMAS A. IDINOPULOS

GERMANY'S METHODICAL LIQUIDATION of 6 million Jewish men, women and children between 1933 and 1945 was not an act of bloodlust or vengefulness, or even of simple hatred. It was an act of terrifying mundaneness, both in itself and in it portents for the future. The standard history of those years—Raul Hilberg's *The Destruction of European Jewry, 1933–1945* (Watts, 1961)— bears ample testimony to the sheer vulgarity of the events that led to the Treblinkas. And Hannah Arendt's *Eichmann in Jerusalem* (Viking, 1963)—significantly subtitled "A Report on the Banality of Evil"—insists that the Nazi actions against Jews were largely "impersonal," the result of decisions dispassionately arrived at, steps in a rationally formulated plan to remove all obstacles to the fulfillment of Germany's destiny as Nazidom's Aryan ideology conceived it. Arendt's best judgment is that Eichmann himself was a rather commonplace fellow who, functioning as a superclerk or technocrat in the scheme, at first planned the expulsion of Jews from Germany to any other country that would have them, but eventually, in obedience to higher orders, arranged the deportation of Jews from all over Europe to the concentration camps and extermination centers in Poland.

Human Beings as Disposable Objects

People who profess to be shocked or even offended at Arendt's finding should admit to a certain romanticism about evil. Seeing ranks of real corpses, they are determined to find ranks of real killers. But alas, the face of modern evil is not Mephistophelian, with a dark will and a twisted imagination; it is more like a vast crater of emptiness opened up by a betrayal of spirit. At the turn of the century Nicolas Berdyaev, influenced in part by Dostoevsky, perceived this evil as the most frightening development of the culture that was emerging in the West. He named it "objectification" and described it variously as the decline of the particular under the oppressive weight of abstractions, the submission of the human instance to the requirements of social organization, and the ascendancy of technique over feeling as our primary resource for acknowledging reality.

The Nazis responsible for the death camps were not the maniacal demons that the fantasies of Hollywood and the potboilers of Leon Uris parade before us. The handful of depraved, demented individuals who operated the torture machines and the gas chambers were real enough. They were almost always assisted by Jewish prisoners whose humanity had been so reduced by starvation and fear that they neither knew nor cared what they were doing. But the vastly more frightening truth is that, for the Heydrichs and Eichmanns who drew up the plans and made the decisions, the deprivation of spirit was so complete that they looked on Jews—and not only Jews but other whole peoples as well—as not in any way human but as mere objects or problems to be neatly and cleanly "disposed of" by way of "a few freight trains, a few engineers, a few chemists" (André Schwarz-Bart). The appalling truth is that the Nazis, practically to a man, regarded gassing as a humane way of exterminating the Jews.

The premise of a recent anthology, *Sanctions for Evil* (edited by Nevitt Sanford and Craig Comstock; Jossey-Bass, 1971), is that the evil which extends from Auschwitz and Hiroshima to My Lai and street crime is rooted in viewing human beings as disposable objects (recall William Calley's telling phrase "waste them"), and—perhaps worse—in society's indifference to and even justification of the dispatch of one group by another. Never forget that if the Germans proved so brilliantly successful in carrying out their Final Solution, it was because this deprivation of spirit equally afflicted the west European peoples whose leaders, when they were not actively cooperating with the Germans in order to solve their own "Jewish problem," condoned by their apathy actions that had the same practical result. One cannot be certain how strong a chain of guilt links 1,900 years of Christian disdain of the Jew to what Nazi Germany did to Jews in the 20th century; but one can be certain that Germany could never have carried out the systematic execution of a whole people without the inner confidence that Western civilization, given its history, could sanction that action. (A footnote to the Holocaust: Jewish leaders approached Churchill and Roosevelt with the request that Auschwitz and the railway tracks leading to it be obliterated by bombing; the request was never honored.)

Reflecting the Shape and Feel of the Truth

The art that has arisen from the ashes of the Holocaust has as its unifying purpose the translation of the abstract into the particular. It takes the number 6 million and transforms it into the story of the living, suffering and dying of each soul. It seeks to discern within abject despair an ultimate significance which can revive the spirit, so that a human being can face the truth and not turn away from it in disgust. The best of this art avoids judgment, whether by praise or by condemnation. Like much other art, it salvages something of worth from the wreckage of human history. As *art*, it does not aim to propagate the truth. The aim of art, Joseph Conrad once said, is to speak "to our capacity for delight and wonder, to the sense of mystery sur-

rounding our lives; to our sense of pity and beauty and pain."
And this the art of the Holocaust does. Investing with significant
form the raw materials of human experience, it gives us on the
outside a relation to what is deeply hidden and mysterious. By
steady reflection not so much on the truth as on the shape and
feel of the truth, this art succeeds in discerning a profound human
tragedy within the crushing mediocrity of the evil it depicts.

I concentrate here on four instances of Holocaust and a series
of eyewitness accounts, a novel, a memoir and a statue. Different
in medium and form, these works all undertake to bring a measure
of humanity to the inhuman. Each makes an effort to depict the
Holocaust from the side of the victim, to reach into the depths
of his or her suffering. Little attention is paid to the assassins, to
their motives or to the politics behind them. What drives the
imagination is a small universe of Jews transformed, in a few
brief months, into columns of white smoke, the sight of which
raises gnawing questions—about innocence and guilt, about God
and his mercy, about a long history brought to an abrupt end,
about cowardliness and defeat and forgiveness, about death and
hope and eternity.

Death-Camp Narratives

I begin by juxtaposing two accounts of the death camps. Both
are taken from an *Anthology of Holocaust Literature* (edited
by Jacob Glatstein et al. [Atheneum, 1971])—a volume made up
of the personal stories of Jews who somehow escaped to record
the suffering they and their fellows endured at Nazi hands. My
first citation is a set of statistics about exterminations:

Chelmno, December 8, 1941–January 18, 1945: 360,000 Jews; 5,000
gypsies from the Lodz Ghetto. Auschwitz, January 1942–November
1944: 2.5 to 4 million Jews. Belzek, March 1942–December 1942:
600,000 Jews. Maidenek, April 1942–July 22, 1944: 500,000 Jews. Sobibor, May 1942–November 1943: 250,000 Jews. Treblinka, July 23,
1942–November 1943: 700,000 Jews, of these 300,000 from Warsaw.

Set against these abstract figures the words of Yankel Wiernik, who escaped from the Treblinka horror camp. His preciseness and restraint arouse our imagination and permit us to feel for an instant what it is for a rationally contrived madness to be visited on each of 6 million souls:

Into the chamber of twenty-five square meters 450 to 500 people were jammed. The congestion was unbelievable. The victims carried in the children, somehow hoping thus to save them from death. On their way to die they were beaten and driven by truncheons and gas pipes. Dogs were set upon them . . . Everyone, eager to escape the blows and the dogs, rushed screaming into the lethal chamber. The stronger pushed the weaker. . . . The doors closed with a clang on the packed chamber. The motor was connected with the inflow apparatus and switched on. In twenty-five minutes . . . all lay dead. But they did not really lie, for they had no room to fall. They died standing, their legs and arms entangled. There were no more screams. Mothers and children were clasped in death's embrace. There was no friend or foe, no envy. No one was more beautiful or ugly—all were suffocated, yellowed by gas. No rich, no poor—all were alike before the Lord.

I take from this anthology one further item—a woman's account of what happened to two Jewish children she tried to help after their parents, along with others, were massacred in their Czech town. Her story shows up the Holocaust as that wedding of reason and madness which is the hallmark of deprivation of spirit.

I managed to leave Lanzut before the massacre. I hid in cornfields and potato patches during the day, or with a friendly peasant. I also was able to hide my sister's two children, a girl of seven and a boy of nine, in the stable of their former home. They were half starved, so I stole vegetables for them from the fields. But in a few days someone denounced them to the Gestapo. They were seized and interrogated, in hopes they would reveal hideouts of other Jews. But the children endured their tormenting and betrayed no one.

As the children were led to the cemetery they were urged not to cry, for they would "go to heaven, and meet their mother, father and aunts." After the children had been shot the Gestapo took their bodies to the circus performing in Lanzut, to be eaten by the beasts.

Identity Through Suffering

André Schwarz-Bart, in his prize-winning novel *The Last of the Just* (Atheneum, 1960), perceives the Holocaust as the culminating event in the long story of Jewish suffering. Ernie Levy, the hero of the novel, stands in a line of "Just Men."

According to [the tradition], the world reposes upon 36 Just Men, the Lamed-Vov, indistinguishable from simple mortals; often they are unaware of their station. But if just one of them were lacking, the sufferings of mankind would poison even the souls of the new born, and humanity would suffocate with a single cry. For the Lamed-Vov are all hearts of the world multiplied, and into them, as into one receptacle, pour all our griefs. . . . the Lamed-Vovnik takes our suffering upon himself . . . and he raises it to heaven and sets it at the feet of the Lord—who forgives. Which is why the world goes on . . . in spite of all our sins.

The first of the Lamed Vov, Rabbi Yom Tov Levy, lived around the year 1000 in the ancient city of York, which was at that time the ecclesiastical capital of northern England. Fleeing from a mob drunk on Christian piety and lusting for Jewish conversions, Rabbi Levy found himself, along with a handful of other Jews, high on a watchtower. The local bishop demanded that they repent for their "perfidy" against the Lord and yield through baptism to the church of Christ. Rather than submit they committed mass suicide. Rabbi Levy carried out the deed of his faithfulness. After dispatching some 40 of his companions—men, women and children—with his dagger, he plunged it into his own throat. Such has been the calling of the Lamed Vov ever since; to act in the fiercest trials so as to preserve a solidarity whose roots are an elementary covenant between the people Israel and the Creator of all that is human. The Lamed-Vovnik shares the sufferings of his people precisely to confirm that they are *a people* and that it is above all by their sufferings that they honor the name of the One who brought them into being.

Schwarz-Bart's hero, Ernie Levy, is the last in the succession of

Lamed-Vov. Born in Germany in the first decade of this century, he emigrates with his family to France in the early years of the Nazi regime, when Jews are being encouraged to leave the country. Ernie finds safety by donning the uniform of the French army. The war begins and France is soon defeated. Ernie looks on helplessly as the French themselves celebrate the German victory by transporting his own and thousands of other Jewish families to extermination camps in Poland. It is then that he comes to understand his vocation on earth. He realizes that survival is fundamentally a matter of the spirit, that in the day of a people's catastrophe the essence of being human may lie not in concealing but in identifying oneself. In the closing scenes of the novel Schwarz-Bart depicts the terror and tenderness which moves Ernie Levy to act (as we know some Jews did indeed act) to gain admission to the gas chambers of the Third Reich.

With the death of Ernie Levy the tradition of the Lamed-Vov has ended. A suffering so great leaves nothing to be redeemed and precious little to forgive or be forgiven. It is not that God died after Auschwitz; it is that he is no longer needed. The covenant has been broken, not by the people but by their Lord. In the words of prayer that end *The Last of the Just*, Schwarz-Bart seems to pronounce a final judgment on what the Holocaust signifies—man's faithfulness and God's unfaithfulness:

And Praised. *Auschwitz.* Be. *Maidenek.* The Lord. *Treblinka.* And Praised. *Buchenwald.* Be. *Mauthausen.* The Lord. *Belzec.* And Praised. *Sobibor.* Be. *Chelmo.* The Lord. *Ponary.* And Praised. *Theresienstadt.* Be. *Warsaw.* The Lord. *Vilna.* And Praised. *Skarzysko.* Be. *Bergen-Belsen.* The Lord. *Janow.* And Praised. *Dora.* Be. *Neuengamme.* The Lord. *Pustkow.* And Praised . . .

Elie Wiesel—no doubt the greatest of Jewish writers on the Holocaust—has said that the efforts of psychologists and historians and jurists to explain the Holocaust are invariable defeated. I would add that they are defeated because the human mind shrinks from the darkest edges of reality; and when apprehesion grows and builds up a more vivid sense of the void, the mind rushes back from the brink, reducing its experience to *questions* in which, it wants to believe, *answers* are implicit.

However the "blame" for the murder of 6 million Jews be assigned, the mystery remains. It is as if in a moment of self-destructive mindlessness the earth had turned on itself and consumed its own progeny. The Holocaust hints at an apocalyptic nihilism out of which may come abominations as terrible or worse.

Both Cursing and Forgiving God

Of the dozen or more books Elie Wiesel has written, none surpasses in power and eloquence his first, the memoir *Night*. It is the story of the year and a half spent as a boy at Auschwitz and Buchenwald. What directs his imagination is not the physical horror he witnessed there, but rather the religious emptiness that horror evidences. Like his later works, *Night* has the form of a spiritual dialectic. He is preoccupied with what he knows to be the impotence or failure of the biblical God in the Holocaust; but he is also struggling with the problem of how he is to lead a life scarred by that knowledge. How he true to the memory of the Holocaust without at the same time being destroyed by that memory? What happened at Auschwitz compels him to reject the religious tradition, but surviving Auschwitz fills him with shame at abandoning the dead—a shame he seems able to come to terms with only through the tradition. Hence, perhaps, the curious tone of his writing: he appears to be cursing God and praying to God at the same moment.

No less than Schwarz-Bart, Wiesel struggles to find a way to be faithful to the dead while burdened by the knowledge of a faithless God. But where Ernie Levy ends his trial of spirit by choosing to join the victims, Wiesel begins his trial by choosing to survive.

Reviewing Wiesel's *Legends of Our Time* in the *New York Times*, Thomas Lask thus aptly sums up the effect on the reader of Wiesel's description of the Holocaust: ". . . pain and death pale before the suffering and humiliation in these events." Wiesel too understands that the ultimate crime of the Holocaust was the crime against the spirit. "Guilt was not invented at Auschwitz," he writes; "it was disfigured there."

In the spring of 1944 the Germans took possession of Sighet—the Transylvanian mountain town that was Wiesel's home—and at once took a major step in accomplishing the degradation that is indispensable to the total destruction of a human being. Some 13 years later, looking back with a mixture of shame and resentment at the naïveté of his elders, Wiesel describes their reaction to the Nazi decree:

. . . a new decree: every Jew must year the yellow star. Some of the prominent members of the community came to see my father—who had highly placed connections in the Hungarian police—to ask him what he thought of the situation. My father did not consider it so grim—but perhaps he did not want to dishearten the others or rub salt in their wounds: "The yellow star? Oh well, what of it? You don't die of it . . ." (Poor Father! Of what then did you die?)

It was not long before the Jews of Sighet (Wiesel among them) were seized to be transported from their sheltered mountain world to an inferno. Herded into sealed cattle cars, driven mad by want of air and water, dying of starvation and dysentery and fear, they prayed for the train to reach its destination. Four days later their prayer was answered. But the relief they felt when they arrived at Auschwitz gave way in an instant to utter horror. The selection process began immediately. Children were parted from their parents, wives from their husbands. Everyone was paralyzed by fear. There was no escape. Most were marked for the gas chambers; only a few strong-looking ones survived—for the time being. In stark and beautiful lines, Wiesel speaks of his first sight of Auschwitz:

Not far from us, flames were leaping up from a ditch, gigantic flames. They were burning something. A lorry drew up at the pit and delivered its load—little children. Babies! Yes, I saw it—saw it with my own eyes . . . those children in the flames. . . .

So this was where we were going. A little farther on was another and larger ditch for adults. . . . Was I still alive? Was I awake? I could not believe it. How could it be possible for them to burn people, children, and for the world to keep silent? No, none of this could be true. It was a nightmare. . . .

Wiesel recognizes the tragic irony of Jewish existence. The God who lies buried under the ashes of 6 million Jews is the same God whose name is blessed in the Jewish prayer for the dead, the Kaddish. The God who is condemned in the Holocaust is also the God without whom the survivor of the Holocaust cannot honor the memory of the dead. At the conclusion of Wiesel's novel *The Gates of the Forest* (Harper & Row, 1966) the hero, Gavriel, finds himself forgiving God; for he knows that unless he overcomes his rage and sorrow he cannot learn to live with the past but will be forever haunted by its ghosts. In both cursing and forgiving God, Wiesel functions in his stories as a kind of priest-poet. His words become a new Kaddish, honoring not the blessed name of God but the sacred names of the Holocaust victims. So, in his practice of the holy art of storytelling, he robs the Holocaust of final victory: silencing the dead in the abstractness of the number 6 million.

God did indeed fail man at Auschwitz. But in his ability to "tell the tale" man possesses the power to overcome the failure— for God's sake as well as for his own. This is the point of the Hasidic legend which Wiesel makes the prologue to his *Gates of the Forest:*

When the great Rabbi Israel Baal Shem-Tov saw misfortune threatening the Jews it was his custom to go into a certain part of the forest to meditate. There he would light a fire, say a special prayer, and the miracle would be accomplished and the misfortune averted.

Later, when his disciple, the celebrated Magid of Mezritch, had occasion, for the same reason, to intercede with heaven, he would go to the same place in the forest and say: "Master of the Universe, listen! I do not know how to light the fire, but I am still able to say the prayer," and again the miracle would be accomplished.

Still later, Rabbi Moshe-Leib of Sasov, in order to save his people once more, would go into the forest and say: "I do not know how to light a fire, I do not know the prayer, but I know the place and this must be sufficient." It was sufficient and the miracle was accomplished.

Then it fell to Rabbi Israel of Rizhyn to overcome misfortune. Sitting in his armchair, his head in his hands, he spoke to God: "I am unable to light the fire and I do not know the prayer; I cannot even find the place in the forest. All I can do is to tell the story, and this must be sufficient." And it was sufficient.

God made man because he loves stories.

Fire, Blood and Tears

Now to my fourth example of Holocaust art. At the Chaim Weizman Institute of Science, near Tel Aviv, stands a granite pillar on which is mounted a large Torah powerfully shaped in bronze. The scroll is torn jaggedly in two, and the viewer gets the impression that some kind of terrible sacrilege has been committed on the holiest book of Jewish faith; that a wound too wide and deep to be easily healed has been inflicted on the body of Israel. The gnarled ridges in the broken Torah repulse, then fascinate. It is only when the viewer is quite near that he discerns, etched on the surface of the metal, numbers upon numbers, covering the whole scroll in what seems a confusing jumble until their significance is borne in on him. They are the identification numbers which the Nazis tattooed on the arms of the inmates of their concentration camps. And the desecrated Torah symbolizes the body of Jewish history broken by the death of 6 million souls in the Holocaust.

In its silence this statue speaks. It cries out powerfully against the enormity that the Holocaust was. It commemorates a loss so deep that the memory of it will remain forever sacred. It is a curse pronounced on the creatures of the earth and no less so on their Creator, and it is a revelation of the ancient solidarity of Jews, affirmed now as then in fire, blood and tears.

Deepening the Mystery of the Holocaust

Does it appear perverse to expatiate on the meaning of a handful of works of art that were inspired by an actual event whose enormity seems to put it beyond the possibility of creative expression? The Holocaust has not been, perhaps cannot be, a popular subject for the artistic imagination. Yet it holds a lesson. Events which lay bare all that is profoundly inhuman uncover the limits of human comprehension and toleration, and therefore cry out all the more for that luminous patterning of which the artist alone is capable. And unless the artist is listened to, we are likely to forget that not the beast but the *human* is both cause and object of the inhuman; and that, finally, human beings alone among the inhabitants of this planet must learn to live with the knowledge of what humans do to each other. Simply stated, the aim of the art of the Holocaust is to show us what is significantly human in the destruction of 6 million people.

Those who have had the patience and the courage to study it agree that the Holocaust cannot be wholly or easily understood. I do not believe that art provides some sort of special understanding where other efforts fail. But then it it is not the purpose of art, as such, to *understand*. The significant form—that is, the *meaning*—which art bestows on the raw materials of experience is compounded of imagination, intelligence, feeling and sheer craftsmanship. The artists I have discussed above succeed in giving meaning to the Holocaust. They do not, for all their art, make us understand what may not be understandable. Nevertheless, what is not understood is shaped by human hands and minds; impenetrable evil is penetrated with meaning in personal accounts, in stories, in sculpture. And we who attend to what these artists have done are, by virtue of our own imagination, feelings and intelligence, put into intimate relationship, as they have been, to what we do not understand. Thus the mystery of the Holocaust is not dissolved; it is deepened, made to be part of our lives.

18

Modern World Literature and the Holocaust

•

HARRY JAMES CARGAS

MIKE ROYKO's biography of Mayor Richard Daley struck one of my students as a work of fiction. "Clearly," the young man said to our class, "the kinds of things described as happening in *Boss* can't be historically true—they must spring from the author's imagination."

Much else in contemporary affairs has been likewise suspect by at least some in our society: Did we really place men on the moon? Can the events of the Watergate affair have actually occurred? Where is Jimmy Hoffa? What's the truth about Mylai? Was there a Howard Hughes? Each of us can, very naturally, assemble a personal roster of such doubts and while a list like this can be an amusement, it has its roots in very serious philosophic ground.

Contemporary literature certainly reflects this. Practitioners of *le nouveau roman* in France are obsessed by the question of how reality is perceived. In a novel like *Jealousy*, Alain Robbe-Grillet can give us detail after descriptive detail and when we close the book we cannot be certain that any of the events related ever happened. Raymond Queneau goes further in, for example, *The Flight of Icarus*, when he has a novelist search for characters he

Reprinted with permission from *Commonweal*, copyright © 1976, Commonweal Publishing Co., 232 Madison Avenue, New York, NY 10016.

has created who have jumped off his page, incarnated themselves, and begun to interact with his real friends. But are the characters any less real than the novelist himself, who is simply a construction of Queneau's? This will remind us of Kurt Vonnegut Jr.'s intrusion into his own novel, *Breakfast of Champions*, in order to give one of the characters, Kilgore Trout, his freedom.

And of course there are so many other writers who can be cited here: There is Argentina's Jorge Luis Borges who, in a parable, "Borges and I," can observe at its conclusion, "I do not know which one of us has written this page." Or there is the Borges of "The Circular Ruins" whose main character is horrified to learn "that he too was a mere appearance, dreamt by another."

Colombia's Gabriel Garcia Marquez, writing in a kind of heightened magical realism, particularly in *One Hundred Years of Solitude* (perhaps Spanish America's greatest novel), must be mentioned. So should Carlos Fuentes of Mexico whose novella, *Aura*, finds a young historian coming to the realization that the young woman he thinks he is making love to in bed is actually his employer, in her nineties, who has projected an image onto him in order to keep him in her employ. We may go to Japan, too, and read Yukio Mishima whose final and major work, the tetralogy titled *The Sea of Fertility*, ends with Honda, the person through whom the action is filtered to us, being staggered concerning the illusoriness of life. When it is suggested that the man whose history Honda was observing, through several incarnations, probably never existed, he utters, in despair: "If there was no Kiyoaki, then there was no Isao. There was no Ying Chan, and who knows, perhaps there has been no I."

The questions proliferate in modern literature concerning the meaning of life, the meaning of humanity. There is one genre, however, which, while also positing doubt, if we may say it that way, by questioning God rather than persons, heaven rather than the world, actually concludes with a kind of hope which may be opposed to the despair of a Mishima, a Vonnegut, or a Robbe-Grillet. This genre has been labeled Holocaust Literature.

The authors of this literature, particularly those who are survivors of the Nazi concentration camps, sometimes demand answers from God, sometimes scold, defy, rebel against God, but most seem to voice their doubts within a context that admits of God's existence. In a way their attitude of faith has been summed up by Elie Wiesel in his cantata *Ani Ma'amin:* ". . . the silence of God is God." Some are more strident, recalling the "atheist" Bendrix in Graham Greene's Catholic novel *The End of the Affair* who, after the woman he loves is lost in death, metaphorically shakes his fist at a God he has been denying and says these words which close the book: "Oh God, You've done enough, You've robbed me of enough, I'm too tired and old to learn to love, leave me alone forever."

We must not conclude, however, that the questions asked of God by Wiesel, Nelly Sachs, Paul Celan, Primo Levi, Jakov Lind, Andre Schwarz-Bart, Emmanuel Ringelblum, Lena Donat, Josef Bor and so many others are necessarily far removed from the doubts of Robbe-Grillet, Nathalie Sarraute, Michael Butor, Jean Cayrol, Robert Antelme, Fuentes, Severo Sarduy, and still others. It may be less than a giant step from doubt in man to faith in God. Perhaps the best illustration of this is found in the work of a man who progressed from the night of Auschwitz to at least the approachables of faith (for, after all, who can say that one truly has belief), Elie Wiesel.

Those who write a type of literature of frustration raise their questions from that frustration. Wiesel and others, on the contrary, see in their queries the very basis of life. Edmond Jabes, a Jew born in Egypt, now writing in Paris, has said so succinctly, "God is a questioning God." Wiesel presents this view in a number of his works. In the autobiographical book *Night*, we read the words of Moché, the mystically mad seer: "Man raises himself toward God by the questions he asks . . ." This same person says a moment later, "I pray to God within me that He will give me the strength to ask Him the right questions."

In a novel, one character insists that "The essence of man is to be a question, and the essence of the question is to be without answer." In another of Wiesel's novels we read, "Only the questions matter." In an interview which forms the basis for my book

Conversations with Elie Wiesel, I asked Wiesel about his idea that questions are more important than answers. Here is his response.

"Yes, they are because the questions remain; the answers change. The questions that Adam asked when he was alive we are still repeating. The basic questions are always the same: What am I doing here? What is the purpose of my life? The purpose of my meeting people? What is the aim, God, death, freedom? All the real questions stay basically the same. The answers change and are being revised. They go and come back and go and come back, to infinity.

"What divides people is not the question, it is the answer. If it hadn't been for answers, there would have been no wars. Question, I think, comes from the word 'quest.' If people were to share their quest and make it a common quest, there could be a better time, a better fate, a better society. But they, for some reason, want to give answers, maybe because we need answers. The answers are all temporary, while those who give the answers see them as eternal. Hence divisions, dissensions, wars, death.

"If I use these ideas so often, it's because I relate them to our generation and to our experience. Those experiences of which I try to speak have no answers, should have no answers. I'm afraid of anyone who comes with a theory, a system, based on that experience. I am suspicious; I don't want theories. I believe the experience was above and beyond theories and systems and philosophies. What remains is the question: How, What and Why. . . ?"

Because answers divide, are incomplete, are lies, one response to the mysteries of existence is silence. This is not something negative but rather a kind of prayer, a listening to God. Wiesel ends one of his non-fiction volumes by saying that silence, ". . . demands to be recognized and transmitted."

The transmission is, of course, of ultimate importance for many survivors of the Holocaust. Eugene Heimler said it remarkably: there were "messages I had to deliver to the living from the dead. . . . Of their dead, burnt bodies I would be the voice." Wiesel too is obsessed with being such a bearer. He feels his responsibility to the dead. He told me, "I don't have the right not to communicate." He fears having said too much, perhaps thus cheapening what he wishes to commemorate; but he nevertheless must not be destructive in a silent way. (In his book *The Jews of Silence* Wiesel distinguishes between constructive silence—illustrated by the praying Jews of Russia—and the destructive silence of Jews throughout the world who refuse to act on behalf of their suffering brothers and sisters.)

This philosophy must inevitably affect the author's style. His has been called a literature of silence. An example or two may be in order. In *Night* Wiesel tells of seeing a young boy hanged. His body was so emaciated that it did not weigh enough to help him to die. For over half an hour he continued swaying, struggling between life and death. About his own reaction the author has but seven words: "That night the soup tasted of corpses." In that same book we read of a cattle car experience. The writer witnesses a son murder his own father in order to steal bread from the old man's mouth. The killer is, in turn, beaten to death by others. Again the reaction: "I was fifteen years old." Silence, for Wiesel, is beyond language, beyond lies.

In his critical work *Language and Silence*, George Steiner parallels Wiesel profoundly: "It is just because we can go no further, because speech so precisely fails us, that we experience the certitude of a divine meaning surpassing and enfolding ours. What lies beyond man's word is eloquent of God."

Not to write, for Wiesel, as for so many other survivors of Hitler's camps, would be a betrayal. How then do they understand this minimal breaking of silence? Again Wiesel provides some clues. He knows what every Jew knows, that for 6,000,000 victims it will be impossible to say the memorial Kaddish at their graves because either the sites are unknown or there are no graves. "My generation has been robbed of everything, even of our cemeteries." (We are grimly reminded of what is probably the best known work by Nobel poet Nelly Sachs, "O, the Chimneys.") So Wiesel says that "the act of writing is for me often nothing more than the secret or conscious desire to carve words on a tombstone: to the memory of a town forever vanished, to the memory of a childhood in exile, to the memory of all those I loved and who before I could tell them I loved them, went away."

Beyond this, Wiesel would agree with Jabes on the seriousness of the writer's work. "I believe in the writer's mission. He receives it from the word, which carries its suffering and its hope within it. He questions the words which question him. He accompanies the words which accompany him." In writing, the contributor to Holocaust Literature is acting out a destiny. As Wiesel has noted in a work composed of spiritual biographies of Hasidic teachers, ". . . some words are as important as deeds—some words *are* deeds." And again, in one of his novels: "In taking a single word by assault it is possible to discover the secret of creation, the center where all threads come together."

Wiesel's works, then, like those of other important Holocaust writers, be they diarists, chroniclers, playwrights, novelists, or poets, are not so much lamentations as they are deeds. They can be distinguished from the writings of Robbe-Grillet, Ionesco, Beckett, and others because they are acts of faith—*even as questions* because those questions are addressed to God rather than being images of absurdity. We are asked to risk *with* Wiesel and the others rather than despair alone. They live out the teaching of the Rabbi in Wiesel's drama *Zalmen, or the Madness of God:* "God requires of man not that he live, but that he choose to live. What matters is to choose—at the risk of being defeated."

Wiesel has chosen, Sachs has chosen, Levi has chosen, Donat has chosen, Bor has chosen . . . the list is at once unfortunately and fortunately very long. These writers intuited what Jesuit critic William F. Lynch has articulated regarding the sanctity of language—language as gift laid at the divine altar.

". . . all language is public and a public act; in all my language I pledge that what I say is what I think; according to the code and game and life of language I make a pledge and expect belief—not belief in what I say, for we expect to find out that we are fools or stupid or mistaken, but belief that what I say is what I think. Language then belongs to the very marrow of the body of faith."

19

How German Thinkers
View the Holocaust

•

ALICE and ROY ECKARDT

"HOLOCAUST" REMAINS AN UNFAMILIAR WORD among Germans, and there is no adequate counterpart in their language. *Christen und Juden,* a new study by the Council of the Evangelical Church in Germany (EKD), recognizes the term, explaining that "Holocaust" means "the extermination of a great part of European Jewry through National Socialism." The French tend to use the simplistic "Auschwitz," though *holocauste* is a French word. The Nazis utilized a particular concept: *die Endlösung,* the "final solution" of the "Jewish question."

The New Anti-Semitism

Is the Holocaust as dead now as the Jews and others who perished in it? For the younger generation in Germany, as elsewhere, the answer is a too-evident Yes. The event is ancient history. An international conference on the Holocaust was held in Hamburg last June—the first such conference on German soil. But the initiative for it was largely non-German, and, significantly, no press representatives appeared. In contrast to North America and

Reprinted with permission from *The Christian Century,* March 17, 1976, copyright © 1976, Christian Century Foundation.

Israel, there is little current published material in Germany and in Europe as a whole on the nature and meaning of the *Endlösung* and the lessons to be learned from it. (Only 30,000 Jews remain in the Bundesrepublik today. The Deutsche-Demokratische Republik [DDR] has a handful. France has upwards of 500,000.)

Nonetheless, certain phenomena reawaken memories of the Holocaust. In the region of Alsace, over a recent period of two years, 15 Jewish cemeteries were desecrated. One group apprehended by the authorities consisted of children aged six to ten. There is a rising to the surface of repressed collective drives. Youth and others among the "new left" in Germany have avidly boarded the bandwagon of anti-Israelism. Many observers find in this development a new incarnation of "death to the Jews."

Jürgen Moltmann of Tübingen has commented that in the new anti-Semitism, self-hatred comes forth. This phenomenon could well entail the subterranean hatred of the previous generation: "You hated; you taught us; we shall excel you; we shall show you by hating even more." Yet a camouflage is needed. It bears the message: "Israel is the militant, aggressive, expansionist tool of the imperialist, reactionary United States." (For the moment, the student "new left" is at a nadir; the students have largely turned inward to problems of academic retrenchment and of expected unemployment.)

The *Spandauer Tagebuch*, a second work by Hitler's own Albert Speer, has quickly gained best-seller status in Germany. The publisher can scarcely keep pace with the demand. Translations are planned in 21 languages. The weekly *Der Spiegel* asks whether the book's popularity somehow reflects a public effort to master the past, or whether Speer is being secretly and longingly turned to in order to "organize" anew an evasion of collective guilt, or whether, for that matter, simple curiosity is the major ingredient.

A Rational or an Irrational Action?

A study of the contemporary impact of the Holocaust presses manifold issues upon us. A few salient ones are here singled out.

1. In Germany and elsewhere there have been substantial changes or developments in the way the Holocaust is perceived—for example, a subsumption of the *Endlösung* under the larger category of Nazi murder policies or the reduction of Jewish suffering to merely one aspect of the general suffering. This very trend is apparent especially in France and Poland but also to some extent within Germany. The government of Poland erected a memorial at Auschwitz bearing the languages of all the victims, with two unbelievable exceptions: Yiddish and Hebrew. Today in eastern Europe the Jewish dead are destroyed a second time through the elimination of their Jewish identity. They become merely "the victims of fascism." The distinctive elements of the mass murder of Jews are obliterated. (By contrast, it may be said, with oversimplification but much truth, that in the DDR one is encouraged to be anti-Zionist but is forbidden to express anti-Semitism in public, whereas in the Bundesrepublik overt anti-Semitism persists while considerable sympathy for Israel remains.)

Is the destruction of European Jewry to be perceived as an irrational action or a rational one? A pastor in Hamburg contends that history never before witnessed a politics of extinction in this measure, one based upon totally irrational motives. Eliezer Berkovits attests that the *Endlösung* was "the ultimate of irrationality. The conscious and radical removal of every vestige of moral restraint on subhuman passions, . . . the extirpation of all human feelings, . . . the religion of brutality . . . was not 'of this world.' "

Heinz Höhne, in direct contrast, distinguishes between the anti-Jewish fanatics and the Social Democratic intellectuals, the latter claiming that their sole object was "to solve the so-called Jewish problem in a cold rational manner." In his new book Speer reinforces the images of passionlessness with his report that Hitler's announcement "I shall destroy the Jews of Europe" was made casually and calmly between the soup and vegetable courses. Again, historian Klaus Scholder of Tübingen identifies Nazism not as nihilism but as a primitive dualistic system of absolute Good and absolute Evil, with all of human history embodying the war of the two forces. Capitalizing upon the powerful presence of traditional anti-Semitism, National Socialism simply and conveniently applied these categories to Germans ("good") and Jews ("evil"). The Nazis saw in the Jews a deadly bacillus threatening the very survival/being of the healthy German/Aryan peoples. One had to be mercilessly objective and exterminate the death-bearing agents.

However, the rationale behind the *Endlösung* transcends Nazi ideology. In the "final solution" there is amassed a wider historical inevitability. For Nazism also built upon the philosophical ideas of great men of Western culture (Voltaire, Nietzsche, Fichte et al.) as well as theological concepts and attitudes central to the long Christian tradition. As some of our German colleagues acknowledge, it is the rationality of the Holocaust that poses an abiding threat to the present and the future.

"Unique Uniqueness"

2. There is the related issue of the Holocaust's uniqueness. Three interpretations vie for attention:

(A) In the first of these, the *Endlösung*, for all its distinctive features, involves essential continuity with other deeds of human genocide—such as the Turkish slaughter of the Armenians.

(B) A second view holds that undoubted uniqueness confronts us in the *Endlösung*, for which *Einmaligkeit* (historical singularity) is the fitting term. Stress falls upon the unparalleled character of the destruction of European Jewry. The combined technological and ideological "perfection" of the destructiveness is often emphasized, together with the obsessiveness of concentration upon the Enemy. This interpretation is widely shared. A Christian theologian in Darmstadt identifies the "final solution" as the singular culminating point of a centuries-prepared denial of Jewish integrity from within the Christian world.

(C) The third possibility is epitomized by the phrase *ganze Einzigartigkeit* (unique uniqueness)—uniqueness not just in the sense of an unparalleled happening, or one that is discontinuous with other genocidal acts, but an Event that twists the human journey through time and space by 180 degrees, a transcendent Event that perhaps even alters the life story of God, that points us inexorably to *Heilsgeschichte* (salvation history), or perhaps to its end; an event that can be compared only with a very small number of other incomparable Events—the Exodus or the giving of Torah. Thus in Elie Wiesel's tale *A Beggar in Jerusalem* the beggar testifies that at Sinai the Lord bestowed the Torah upon Israel, but then in "the kingdom of night," in the flames of the "final solution," God took back his Torah. Such radicalization of uniqueness in effect places the *Endlösung* (together perhaps with its sequel, the Third Jewish Commonwealth, the State of Israel) within a frame of reference like unto the break between B.C. and A.D. or, in Islam, between B.H. and A.H. We should then have this symbolism: B.E., before the *Endlösung*, the event that ended the Covenant ("ended" perhaps suggesting *telos* as well as *finis*, goal as well as finish); and A.E., after the *Endlösung*, the epoch beyond covenantal demands, the post-Covenant time; i.e., the time of Jewish normalization.

Presumably, one may reject this third treatment of uniqueness by rejecting all transcendent, *heilsgeschictliche* events. Then there is no argument. But if the rejection comes from someone who demands *heilsgeschichtliche* responses to *alternative* events (Exodus, Calvary, Resurrection), we may have to answer (as a German saying has it), "The one ass is calling the other ass 'Long-ears.' "

3. There is the shattering question of the redeeming of the past. In German literature one recurrently meets the phrase *die unbewältigte Vergangenheit*, the yesterday that remains unmastered. The expression has become, indeed, almost banal. In his book *Die Unfähigkeit zu Trauern* ("The Inability to Mourn"), Alexander Mitscherlich argues, from a depth-psychological perspective, that in the Bundesrepublik since 1945, a repentant working-through of the guilt of the Third Reich has not taken place in any measure worthy of celebration. Jürgen Moltmann voices concern that the German people have repressed and suppressed the dark history: "The guilt was never given expression, and so it could not be forgiven."

At least two complications enter. There is, for one thing, the moral fact of world guilt. When, for example, President Franklin D. Roosevelt was asked, five days after the November 9, 1938, pogrom, whether U.S. immigration restrictions against Jews would be eased, he replied with a sharp and unqualified No. Second, as Reinhold Niebuhr was always insisting, nations as such do not repent—although this does not rule out subnational efforts at repentance within given nation-states.

In order to cope with the massive data within this third question, we offer a working typology:

(A) The first model: descriptively the Holocaust is treated here, tacitly, as a nonevent; evaluatively, Christians remain prisoners of the past. Large numbers of persons, within Germany as outside, live quite unaffected by the "final solution." They think and behave just as though there had been no kingdom of night. Nothing essential is learned or changed.

A ready illustration is Friedrich Greunagel's small book *Die Judenfrage* ("The Jewish Question"). At the outset the author prompts high expectations by lamenting "the yesterday that remains unmastered" and calling for Jewish-Christian reconciliation. But before long Greunagel explodes into anti-Jewish sentiments, wherein certain reputedly enduring, fundamental Jewish sins are catalogued. These center upon hardheartedness and nationalism. In fact, we are assured that the National Socialist adaptation of the claim to election simply reincarnated the mentality of Jews. Today, Jews and Israelis stand in the dangerous situation of claiming a monopoly upon the blessings of God, who makes them victorious at the expense of other peoples.

For Greunagel, as matters develop, the only real fault of the Christian church in the entire relationship is its failure to bring the Jews to Christ, their Savior from the Law, nationalism and other evils. Anti-Semitism becomes basically a matter of Jewish culpability, due to Jewish hardness of heart. In effect, only when Jews conquer their sins will anti-Semitism be overcome and Christians and Jews reconciled.

Greunagel's diatribe brings forcibly to mind a concept that is argued over today in German church circles: *eine geistliche*

Endlösung, a spiritual final solution. In the last resort, no real practical difference obtains between stuffing Jews into furnaces and subverting their religious and human integrity. Within the first rank of concerned Christian scholars in Germany today stands Rudolf Pfisterer of Schwäbisch Hall, who emphasizes that the Christian mission to the Jews is the continuing work of the Holocaust. Yet there are other effective means of subverting Jewish rights. As a substitute for "non-event," we may speak of the *Endlösung* as a perpetuating event—an event that serves to give continuing life to certain stereotypes and prejudices, which in turn provide an atmosphere conducive to future Holocausts.

Conflict over the *"Judenmission"*

(B) In a second model the Holocaust becomes, descriptively, a partial event ("partial" in its semidecisiveness); evaluatively, Christians are started along the path to liberation. An example is the current official pronouncement *Christen und Juden*, which goes further theologically and morally than the EKD has ever gone before. The members preparing the statement remain acutely aware of the *Endlösung;* it is much on their conscience. They speak of the deep trauma that the event created for Christians, of our faith's latter-day rediscovery of its Jewish roots, and of the abiding integrity of Judaism. They confess the dreadful role of the Christian world in the historic persecution of Jews, including the contribution of Christian anti-Semitism to the annihilation of the Jews of Europe. The authors stress that the Christians of Germany are charged with a special duty to oppose the new anti-Semitism that appears in the form of politically and socially motivated anti-Zionism. Christians have a particular obligation to support the independence and security of Israel—not alone as a political entity or achievement but also within the framework of the history of the people of God.

Yet after declaring these things, the pronouncement mirrors the conflict over the *Judenmission*—a conflict that continues to divide the Protestant churches in Germany. The authors raise the question of how the Christian is to bear witness to the Jew. Declaring that Christ is the "Saviour of all men," they insist that while certain current missionary practices have given Jews reason for mistrust, Christians cannot remain silent concerning the ground of their hope and faith. Thus, in the end, the EKD is not unqualifiedly ready to accept Jews as equals.

Further, *Christen und Juden* fails to surmount or exclude the ancient canard of Jewish responsibility, or co-responsibility with the Romans, for the execution of Jesus. Even if such responsibility in fact existed—it never did—the moral and psychological question remains: Why must this charge receive wearisome repetition in a church statement reputedly devoted to Christian-Jewish reconciliation? In a word, the EKD is living, simultaneously, a post-Holocaust life and a pre-Holocaust life.

Accepting Ourselves, Accepting the Other

(C) In the third model, descriptively the Holocaust becomes *metanoia*, total revolution; evaluatively, Christians are granted the power and joy of liberation. Liberation means not alone total self-acceptance but freedom from the idolatry of triumphing over the other. When we can accept ourselves, we are enabled to accept the other. And in accepting the other, we accept ourselves. Jesus is "the man for others." Such deliverance may be approximated collectively as well as individually.

In the *Journal of the History of Ideas* Emil L. Fackenheim poses the question of whether the link between Christian affirmation and Christian anti-Semitism has become, "after Auschwitz," *the* question for Christianity. In *Faith and Fratricide* Catholic theologian Rosemary Ruether finds the resolution of the moral-theological problem only in the church's unequivocal repudiation of its original sin, that is, its antithetical theology (*gegensätzliche Theologie*) and its "realized eschatology." Ruether asks, "Is it possible to say 'Jesus is Messiah' without, implicitly or explicitly, saying at the same time 'and the Jews be damned'?" She answers: "It is possible only if the Christian affirmation is 'relativized' into a 'theology of hope' which will free it of anti-Jewish imperialism, and indeed of all religious imperialism."

In Germany as abroad, the "theology of hope" is linked to the name of Jürgen Moltmann. However, from Ruether's standpoint, Moltmann's recent study *The Crucified God* embodies very largely a theology of hopelessness, a Lutheran-Pauline, gospel-versus-law line which is very much pre-Holocaust in its content and thrust. In great measure, the Christian is confirmed in his servitude rather than being offered liberation. (Moltmann is Reformed, but, as Wilhelm Pauck once remarked, it is the fate of German theologians to retain an umbilical attachment to Martin Luther.)

In some contrast, within Moltmann's latest book, *Kirche in der Kraft des Geistes* ("The Church in the Power of the Spirit"), some significant changes are evident, as in the author's celebration of Jewish adherence to Torah, his stress upon the great need for the church to return to its foundations in Israel, his insistence that prerequisite to the victory over Christian triumphalism is the acceptance of Israel as equal partner with the church, and his emphasis upon the integrity of the State of Israel. The views of Franz Rosenzweig gain a consequential role. On the other hand, Moltmann is inconsistent. He is as yet incapable of overcoming the claim that, *practically* construed, the church has replaced Israel in the work of salvation. The church remains, in Moltmann's view, the (round-about) instrument of the salvation of Israel. And with the parousia of Christ will come the fulfillment not only of the Christian hope, but of the Jewish hope, for then will Christ manifest himself as the Messiah of Israel. Thus it turns out that the only major substantive difference between *The Crucified God* and *Kirche in der Kraft des Geistes* is that the latter propounds what we might call "postponed triumphalism," in partial distinction from "pure" triumphalism.

The happy truth abides that Jürgen Moltmann has taken the Holocaust to heart; accordingly, we may hope for added transformations within his developing theology. However, we may not expect any immediate assent by him to Rosemary Ruether's word of final Christian liberation: "The self-infinitizing of the messianic sect that empowers itself to conquer all mankind in the name of the universal" is essentially "a false messianism. What Christianity has in Jesus is not the Messiah but a Jew who hoped for the coming of the Kingdom of God and who died in that hope."

Ruether is giving voice to a true theology of hope, of liberation, wherein lies ultimate Christian deliverance from complicity in the "final solution." The obvious question arises: Have any Christian thinkers in Germany been saved? Yes, a few. To Reinhold Mayer of Tübingen the *Judenmission* is a degradation (*Judentum und Christentum*). For Rolf Rendtorff, professor of Old Testament at Heidelberg, Jews are not to be treated as potential Christians; they possess their own inner integrity (in the journal *Evangelische Kommentare*). And to Heinz Kremers we are called, as Pope John said, simply to accept Jews as equal brothers. The clear implication is the unqualified right of the Jewish people, with other human collectivities, to work out their destiny freely. This entails, among other means, the exercise of sovereignty.

Re-enactment of the "Final Solution"

To spend time in the country of the "final solution" is to be made especially sensitive to the potential for that event's repetition. A closing judgment is prompted by current world events. The phases of the Nazi program—the identification of Jews as a threatening "race," the boycott, the undermining of Jewish integrity and of respect for Jews as human beings, the isolating and excluding of Jews from the human community, their eventual destruction—are being replicated today. But the process now takes place upon a world scale, not just upon a German or European scale. Before our eyes the *Endlösung* is beginning to be re-enacted. Accordingly, we Christians, with others, are asked in the name of Jesus the Jew: Is it nothing to you, all you who pass by?

Epilogue

HARRY JAMES CARGAS

SUCH CARE IS BEING TAKEN to hang this woman properly. Look at the expressions of each of these men. They are paying such close attention to every last detail. They perform rather artistically for the photographer here, each relating so intently to a particular aspect of the unholy task literally *at hand!* Note how well dressed the men are. The executioner on the left wears trousers that have been carefully creased. (This was long before the invention of permanent press.) And how about the man working from above, with tie and hat. When he left home, did his neighbors think he was heading for the office? Did he ask his wife, "What's for dinner tonight?" thinking that today's work would not interfere with a hearty appetite?

But we cannot consider only the killers. Our eyes are continually brought back to the woman who is soon to die. She seems hardly to pose a threat. She looks like my grandmother, is undoubtedly somebody's grandmother. What is she thinking? Is she praying? How frightened is this woman? Does she hope for some miracle to save her, or does she despair because she knows that a tremendous human slaughter is taking place, that she is only a single unit in an overwhelming event that will number

50,000,000 units? She may be almost at peace; somehow the camera suggests this. How many has she seen hanged before her?
The corpse on the right suggests that there may have been
several. How long will she be able to maintain a certain dignity,
before the bulk of her body, in opposition to her neck, will force
her to attempt to flail her legs and arms in some futile gesture
toward life? Did she know the shrouded victim? Was it her
husband or a child of hers? Did she die quickly?

However we define Hope, we see here a man who has none. His anguish is not superficial; it has penetrated his soul. To speculate on the cause of this victim's condition might be to dishonor him. But we may wonder if he survived the moment. His pain seems too complete, so overwhelming that this may have been the final expression of his life. Jewish psychiatrists who themselves had concentration camp experiences have written about how some (of the few) who survived the death camps were able to do so. Bruno Bettelheim suggests that certain men and women took on the personalities of their aggressors in order to get through alive. Leo Eitinger, after having analyzed many patients who, like himself, barely outlived Auschwitz and other camps, feels that one almost indispensable element to the survival of many was having a close relative sharing the atrocious experiences. Those who lost their entire families or who were separated from them in a kind of absolute way did not have this opportunity. Viktor Frankl, the founder of logotheraphy, a psychiatric approach based on hope—the hope of being reunited with a loved one, of completing a particular project—saw this as being important to a relatively large number of survivors. But the man in this photograph seems to have none of these. His posture is hardly that of one who is aggressive in any form. Furthermore, here he seems so alone that abandonment by family, friends, even God, appears to be reflected in his cry. And it is despair, not hope, which is reflected in his face, a despair that may have come from a realization that he is a creature suspended on earth, with ties to no one, no thing. Nor are we taking into account any physical pain this person is suffering. How cold is he? How long has it been since he has eaten? Is disease ravaging his body the way it did nearly all who lived for any length of time in the death camps? In a culture saturated with the false emotions of Hollywood, television soap operas, advertisers, self-pitiers and sycophants in general, can we long contemplate the true emotion of this miserable, miserable human being? We must.

How old is the little boy in this photograph? Perhaps seven.
But his eyes contain centuries. What a pitiful incongruity. Innocence, by its very nature, does not encompass experience. But
then this photograph is of a situation that is not consistent with
nature. The Holocaust was, by every civilized measure, anti-
natural. The boy intuits this. Something is horribly topsy-turvy,
terribly frightening. A man is holding a weapon on him, during
this roundup of Jews in Warsaw. For what reason? No reason
could ever be invented to justify what is happening in this scene,

and the real cause is ludicrous in the root sense of that word. This boy is being taken to his death because he has been judged a danger to European equilibrium. He is a Jew. That is crime enough in some people's minds. And while we could focus our attention exclusively on him in this picture, there are others who need to be considered. For instance, the child with his hands raised isn't even the youngest Pole in the group. Just above his right shoulder we see another who is about four or five years old. Another threat, another Christ-killer to some. A second boy to the left of center, looking off to his right, also exhibits in his eyes a terror no child should know. Eyes, in fact, can be considered a theme, if we dare to be academic about this setting. The camera's eye must be considered. It *must* be. Who has dared to take this photograph? For what purpose? Why memorialize this sin? What is the intended audience? Who will enjoy viewing this? Clearly this picture could *not* have been made without official permission. The victims were not snapping shutters. No, the persecutors were. Note that no eyes of the prisoners are looking at the camera. Those eyes are concentrated on something other than publicity. There is one, however, who is looking directly into the lens: the guard who has his gun directed at the little boy up front. We may take it that he is posing for this photographer. Why? Is he proud of what he is doing? Is he pleased to be carrying out his government's policy concerning Jews? Did he request a copy of the photo to show his friends and family? I have heard that after this photograph became famous, this guard was found as a civilian. I do not know the accuracy of this, but if true, he really has seen *himself* in this situation. How does he feel about it? Does he ever wonder if God's eye has recorded the same event? Does he have some thoughts about Judgment Day? What else did he do in the war that is memorable?

This was a face. It is grotesque, reminding us of novelist Flannery O'Connor's reply to a question about the bizarre situations and characters she rendered to present her theological viewpoint. She insisted that to the hard of hearing you have to shout. The photograph here is a response to those who would hail war as a noble effort, or worse, who would deny that the Holocaust ever really happened. Since over forty books in Europe and the

United States have been published denying the actuality of Nazi tortures, let the authors study this picture. This man was beaten to death with a hammer. Who was he? When he was nursing in his mother's arms, what hopes did she have for him when he reached maturity? Did she dream that he would become a medical doctor who might perform heroic acts of healing? Perhaps she hoped that her baby would become a rabbi and attend the spirit rather than the body. Possibly the boy would be trained as a scientist, become a good family man. He may have been a father. It is not impossible that a son of his saw him being bludgeoned to death. Surely the mother could not have dared to imagine her son's cruel end; he has become, for the world, only a victim, his face and head bones crushed because some guard was somehow irritated with him. And what of the guard? Was he mad or sane in the way the world ordinarily judges? When he finished his human massacre, was he able to look upon his effort or did it disgust him? Did he brag about his heroics or was he as ashamed of himself as we are of him now? This was a face, the face of a man who lived and dreamed and died a ghastly death. We cannot look at this face—and yet we dare not avert our eyes lest . . .

Bibliography

In 1977 I published *The Holocaust: An Annotated Bibliography* (Haverford, Pennsylvania: Catholic Library World) in which 425 books and articles on the subject and its history are described. While some will still find that document of value, it has become somewhat dated now. Below is a current bibliography (1981), based on my previous work but limited to books only. Of course, not every existing volume published in the United States is listed. I deliberately do not name the writings of Bruno Bettelheim, whose observations on the Holocaust seem to me to be clearly wrongheaded, nor do I regard William Styron's novel *Sophie's Choice* as belonging on this list. Some have disagreed with me but others may compile their own rationales. A bibliography hardly seems to be the place to throw out the challenge for a debate. The Bettelheim issue seems to me to have been settled authoritatively by Terrence Des Pres in his article, "The Bettelheim Problem," *Social Research* XLVI (Winter 1979), pp. 619–647. The discussion about *Sophie's Choice* continues.

A. *Historical Works about Nazi Germany* (Basically overviews)

Abel, Theodore. *The Nazi Movement.* New York: Atherton, 1966.
On Hitler's coming to power.
Allen, William Sheridan. *The Nazi Seizure of Power.* New York: New Viewpoints, 1965.
A single German town's experience, 1930–1935.
Arendt, Hannah. *The Origins of Totalitarianism.* Cleveland: World Publishing Co., 1958.
On Nazi and Stalinist totalitarianism.
Baumont, Maurice; Fried, John H. E.; and Vermeil, Edmond, eds. *The Third Reich.* New York: Praeger Publishers, 1955.
Important on anti-Semitism, racialism, and Hitler's SS troops.
Crankshaw, Edward. *The Gestapo: Instrument of Tyranny.* New York: Viking Press, Inc., 1956.
About one of the most notorious institutions in history.
Dawidowicz, Lucy S. *The War Against the Jews 1933–1945.* New York: Holt, Rinehart and Winston, 1975.
Shows that Nazis were more concerned with killing Jews than victory in World War II.

Delarue, Jacques. *The Gestapo: A History of Horror.* New York: William Morrow and Co., Inc., 1964.
A solid history.
Fest, Joachim. *The Face of the Third Reich.* New York: Pantheon Books, Inc., 1970.
Portraits of Nazi leadership.
Hilberg, Raul. *The Destruction of the European Jews.* New York: Quadrangle, 1961.
One of the finest of the histories.
———, ed. *Documents of Destruction.* New York: Quadrangle, 1971.
An important companion volume to Hilberg's great history.
Hillel, Marc, and Henry, Clarissa. *Of Pure Blood.* New York: McGraw-Hill, 1977.
On an attempt to breed a super race.
Jarman, T. L. *The Rise and Fall of Nazi Germany.* New York: New York University Press, 1956.
A good scholarly appraisal.
Jewish Black Book Committee. *The Black Book, The Nazi Crime Against the Jewish People.* New York: Duell, Sloan and Pearce, 1946.
A valuable, very early study.
Levin, Nora. *The Holocaust.* New York: Schocken Books, Inc., 1968.
The most readable of the important one-volume histories.
Manvell, Roger. *S.S. and Gestapo.* New York: Ballantine Books, Inc., 1969.
Those who most seriously implemented Hitler's plans.
Manvell, Roger, and Fraenkel, Heinrich. *The Incomparable Crime.* New York: G. P. Putnam's Sons, 1967.
Genocide and its roots.
Mitscherlich, Alexander, and Mielke, Fred. *Doctors of Infamy.* New York: H. Schuman, 1960.
Nazi medical crimes.
Moose, George, ed. *Nazi Culture.* New York: Grosset and Dunlap, Inc., 1968.
Intellectual, cultural, and social origins of the Third Reich.
Newmann, Robert. *The Pictorial History of the Third Reich.* New York: Bantam Books, Inc., 1962.
Strong emotional impact.
Noakes, Jeremy, and Pridham, Geoffrey, eds. *Documents on Nazism, 1919–1945.* New York: Viking Press, Inc., 1975.
The title is properly descriptive.
Orlow, Dietrich. *A History of the Nazi Party, 1919–1933.* Pittsburgh, PA: University of Pittsburgh Press, 1969.
The beginnings of the Nazi party.

Pilch, Judah, ed. *The Jewish Catastrophe in Europe.* New York: American Association for Jewish Education, 1968.
A handbook approach.

Poliakov, Leon. *Harvest of Hate.* Syracuse, NY: Syracuse University Press, 1954.
The Nazi program of annihilation.

Reitlinger, Gerold. *The Final Solution.* New York: Beechhurst, 1953.
On the administrative machinery of mass murder.

———. *The SS: Alibi of a Nation, 1922–1945.* New York: Viking Press, Inc., 1957.
Perhaps the best history of the SS.

Remak, Joachim, ed. *The Nazi Years.* Englewood Cliffs, NJ: Prentice-Hall, Inc., 1969.
Documents and speeches.

Roper, Edith, and Leiser, Clara. *Nazi Justice.* New York: E. P. Dutton and Co., 1941.
The perversion of justice by the Nazis.

Russell, Lord of Liverpool. *The Scourge of the Swastika.* New York: Ballantine Books, Inc., 1956.
Short history of Nazi crimes.

Rutherford, Ward. *Genocide.* New York: Ballantine Books, Inc., 1973.
Grim illustrations mark this introductory work.

Schleunes, Karl A. *The Twisted Road to Auschwitz.* Urbana, IL: University of Illinois Press, 1970.
The early Nazi policy toward Jews.

Schuman, Frederick Lewis. *The Nazi Dictatorship.* New York: Alfred A. Knopf, 1936.
A study in social pathology.

Shirer, William L. *The Rise and Fall of the Third Reich.* New York: Simon and Schuster, 1960.
Perhaps the most comprehensive history.

Shub, Boris, ed. *Hitler's Ten Year War on the Jews.* New York: Institute of Jewish Affairs, 1943.
With firsthand reports, written in the midst of the atrocities.

Stein, George. *The Waffen SS.* Ithaca, NY: Cornell University Press, 1970.
Hitler's unique guard at war.

Stochura, Peter D. *Nazi Youth in the Weimar Republic.* Santa Barbara, CA: Clio Press, 1975.
How the young were used.

Thalman, Rita, and Feinermann, Emmanuel. *Crystal Night.* New York: Coward, McCann & Geoghegan, 1974.
The organized Nazi terror of November 9–10, 1938.

Thomas, Gordon and Witts, Max Morgan. *Voyages of the Damned.*
New York: Fawcett, 1975.
On 937 Jews trying to escape Nazi terror.

Wheaton, Eliot Barculo. *The Nazi Revolution 1933–1935.* New York:
Anchor, 1969.
Concentrates on a brief period before the war.

B. *Adolf Hitler and Associates* (On the men behind the movement)

Boelcke, Willi A. *The Secret Conferences of Dr. Goebbels.* New
York: E. P. Dutton & Co., 1970.
A view of the Nazi propaganda machine.

Bramsted, Ernest K. *Goebbels and Nationalist Socialist Propaganda.*
East Lansing, MI: Michigan State University Press, 1965.
Shows how truth is a casualty of war.

Bullock, Alan. *Hitler: A Study of Tyranny.* New York: Harper and
Row, 1964.
A historical and psychological portrayal.

Fest, Joachim. *Adolph Hitler.* New York: Harcourt Brace Jovanovich,
1974.
Better than adequate biography.

Friedlander, Saul. *Kurt Gerstein: The Ambiguity of Good.* New York:
Alfred A. Knopf, 1969.
An SS officer: hero or demon?

Goebbels, Joseph. *Final Entries 1945.* New York: G. P. Putnam's Sons,
1978.
Contains valuable insights into the workings of the Nazi mind.

———. *The Goebbels Diaries.* Westport, CT: Greenwood (reprint of
1948 edition).
A major source work.

Gordon, Harold J., Jr. *Hitler and the Beer Hall Putsch.* Princeton,
NJ: Princeton University Press, 1972.
The rise of the dictator.

Heiden, Konrad. *Der Fuehrer: Hitler's Rise to Power.* Boston: Beacon
Press, 1969.
A biographical study of Nazism.

Herzstein, Edwin. *Adolph Hitler and the German Trauma, 1913–1945.*
New York: G. P. Putnam's Sons, 1974.
A well-balanced introduction.

Hitler, Adolph. *Mein Kampf.* Boston: Houghton Mifflin Co., 1943.
The self-pronounced plan of terror.

Hoess, Rudolf. *Commandant of Auschwitz.* Cleveland: World Publishing Co., 1960.
By the man responsible for two million murders.

Hohne, Heinz. *The Order of the Death's Head*. New York: Coward, McCann & Geoghegan, 1970.
The SS story.

Jackel, Eberhard. *Hitler's Weltanschauung*. Middletown, CT: Wesleyan University Press, 1972.
Subtitled "A Blueprint for Power."

Manvell, Roger, and Fraenkel, Heinrich. *Dr. Goebbels: His Life and Death*. New York: Simon and Schuster, 1960.
Life of the propaganda minister.

Maser, Werner, ed. *Hitler's Letters and Notes*. New York: Harper and Row, 1974.
Revealing private papers.

Miale, Florence, and Selzer, Michael. *The Nuremberg Mind*. New York: Quadrangle, 1975.
The psychology of Nazi leaders.

Mosley, Leonard. *The Reich Marshall*. New York: Dell, 1975.
Biography of Hermann Goering.

Neumann, Peter. *Black March*. New York: William Sloan Associates, 1958.
Training and personality of a Gestapo officer.

Robertson, Esmonde M. *Hitler's Pre-War Policy and Military Plans 1933–1939*. Secaucus, NJ: Citadel Press, Inc., 1967.
The title is descriptive.

Sereny, Gitta. *Into That Darkness*. New York: McGraw-Hill, 1974.
Mass murderer Franz Stangl's deathbed confession.

Smith, Bradley. *Adolph Hitler*. Stanford, CA: Hoover Institution Press, 1967.
The young Hitler.

———. *Heinrich Himmler*. Stanford, CA: Hoover Institution Press, 1971.
About a Nazi in the making.

Snyder, Louis L. *Hitler and Nazism*. New York: Bantam Books, Inc., 1971.
How Hitler shaped the movement in his own image.

Speer, Albert. *Inside the Third Reich*. New York: Macmillan Publishing Co., Inc., 1970.
Self-serving account by Hitler's architect.

———. *Spandau*. New York: Macmillan Publishing Co., Inc., 1976.
From the diaries of a Nazi who does not admit his own guilt.

Taylor, Telford. *Sword and Swastika*. New York: Simon and Schuster, 1952.
Of generals and other Nazis.

Toland, John. *Adolf Hitler*. New York: Doubleday & Co., Inc., 1976.
An excellent volume.

Trevor-Roper, H. R. *The Last Days of Hitler*. New York: Macmillan Co., 1947.
A detailed account.

Waite, Robert G. L. *The Psychopathic God*. New York: Basic Books, Inc., 1977.
Powerful dissertation on the Hitler psyche.

Wighton, Charles. *Heydrich: Hitler's Most Evil Henchman*. Radnor, PA: Chilton Book Co., 1962.
Biography of a man of evil who may have been a Jew.

C. *Regional Events* (Events in individual nations)

Apenszlak, Jacob, ed. *The Black Book Polish Jewry*. New York: The American Federation for Polish Jews, 1943.
On the martyrdom of Polish Jews.

Braham, Randolph L. *The Politics of Genocide* (two volumes). New York: Columbia University Press, 1981.
Documentary account of what befell Hungarian Jews.

Chary, Frederick B. *The Bulgarian Jews and the Final Solution, 1940–1944*. Pittsburgh, Pa: University of Pittsburgh Press, 1972.
Deportations and legislation against the Jews are the subjects of this volume.

Flender, Harold. *Rescue in Denmark*. New York: Simon and Schuster, 1963.
An exciting story.

Katz, Robert. *Black Sabbath*. New York: Macmillan Publishing Co., Inc., 1969.
Concerning the deportation of Jews from Rome.

Levy, Claud, and Tillard, Paul. *Betrayal at the Vel d'Hviv*. New York: Hill & Wang, Inc., 1969.
On the deportation of Paris Jews.

Presser, Jacob. *The Destruction of the Dutch Jews*. New York: E. P. Dutton & Co., 1969.
Part history, part memoir.

Ringelblum, Emmanuel. *Polish-Jewish Relations During the Second World War*. New York: Howard Fertig, Inc., 1976.
Immensely valuable, by an eyewitness who did not survive.

Ross, Robert W. *So It Was True*. Minneapolis: University of Minnesota Press, 1980.
How the American Protestant press reacted to the Nazi persecution of the Jews.

D. *Resistance* (Jewish resistance during the Holocaust)

Ainsztein, Reuben. *Jewish Resistance in Nazi Occupied Eastern Europe*. New York: Barnes and Noble, 1975.
Gives the lie to the notion that Jews did not resist the Nazis.
Barkai, Meyer, ed. *The Fighting Ghettos*. Philadelphia: J. B. Lippincott Co., 1962.
A series of essays on Jewish resistance.
Elkins, Michael. *Forged in Fury*. New York: Ballantine Books, Inc., 1971.
A chronicle of Jews who fought back.
Garlinski, Josef. *Fighting Auschwitz*. New York: Fawcett, 1976.
Compiled from diaries and records.
Suhl, Yuri, ed. *They Fought Back*. New York: Schocken Books, Inc., 1967.
On Jewish resistance groups in nearly every ghetto and camp.
Trunk, Isaiah. *Jewish Responses to Nazi Persecutors*. New York: Stein and Day Publishers, 1979.
Filled with information.
Tushnet, Leonard. *To Die with Honor*. Secaucus, NJ: Citadel Press, Inc., 1965.
The Jewish uprising in the Warsaw Ghetto.
Yahil, Leni. *The Rescue of Danish Jewry*. Philadelphia: The Jewish Publication Society of America, 1969.
A closely researched volume.
Zuckerman, Isaac, ed. *The Fighting Ghettos*. New York: Belmont-Tower Books, Inc., 1971.
Resistance in the ghettos and forests of Eastern Europe.

E. *Ghettos, Camps, and Eyewitness Accounts* (On specific locales)

Amery, Jean. *At the Mind's Limit*. Bloomington, IN: Indiana University Press, 1980.
Profound reflections on torture.
Berg, Mary. *Warsaw Ghetto—A Diary*. New York: L. B. Fischer, 1945.
One of the first accounts.
Birenbaum, Halina. *Hope Is the Last to Die*. New York: Twayne Publishers, Inc., 1971.
A personal documentation of Nazi terror.
Bor, Josef. *Terezin Requiem*. New York: Alfred A. Knopf, 1963.
About a famous act of spiritual resistance.

Cohen, Elie A. *Human Behavior in the Concentration Camp.* New York: W. W. Norton & Co., 1953.
A psychological perspective.
———. *The Abyss.* New York: W. W. Norton & Co., 1973.
By a Dutch doctor who survived several camps.
Delbo, Charlotte. *None of Us Will Return.* Boston: Beacon Press, Inc., 1978.
Brief and very powerful.
D'Harcourt, Pierre. *The Real Enemy.* New York: Charles Scribner's Sons, 1967.
By an imprisoned Christian.
Donat, Alexander. *The Holocaust Kingdom: A Memoir.* New York: Holt, Rinehart and Winston, 1965.
Of a Polish Jewish family that survived.
Dribben, Judith Strick. *A Girl Called Judith Strick.* Chicago: Cowles, 1970.
Autobiography of a survivor of the underground, prison, Auschwitz, and the Soviet army.
Edelman, Marek. *The Ghetto Fights.* New York: American Representation of the General Jewish Workers' Union of Poland, 1946.
A small pamphlet concentrating on the Warsaw Ghetto.
Fenelon, Fania. *Playing For Time.* New York: Atheneum Publishers, 1977.
The famed story of personal courage.
Frank, Anne. *The Diary of a Young Girl.* New York: Pocket Books, Inc., 1965.
The classic memoir.
Friedman, Philip. *Martyrs and Fighters.* New York: Praeger Publishers, Inc., 1954.
Heroism of the Warsaw Ghetto.
Goldstein, Bernard. *The Stars Bear Witness.* New York: Viking Press, Inc., 1949.
Personal narrative of a Warsaw Ghetto survivor.
Goldstein, Charles. *The Bunker.* Philadelphia: The Jewish Publication Society of America, 1970.
How seven survived the Warsaw Ghetto.
Grossman, Mendel. *With a Camera in the Ghetto.* New York: Schocken Books, Inc., 1977.
Photographs from the Lodz Ghetto.
Heimler, Eugene. *Concentration Camp.* (Original title: *Night of the Mist,* 1960.) New York: Pyramid Books, 1961.
Author sees himself as a messenger from the dead.

Hermanns, William. *Holocaust.* New York: Harper and Row, 1972.
By a survivor from Verdun.

Hersh, Giselle, and Mann, Peggy. *Giselle, Save the Children.* New York: Everest House Publishers, 1980.
Moving account by a Hungarian victim.

Hilberg, Raul, *et al.*, eds. *The Warsaw Diary of Adam Czerniakow.* New York: Stein and Day Publishers, 1979.
The daily record of one of the most tragic of Holocaust figures.

Hyams, Joseph. *A Field of Buttercups.* Englewood Cliffs, NJ: Prentice-Hall, Inc., 1968.
About Janusz Korczak, who volunteered his death to aid children.

Kantor, Alfred. *The Book of Alfred Kantor.* New York: McGraw-Hill, 1971.
Profound visual impression of Holocaust life.

Kaplan, Chaim A. *The Scroll of Agony.* Translated and edited by A. Katsh. (Reprinted as *The Warsaw Diary of Chaim Kaplan.*) New York: Macmillan Publishing Co., Inc., 1965.
The account by one who perished in 1942.

Katz, Alfred. *Poland's Ghettos at War.* New York: Twayne Publishers, Inc., 1970.
An in-depth treatment.

Kessel, Sim. *Hanged at Auschwitz.* New York: Stein and Day Publishers, 1972.
A personal narrative.

Klein, Gerda. *All But My Life.* New York: Hill & Wang, Inc., 1957.
By a slave laborer.

Koestler, Arthur. *Scum of the Earth.* New York: Macmillan Publishing Co., Inc., 1968.
On the concentration camps and those who worked them.

Kogon, Eugen. *The Theory and Practice of Hell.* New York: Farrar, Straus and Cudihy, 1950.
The system behind the camps.

Korczak, Janusz. *Ghetto Diary.* New York: Schocken Books, Inc., 1978.
The record of a true hero.

Kurzman, Dan. *The Bravest Battle.* New York: G. P. Putnam's Sons, 1976.
The 28 days of the Warsaw Ghetto.

Leitner, Isabella. *Fragments of Isabella.* New York: Crowell, 1978.
A moving, at times angry, eyewitness view.

Levi, Primo. *If This Man Is a Man*. Willows, CA: Orion, 1959. (Later
published as *Survival in Auschwitz*.)
How the author and others survived.

Lewinska, Pelagia. *Twenty Months at Auschwitz*. Secaucus, NJ: Lyle
Stuart, Inc., 1968.
A terrible story of incarceration.

Mark, Ger. *Uprising in the Warsaw Ghetto*. New York: Schocken
Books, Inc., 1975.
The major revolt of the Jews.

Maurel, Michelen. *An Ordinary Camp*. New York: Simon and Schuster, 1958.
What a death camp is like.

Michel, Jean. *Dora*. New York: Holt, Rinehart and Winston, 1980.
A look at the horrible camp.

Minco, Marga. *Bitter Herbs*. New York: Oxford University Press,
1960.
A memoir of Dutch-Jewish childhood.

Muller, Filip. *Eyewitness Auschwitz*. New York: Stein and Day Publishers, 1979.
One of the most terrifying of eyewitness commentaries.

Naumann, Bernd. *Auschwitz*. New York: Praeger Publishers, Inc.,
1966.
Contains testimony and relevant documentation.

Newman, Judith Sternberg. *In the Hell of Auschwitz*. Jericho, NY:
Exposition Press, Inc., 1963.
An eyewitness account of horror.

Novitch, Miriam. *Sobibor*. New York: Schocken Books, Inc., 1980.
Based on hundreds of eyewitness accounts.

Nyiszli, Miklos. *Auschwitz*. New York: Frederick Fell, Inc., 1960.
A doctor's eyewitness account.

Perl, Gisella. *I Was a Doctor in Auschwitz*. New York: International
Universities Press, Inc., 1948.
A unique viewpoint of a death camp.

Pinkus, Oscar. *The House of Ashes*. Cleveland: World Publishing Co.,
1964.
The reminiscence of a Polish Jew makes up the chief portion of
this work.

Ringelblum, Emmanuel. *Notes from the Warsaw Ghetto*. New York:
McGraw-Hill, 1958.
The classic day-by-day account.

Rosen, Donia. *The Forest, My Friend*. New York: World Federation
of Bergen-Belsen Associates, 1971.
Survival of a six-year-old Ukrainian girl.

Rousset, David. *The Other Kingdom*. New York: Reynal and Hitchcock, 1947.
The concentration camp universe.

Salomon, Charlotte. *Charlotte: A Diary in Pictures*. New York: Harcourt Brace, 1963.
Drawings by a young Jewish girl.

Schoenberner, Gerhard. *The Yellow Star*. New York: Bantam Books, Inc., 1973.
Mixes official and personal documents on the persecution of Jews.

Senesh, Hannah. *Hannah Senesh—Her Life and Diary*. New York: Schocken Books, Inc., 1972.
Portrait of a Jewish martyr.

Shapell, Natham. *Witness to the Truth*. New York: David McKay Co., Inc., 1974.
By a survivor of Auschwitz.

Smith, Marcus J. *The Harrowing of Hell: Dachau*. Albuquerque: University of New Mexico Press, 1972.
The fight to save Dachau's survivors by a doctor.

Stroop, Juergen. *The Stroop Report*. New York: Pantheon Books, Inc., 1979.
A Nazi account of the Warsaw Ghetto.

Szmaglewska, Seweryna. *Smoke Over Birkenau*. New York: Holt, 1947.
A personal narrative of the infamous camp.

Wells, Leon W. *The Death Brigade*. New York: Schocken Books, Inc., 1978.
Gripping account by one who testified at the Nuremberg Trials.

Wiechert, Ernst. *The Forest of the Dead*. New York: Greenberg, 1947.
Thinly veiled autobiography of concentration camp experience.

Wiesel, Elie. *Night*. New York: Hill & Wang, Inc., 1960.
Perhaps the most eloquent of autobiographies of the Holocaust experience.

Zylberberg, Michael. *A Warsaw Diary*. Bridgeport, CT: Hartmore House, 1969.
An eyewitness account.

F. *Samaritans* (Of those who aided Jews)

Bartoszewski, Sladyslaw. *The Samaritans*. New York: Twayne Publishers, Inc., 1970.
Poles who risked their lives to save Jews.

Bertelsen, Aage. *October '43*. New York: G. P. Putnam's Sons, 1954.
The rescue of Danish Jews.

Boehm, Eric H., ed. *We Survived*. New Haven: Yale University Press, 1949.
Stories of persons hidden and hunted in Nazi Germany.

Brand, Joel. *Desperate Mission*. New York: Criterion Books, 1958.
Of negotiations to ransom Jews.

Friedman, Philip. *Their Brothers' Keepers*. New York: Crown Publishers, Inc., 1957.
Stories of some who shielded and befriended Jews.

Horbach, Michael. *Out of the Night*. New York: Frederick Fell, Inc., 1967.
On Germans who rescued Jews.

Iranek-Osmecki, Kazimierz. *He Who Saves One Life*. New York: Crown Publishers, Inc., 1971.
The definitive volume on Polish samaritans.

Leboucher, Fernande. *Incredible Mission*. New York: Doubleday & Co., Inc., 1969.
About a heroic French priest.

Mann, Peggy, and Kluger, Ruth. *The Last Escape*. New York: Doubleday & Co., 1973.
Thrilling story of one who helped thousands to escape.

Masters, Anthony. *The Summer That Bled*. New York: St. Martin's Press, Inc., 1972.
Attempts to rescue Hungarian Jews.

Papanak, Ernst, with Edward Linn. *Out of the Fire*. New York: Morrow, 1975.
On the author's work to save Jewish children.

Zahn, Gordon C. *In Solitary Witness*. New York: Irvington, 1964.
The life of a Christian martyr who refused to serve the Nazis.

G. *Justice* (War crimes/trials)

Arendt, Hannah. *Eichmann in Jerusalem*. New York: Viking Press, Inc., 1964.
Reportage of a trial.

Bosch, William J. *Judgement at Nuremberg*. Chapel Hill, NC: University of North Carolina Press, 1970.
American attitudes toward the war crimes trials.

Comer, Clarke. *Eichmann: The Man and His Crimes*. New York: Ballantine Books, Inc., 1960.
The story of an infamous mass murderer.

Davidson, Eugene. *The Trial of the Germans*. New York: Macmillan Publishing Co., Inc., 1966.
A demoniacally fascinating record.

Gilbert, G. M. *Nuremberg Diary*. New York: Farrar, Straus, and Giroux, 1947.
By a prison psychologist.

Glock, Charles; Selznick, Gertrude; and Spaeth, Joe. *The Apathetic Majority*. New York: Harper and Row, 1966.
On public responses to the Eichmann trial.

Harris, Whitney R. *Tyranny on Trial*. Dallas: Southern Methodist University Press, 1954.
An analysis of the evidence of the Nuremberg Trials.

Hausner, Gideon. *Justice in Jerusalem*. New York: Harper and Row, 1966.
On the capture and trial of Eichmann.

Klarsfield, Beate. *Wherever They May Be*. New York: Vanguard Press, Inc., 1974.
Story of a Christian woman engaged in hunting Nazi war criminals.

Pearlman, Moshe. *The Capture and Trial of Adolf Eichmann*. New York: Simon and Schuster, 1963.
The title here is descriptive.

Robinson, Jacob. *And the Crooked Shall Be Made Straight*. New York: Macmillan Publishing Co., Inc., 1965.
A critical response to Hannah Arendt.

Smith, Bradley. *Reaching Judgment at Nuremberg*. New York: Basic Books, Inc., 1976.
How the Nazi war crimes were judged.

Wiesenthal, Simon. *The Murderers Among Us*. New York: McGraw-Hill, 1967.
Memoirs of a Nazi hunter.

Zeiger, Henry A., ed. *The Case Against Adolf Eichmann*. New York: New American Library, Inc., 1960.
From documents and eyewitness accounts.

H. *Reflections, Interpretations*
(Theological, philosophical, psychological)

Beradt, Charlotte. *The Third Reich of Dreams*. New York: Quadrangle, 1968.
Important record of dreams of citizens of the Third Reich.

Berkovitz, Eliezer. *Faith after the Holocaust*. New York: KTAV Publishing House, Inc., 1973.
A powerful discussion.

Cargas, Harry James. *A Christian Response to the Holocaust.* Denver: Stonehenge, 1981.
A backward and forward look.

Cohen, Arthur A. *Arguments and Doctrines.* New York: Harper and Row, 1970.
A collection of responses by Jewish thinkers.

Conway, John. *The Nazi Persecution of the Churches.* New York: Macmillan Publishing Co., Inc., 1969.
Nazi policy on Protestant and Catholic churches.

Eckardt, A. Roy. *Elder and Younger Brothers.* New York: Charles Scribner's Sons, 1967.
On the encounter of Jews and Christians.

Fackenheim, Emil. *God's Presence in History.* New York: New York University Press, 1970.
On the survival of Judaism as an essential commandment.

Falconi, Carlo. *The Silence of Pius XII.* Boston: Little, Brown, 1970.
On a tragic topic.

Flannery, Edward H. *The Anguish of the Jews.* New York: Macmillan Publishing Co., Inc., 1965.
A priest's study of anti-Semitism.

Fleischner, Eva, ed. *Auschwitz: Beginning of a New Era?* New York: KTAV Publishing House, Inc., 1977.
A collection of thoughtful essays from a series of perspectives.
————. *Judaism in German Christian Theology since 1945.* Metuchen, NJ: Scarecrow Press, Inc., 1975.
By a leading Christian theologian.

Frankl, Viktor. *Man's Search for Meaning.* (Original title: *From Death-Camp to Existentialism,* 1959.) Boston: Beacon Press, 1963.
Psychiatric theory by a survivor.

Friedlander, Saul. *Pius XII and the Third Reich: A Documentation.* New York: Alfred A. Knopf, 1966.
A critical view.

Hay, Malcolm. *Thy Brother's Blood.* New York: Hart Publishing Co., Inc., 1975.
Roots of Christian anti-Semitism.

Isaac, Jules. *The Teaching of Contempt.* New York: Holt, Rinehart and Winston, 1964.
Profound view of Christian anti-Semitism.

Jaspers, Karl. *The Question of German Guilt.* New York: Dial Press, Inc., 1947.
By Germany's foremost modern philosopher.

Lewy, Gunter. *The Catholic Church and Nazi Germany.* New York: McGraw-Hill, 1964.
Important insights.

Littell, Franklin H. *The German Phoenix*. New York: Doubleday & Co., Inc., 1960.
A history of protest and resistance.

———, ed. *The German Church Struggle and the Holocaust*. Detroit: Wayne State University Press, 1974.
Important essays wonderfully synthesized by the editor.

———. *The Crucifixion of the Jews*. New York: Harper and Row, 1975.
By one of the world's leading Protestant scholars on the Holocaust.

McGarry, Michael B. *Christology After Auschwitz*. Paramus, NJ: Paulist Press, 1977.
A penetrating summation.

Meinecke, Fredrich. *The German Catastrophe*. Gloucester, Mass: Peter Smith, 1963.
Reflections on a German tragedy.

Mitscherlich, Alexander and Margareta. *The Inability to Mourn*. New York: Grove Press, 1975.
Psychiatric analysis of postwar German reactions.

Pawelczynska, Anna. *Values and Violence in Auschwitz*. Berkeley: University of California Press, 1979.
By a Polish sociologist.

Prager, Moshe. *Sparks of Glory*. New York: Shengold Publishers, Inc., 1974.
Jews who continued in their faith through the Holocaust.

Rosenbaum, Irving. *The Holocaust and Halakhah*. New York: KTAV Publishing House, Inc., 1976.
On conforming to Jewish law.

Roskies, David, ed. *Night Words: A Midrash on the Holocaust*. Washington, DC: B'nai B'rith Hillel Foundations, 1971.
Composed of traditional and modern texts.

Rubenstein, Richard L. *After Auschwitz*. Indianapolis: Bobbs-Merrill Co., 1966.
A controversial theological reflection demanding a response.

Ruether, Rosemary R. *Faith and Fratricide*. New York: Seabury Press, Inc., 1974.
On the theological roots of anti-Semitism.

Samuel, Maurice. *The Great Hatred*. New York: Alfred A. Knopf, 1948.
On Christian and Nazi hatred of Jews.

Snell, John L., ed. *The Nazi Revolution—Germany's Guilt or Germany's Fate?* Lexington, Mass: D. C. Heath Company, 1959.
Nineteen investigative essays.

Viereck, Peter. *Metapolitics.* New York: Capricorn, 1961.
The roots of the Nazi mind.
Zahn, Gordon C. *German Catholics and Hitler's Wars.* New York: Sheed & Ward, Inc., 1962.
An authoritative investigation.

I. *The Arts* (Fiction, poetry, drama, and interpretive literature.
This segment is not annotated because of the extreme subjectivity of such an exercise.)

Aichinger, Ilse. *Herod's Children.* New York: Atheneum Publishers, 1963.
Andersch, Alfred. *Efraim's Book.* New York: Doubleday & Co., Inc., 1970.
Arnold, Elliott. *A Night of Watching.* New York: Fawcett, 1967.
Becker, Jurek. *Jacob the Liar.* New York: Harcourt Brace Jovanovich, 1975.
Berger, Zdena. *Tell Me Another Morning.* New York: Harper and Row, 1961.
Blagowidow, George. *The Last Train from Berlin.* New York: Doubleday & Co., Inc., 1977.
Borowski, Tadeusz. *This Way for the Gas, Ladies and Gentlemen.* New York: Viking Press, Inc., 1967.
Cargas, Harry James. *Harry James Cargas in Conversation with Elie Wiesel.* Paramus, NJ: Paulist/Newman Press, 1976.
Eisner, Jack. *The Survivor.* New York: Morrow, 1980.
Gershan, Karen. *Selected Poems.* New York: Harcourt, Brace and World, 1966.
Green, Gerald. *The Artists of Terezin.* New York: Hawthorn Books, Inc., 1969.
Habe, Hans. *The Mission.* New York: Coward, McCann & Geoghegan, 1966.
Halperin, Irvin. *Messengers from the Dead.* Philadelphia: Westminster Press, 1970.
Heartfield, John. *Photomontages of the Nazi Period.* New York: Universe Books, 1977.
Heimler, Eugene. *The Storm.* Seattle: Serendipity, 1976.
Hersey, John. *The Wall.* New York: Alfred A. Knopf, 1950.
Heyen, William. *The Swastika Poems.* New York: Vanguard Press, Inc., 1977.
Hilsenrath, Edgar. *The Nazi and the Barber.* New York: Doubleday & Co., Inc., 1971.
Hochhuth, Rolf. *The Deputy.* New York: Grove Press, 1964.

Hull, David Stewart. *Film in the Third Reich*. New York: Simon and Schuster, 1973.

Jacot, Michael. *The Last Butterfly*. New York: Indianapolis: Bobbs-Merrill Co., 1974.

Karmel, Ilona. *An Estate of Memory*. Boston: Houghton Mifflin Co., 1969.

Karmel-Wolfe, Henia. *The Baders of Jacob Street*. Philadelphia: J. B. Lippincott Co., 1970.

Ka-tzetnik. *Atrocity*. Secaucus, NJ: Lyle Stuart, Inc., 1963.

———. *House of Dolls*. New York: Pyramid, 1960.

Kosinski, Jerzy. *The Painted Bird*. New York: Pocket Books, Inc., 1966.

Kuper, Jack. *Child of the Holocaust*. New York: Doubleday & Co., Inc., 1968.

Kuznetsov, Anatoly. *Babi Yar*. New York: Farrar, Straus and Giroux, 1970.

Langer, Lawrence L. *The Holocaust and the Literary Imagination*. New Haven: Yale University Press, 1975.

Langfus, Anna. *The Whole Land Brimstone*. New York: Pantheon Books, Inc., 1962.

Leiser, Erwin. *Nazi Cinema*. New York: Macmillan Publishing Co., Inc., 1975.

Levin, Meyer. *Eva*. New York: Simon and Schuster, 1959.

Lind, Jakov. *Landscape in Concrete*. New York: Grove Press, 1966.

———. *Soul of Wood and Other Stories*. New York: Fawcett, 1966.

Lustig, Arnost. *A Prayer for Katerina Horovitzova*. New York: Harper and Row, 1973.

———. *Darkness Casts No Shadow*. Washington, DC: Inscape Corp., 1976.

———. *Night and Hope*. Washington, DC: Inscape Corp., 1976.

———. *Diamonds of the Night*. Washington, DC: Inscape Corp., 1978.

Napora, Paul. *Auschwitz*. San Antonio, TX: Naylor Co., 1967.

———. *Death at Belsen*. San Antonio, TX: Naylor Co., 1967.

Rawicz, Piotr. *Blood from the Sky*. New York: Harcourt, Brace and World, 1964.

Sachs, Nelly. *O The Chimneys*. New York: Farrar, Straus and Giroux, 1967.

Schaeffer, Susan Fromberg. *Anya*. New York: Macmillan Publishing Co., Inc., 1974.

Schwarz-Bart, André. *The Last of the Just*. New York: Bantam Books, Inc., 1960.

Semprun, Jorge. *The Long Voyage*. New York: Grove Press, 1964.

Sperber, Manes. . . . *Than a Tear in the Sea.* New York: World Federation of Bergen-Belsen Associations, 1967.

Steiner, Jean-Francois. *Treblinka.* New York: Simon and Schuster, 1967.

Tomkiewicz, Mina. *Of Bombs and Mice.* Cranbury, NJ: A. S. Barnes & Co., 1970.

Volavkova, H., ed. *I Never Saw Another Butterfly.* New York: McGraw-Hill, 1964.

Ziemian, Joseph. *The Cigarette Sellers of Three Crosses Square.* Minneapolis: Lerner, 1970.

J. *Miscellaneous* (Everything else)

Bauer, Yehuda. *The Holocaust in Perspective.* Seattle: University of Washington Press, 1978.
A philosopher's account.

Brenner, Reeve Robert. *The Faith and Doubt of Holocaust Survivors.* New York: Free Press, 1980.
On what happened to their personal religious beliefs.

Dawidowicz, Lucy S., ed. *A Holocaust Reader.* New York: Behrman House, Inc., 1976.
A good anthology.

Des Pres, Terrence. *The Survivor.* New York: Oxford University Press, 1976.
A brilliant analysis of survivors.

Feingold, Henry. *The Politics of Rescue.* New Brunswick, NJ: Rutgers University Press, 1970.
Charging America's failure to help.

Friedlander, Albert H., ed. *Out of the Whirlwind.* New York: Schocken Books, Inc., 1976.
Perhaps the best existing anthology.

Friedman, Saul S. *No Haven for the Oppressed.* Detroit: Wayne State University Press, 1973.
On U.S. policy toward Jewish refugees.

Glatstein, Jacob; Knox, Israel; and Margoshes, Samuel, eds. *Anthology of Holocaust Literature.* Philadelphia: The Jewish Publication Society of America, 1969.
Valuable for containing writings by lesser known authors.

Gollwitzer, Helmut; Kuhn, Kathe; and Schneider, Reinhold, eds. *Dying We Live.* New York: Pantheon Books, Inc., 1956.
Last words of martyrs and victims.

Korman, Gerd, ed. *Hunter and Hunted: Human History of the Holocaust.* New York: Viking Press, 1973.
Essays by survivors and scholars.

Merkl, Peter H. *The Making of a Stormtrooper.* Princeton, NJ: Princeton University Press, 1980.
Analysis of the "typical" stormtrooper.

Morley, John F. *Vatican Diplomacy and the Jews During the Holocaust, 1939–1943.* New York: KTAV Publishing House, Inc., 1980.
A careful scholarly analysis by a priest.

Morse, Arthur D. *While Six Million Died.* New York: Random House, 1967.
The story of American apathy.

Rabinowitz, Dorothy. *New Lives.* New York: Alfred A. Knopf, 1976.
Biographical accounts of survivors' lives.

Robinson, Jacob, and Bauer, Yehuda, eds. *Guide to Unpublished Material of the Holocaust Period.* Jerusalem: "Ahva" Cooperative Press, Vol. I, 1970; Vol. II, 1972; Vol. III, 1975.
Invaluable tool.

Snyder, Louis L. *Encyclopedia of the Third Reich.* New York: McGraw-Hall, 1976.
A solid compendium of information.

Trunk, Isaiah. *Judenrat.* New York: Macmillan Publishing Co., Inc., 1972.
On Jewish "self-government."

Tushnet, Leonard. *The Pavement of Hell.* New York: St. Martin's Press, Inc., 1972.
On the acts of Jewish leaders.